Choice of Law

Choice of Law

Edmund B. Spaeth, Jr.

*To Nancy,
the light of my life.*

Acknowledgment

I am particularly grateful to Gussella W. Gelzer, my secretary for many years, both when I was a judge and later when I was a lawyer. Not only did she type the entire manuscript, she did it by reading my execrable handwriting.

Chapter 1

May 30, 2002

Dear Judge:

Please excuse me for writing you. I called chambers and asked Mrs. B when you would be back from Maine and she said she wasn't sure—not till late next week, or maybe later.

The reason I'm writing is that Littleton Jones has just made me an offer to be an associate there, starting in September, after Labor Day, and I should let them know soon. I know it's supposed to be one of the best firms in the city—country, I guess. Also, as I think you know, I worked there the summer before my last year in law school, and I liked the lawyers I worked with a lot. The problem is, in the last few months I've begun to wonder whether I want to be a lawyer. I would really value your advice.

Thank you again, and please thank Mrs. Green, for inviting me to Squirrel Island over Memorial Day weekend. It is a very beautiful place, and I will never forget the wonderful time I had. It was a perfect way to end my year as your law clerk. I won't try again to say how much I learned that year.

Love,
Sally

Chapter 2

Neither would Judge Green—more properly, The Honorable James Green, Chief Judge of the Supreme Court—ever forget the weekend Sally Link had spent with him and his wife, Emily, at their cottage on Squirrel Island, off the coast of Maine.

It had been a glorious weekend—"one perfect Maine day after another," Emily had said. (In fact, the judge thought, "perfect Maine day" didn't make much sense, even though people who vacationed in Maine liked to say it. Especially early in the season, a Maine day was likely to be cold and gray, with fog or rain and a northeast wind. But then would come a day for which "perfect" wasn't too strong a word, the air like chilled white wine, the colors squeezed right out of the tube.)

On Memorial Day, the judge had suggested, "Let's take a spin in the *Emily*," to which the live Emily had replied, "Why don't just you and Sally go? I'm in the middle of this rhubarb pie." And so they had gone.

Emily was a reproduction of a nineteenth century lobster boat known as a "Hampton," a broad-beamed boat some twenty feet long, with a high bow to handle the seas and keep the lobster-man dry, and a low stern to make it easy for him to pull his traps—still the distinctive silhouette of lobster boats. Unlike modern lobster boats, *Emily* was an open boat. Some shelter from rain or dirty seas could be gained by rigging a canvas dodger. This was done by fitting two pieces of wood together to form a vertical triangle across the middle of the boat, then fitting another, longer piece of wood from the bow to the peak of the triangle, and clipping a heavy brown tarpaulin over the resulting framework.

Emily's hull was painted gleaming white, her gunwales and transom were natural pine, varnished to a mirror's glitter, her name, across the transom, was in brass letters. Whenever the judge walked by the cove he looked out to *Emily* riding on her mooring. Even in a running sea she didn't strain but rose and fell gently, like a resting gull. It wasn't unusual for a lobster man to give *Emily* a wave—a tribute rarely tendered a pleasure boat. Once Judge Green had remarked to a friend that he knew it was wrong to love a material object. "*Emily*," the friend had replied, "isn't a material object."

Emily was not only beautiful but tough. The judge had watched her being built, in the same way the original Hamptons had been built. Long clear strips of white pine were laid one on top of another and nailed together, then nailed to oak frames. ("Strip-planking," the builder told him. "No one does it anymore.") The result was a massive, tight hull, which needed no caulking. *Emily's* power was a twenty-five horsepower diesel engine, and though she wasn't fast she was quiet and would run an hour on a gallon of fuel. When the judge told the builder he was worried about his ability to handle *Emily* ("I've never done much with motor boats"), the builder replied, "'Don't worry. She'll teach you how." And so it had proved. *Emily* adjusted herself easily to all sorts of seas, never losing her balance. Her large rudder provided a tight turning circle, and she tracked beautifully. In quiet water, the judge steered with a finger, and often took his hands off the wheel.

Judge Green's plan was to take Sally out to the islands that lay between Squirrel and the open sea—Fisherman's and Damariscove, and beyond them, Outer Heron. As they entered the passage between Fisherman's and Damariscove, he cut *Emily's* speed. Fisherman's to port, and Damariscove to starboard, stretched in a long generally north-to-south line, rocky, gaunt, bare of trees. On the high point of Fisherman's stood a house that looked like a setting for *Wuthering Heights* or *The Hound of the Baskervilles*. It was built of boulders, with leaded windows, oak beams and a fireplace a man could stand in. The judge believed that once the house had been a ministers' place of retreat; who owned it now he didn't know.

Damariscove had been bought by The Nature Conservancy. From April to October, two friendly serious young people lived in what had been a fisherman's shack, kept records of the wildlife, and shooed visitors away from the common eider duck breeding area at the northern end. At the southern end of Damariscove was a cove, entered by carefully steering past a large rock always covered with boiling surf and called The Motions. Inside the cove were the granite remains of a wharf dating back to the sixteenth and seventeenth centuries, when Damariscove had been the busiest port on the northeast coast, with as many as a hundred vessels off its shore. The fishermen on Damariscove had provided supplies to the starving Plymouth colony.

Ahead lay Outer Heron, beyond it, the open sea. Even on a sparkling day Outer Heron was a foreboding mass of granite covered with spruce. Its shores were steep walls of jagged rocks, generally inaccessible from the water except for a cove at the seaward end, and, preferred by the judge, a fault on the western shore, which, when filled by the high tide gave snug shelter. If you were willing to put up with being scratched by brambles and dead spruce and bitten by mosquitoes, you could push and stumble your way through the woods to a great blue heron colony. Somewhere in the woods an Englishman who died at sea was supposed to be buried, but no one had ever found his grave.

Until a few years ago, a gnarled oak, its trunk easily ten feet around, had clung to a rocky promontory on Outer Heron's seaward end, alone, defying the storms. The judge had used it as a navigation mark. Often, he had thought, he saw beneath it, close to the water, a mermaid combing her golden hair, but as he approached she always disappeared. He supposed but was unwilling to accept that she was only sun glistening from sea-polished stone.

"I call these waters The Sacred Sector, Sally. As long as I can get here, I figure I'll be all right the rest of the year." Sally, who had been looking through binoculars in search of an eagle's nest reported to be on Outer Heron, looked up, surprised. She had never heard the judge make so introspective a remark, and she realized that even after working with him for a year she didn't know him very well—really, hardly at all.

Judge Green was a big man—six three or four, something over two hundred pounds, in his fifties, maybe early sixties, Sally guessed, gray hair, ruddy face. In chambers, he was always formal. Although he sometimes worked in his shirt sleeves, when he met with lawyers he wore a jacket, often with a vest, a quiet, reserved man.

Once Sally had attended a training session for law students who had volunteered to work with the homeless. In explaining how rotten homeless persons feel about themselves, the leader of the session had asked each student to think of the single word that would best describe him or herself. At the time, Sally thought this a silly exercise, but later she found herself using it. It made her think of all of a person's qualities, and, by sorting them out, decide what the person was really like. For Judge Green, she had decided, the word would be "kind," or perhaps "decent."

He didn't fit her notion of a judge, except that he looked like a casting director's choice to act the part. He was not authoritative and seemed diffident in presiding over the Supreme Court's argument sessions, unable or unwilling to rein in an abrasive or loquacious lawyer. And he seemed hesitant in forming a judgment, less than crisp in questioning lawyers or in correcting or changing draft opinions Sally submitted him.

The word Sally had picked to describe herself was "saucy." She loved repartee, and had a playful, quicksilver mind. Sometimes, working with the judge, she felt like some sort of wood nymph dancing around an old bear. This weekend, though, Sally had seen a man she didn't know, starting with when the judge rowed her out to *Emily*. With no grunting or apparent effort, he pushed the skiff smoothly through the water, feathering the oars with the ease of a fisherman filleting his catch, no splashing, his course straight as a string. And he handled *Emily* as though he were part of her. He was big, but he moved like a cat, so smoothly you didn't realize how fast he was. No missteps, no tangled lines. "Tell you what, Sally. Just stay there a moment." Ignition on. Skiff carried forward, secured to mooring. Mooring dropped. *Emily* backed off. "OK. We're on our way!" Sally, staying put as directed, had watched with admiration. The judge certainly didn't handle his courtroom the way he did his boat. And now this introspective remark about a "sacred sector." Sally returned to scanning Outer Heron through the binoculars.

"Judge! That boat seems to be drifting. I don't think there's anyone in it."

Judge Green turned to where Sally pointed. He recognized the little sailboat as like those the local yacht club used in its sailing classes.

Its sails were furled. It was drifting. And no one was in it. "Let's check it out."

As *Emily* turned towards the drifting boat, Sally called out again. "Judge! There's someone swimming. Trying to catch the boat, it looks like. See, about a hundred yards in back of it?" Without the binoculars, the judge couldn't see any swimmer, but he veered *Emily* in the direction Sally pointed and pulled back hard on the throttle. "We'd better get to him fast. You don't last long in this water."

As they approached the swimmer, the judge put *Emily* up-wind and cut her speed. When they were within a few feet, he put *Emily* in idle. "Sally, take the wheel, please. Just hold her steady." The judge went to the stern, and as the wind carried *Emily* down to the swimmer, he leaned over and reached out his hands.

It was just a boy—fourteen, fifteen at most—so tired and weak he could hardly grip the judge's hands. The judge pulled the boy close to *Emily*, heaved him up, a limp dead weight."Sally, give me a hand, please." Sally let go of the wheel, and together, she and the judge hauled the boy into the boat. He was dead white and shivering violently. "Get his clothes off. Here's my sweater. Rub him dry. Or as dry as you can." The judge went forward, put *Emily* hard over and headed for the harbor, full throttle.

"May Day! May Day!. This is the motor boat *Emily*. We just picked up a swimmer off Outer Heron. I think he's in hypothermia. We're headed for Saint Andrews Hospital, but I can't do better than ten knots. Can some one meet us and take him in? Over." "Motor boat *Emily*. This is the Coast Guard. We'll meet you. State your position and course and what you look like. Over." "Coast Guard. This is *Emily*. We're just about to run between Fisherman's and Damariscove. Course zero one zero. Twenty two foot white open boat. Looks like an old fashioned lobster boat. Over." "*Emily*. Hold your course and speed. We're on the way. Try to get him warm and dry. Over and out."

"Help me get your clothes off. We've got to get you dry. Just pretend I'm a nurse." The boy was too weak to help Sally, but he didn't resist. "Way to go. Now, then, roll over." Sally rubbed him furiously with the judge's sweater. "Oh, judge, he's still wet and shivering like anything. And now your sweater's soaked." "Hit him with the edges of your hands, Sally, the way trainers do." Instead, Sally straightened up and pulled off her own sweater—a heavy woolen sweater made in Ireland or the

Hebrides, or some such place, the judge supposed—and resumed her furious rubbing of the boy. From the corner of his eye, the judge saw that Sally had been wearing no blouse under her sweater, only a bra.

They heard the siren first, then saw the Coast Guard cutter, its bow angled high between two sheets of white water, the plume of its rooster tail arched above its wake. The judge squeezed the handle of *Emily's* compressed air fog horn and held it down, producing a sustained blast In response, the cutter altered course to head straight for them.

"Sally, stand by the stern. They'll be throwing us a line." The judge cut *Emily's* speed as the cutter came alongside. Lines were tossed, the vessels were lashed together, and two sailors jumped aboard *Emily.* "Easy does it, fella." The sailors rolled the boy onto a stretcher, wrapped him in a blanket, and strapped him down. "Steady now." Hands reached out, the boy was lowered onto the cutter's deck, the sailors jumped back on to the cutter.

As the cutter had approached and swung alongside *Emily,* Sally had become conscious of the fact that she was, nearly, half naked. Sensing her embarrassment, the judge had tried to stand between her and the sailors. When the boy had been transferred to the cutter and the cutter's captain sang out, "Cast off!," the judge stepped over to help with the lines. "Wait!" Sally called. "He'll need these." She picked up the boy's sneakers and clothes, and, flushed brick red, handed the soggy bundle across to one of the sailors.

"Well done, *Emily,*" the captain called. "He'll be all right." The cutter leapt away, siren wailing, white water flying. The transfer hadn't taken more than five minutes. "Look at them go, Sally." The judge turned to take *Emily's* wheel. "Oh judge! We did it! I mean, you did." Sally threw her arms around the judge's neck.

Sally's sudden embrace surprised Judge Green, but then, she had surprised him before, starting with when she had become his law clerk. When Sally had applied to be his clerk, he had asked her why. Her resume reflected that she was editor-in-chief of the law review, and had maintained one of the highest averages in the law school's history; her professors' letters of reference described her in superlatives. "I should think you'd apply to a federal court of appeals judge, or even a justice of the United States Supreme Court. Why me?"

Sally lifted her chin, in a way the judge came to know, and flushed. She hadn't expected either the question or the self-deprecation it implied. "I did apply, but"—her flush grew deeper—"but . . . well, I'm more interested in state law. I don't mean federal law isn't important but for most people, I think, state law is more important. Questions like whether they're entitled to damages for personal injury, or who gets custody of a child, are decided by state law. I thought a clerkship with you would help me learn how state law develops."

Sally became silent. She was sure that the big gray haired man sitting quietly across the desk knew there was more than that to why she had applied to him for a clerkship, but she hadn't known how to explain her application without sounding cocky and disrespectful of persons and institutions law students were supposed to respect, in particular, the United States Supreme Court.

She regarded the five justice majority that dominated that court as cruel and arrogant, and their protestations that they were strictly adhering to the Constitution as hypocritical. Even so, Sally had applied to two judges of the federal court of appeals whose chambers were in the city, but the experience only confirmed her determination not to seek a federal clerkship, and although both judges had been courteous and encouraging, she withdrew her applications.

To begin with, Sally hated the federal court house, a massive high rise of black and white marble. Hated having to enter through detectors, after emptying her pocketbook into a tray and surrendering her brief case for inspection. Hated the hushed corridors, the antiseptic courtrooms, the judges' luxurious chambers, the flags and seal of the United States everywhere she looked. No doubt, Sally thought, these surroundings were meant to impress all who entered with the majesty of the law, its serene impartiality, its indifference to whether weak or powerful stood before the bench. But for Sally, the courthouse brayed power—and Sally had her doubts about that power.

Sally revered Chief Justice Marshall for his decisions laying the foundations of the nation, and yet, she had begun to question one of Marshall's greatest achievements, his establishment of the federal courts' power to declare an act of Congress unconstitutional and therefore void. The justification of that power was that judges would be wise—and Marshall had been wise, and so had other judges. Sally could quote Holmes:

> [W]hen men have realized that time has upset many fighting faiths, they may come to believe even more than they believe the very foundations of their own conduct that the ultimate good desired is better reached by free trade in ideas—that the best test of truth is the power of the thought to get itself accepted in the competition of the market . . . .

And Brandeis:

> The makers of our Constitution undertook to secure conditions favorable to the pursuit of happiness. They recognized the significance of man's spiritual nature, of his feeling and of his intellect. They knew that only a part of the pain, pleasure and satisfaction of life are to be found in material things. They sought to protect Americans in their beliefs, their thoughts, their emotions and their sensations. They conferred, as against the government, the right to be let alone—the most comprehensive of rights and the right most valued by civilized men.

And Cardozo:

> Delicate enough and subtle is the inquiry . . . . There must be no blurring of the issues by evidence illegally admitted and carrying with it in its admission an appeal to prejudice and passion . . . . In a very real sense, a defendant starts his life afresh when he stands before a jury, a prisoner at the bar.

And Sally could call as a roll of honor the great decisions of the Warren Court protecting the weak and despised—black children herded into rundown schools declared, with no shame, to be equal to the schools white children attended; persons accused of crime and too poor to afford a lawyer. Gentle Harry Blackmun, whose opinion in *Roe v. Wade* established a woman's right to an abortion, was one of Sally's heroes.

But if some judges were wise and generous spirits, others were cold, narrow, cruel. How else, Sally asked herself, to describe the Taney Court's decision in *Dred Scott,* holding that Congress had no power to bar slavery from the territories, that slaves were property that couldn't be taken away from their owners, that no descendant of a slave could ever become a citizen of the United States? How else describe judges who were blind to the misery, the despair and loss of hope, of millions, judges whose niggardly reading of Congress's power to regulate commerce threatened the New Deal? If pressed to say whether the United States Supreme Court, on balance, had done more to advance than retard building a fair and democratic society, Sally would have fumbled for an answer.

She would not have hesitated a second, however, in saying where in the ebb and flow of the search for justice the Rehnquist Court belonged: it belonged with the Taney Court. The greatest achievement of Congress, certainly since the Civil War, was the 1964 Civil Rights Act, upheld as constitutional by the Warren Court. Now, in a series of decisions filed while Sally was in law school, a relentless five-justice majority of the Rehnquist Court had embarked on a crusade to limit, if not deny, Congress the power to protect civil rights. Reading those decisions, with their theological invocation of the "sovereignty" and "dignity" of the states, had revived in Sally's mind doubts about the wisdom of judicial review—doubts she thought she had overcome. According to the Rehnquist majority, Congress was powerless to provide that a state was liable for damages when it discriminated against elderly employees, or disabled employees; a state university was not liable when it refused to discipline members of the football team who gang raped a freshman. If you want to work for justice, Sally thought, maybe you shouldn't be a lawyer but a teacher, or social worker, or politician. In any event, she despised the Rehnquist Court and wanted nothing to do with it or with the judicial system over which it presided.

But if Sally hated the federal court house as embodying the unfeeling arrogance of the United States Supreme Court, she loved old City Hall, where the state Supreme Court sat and where Chief Judge Green's chambers were.

City Hall was a huge pile of a building. The largest building in the United States, or so Sally had read, with no structural framework, it was simply one massive block of granite piled on top of another. Built around a courtyard entered through four arches, one with "Justice" engraved over it, with mansard roofs and dormers, tall windows, lofty ceilings, endless corridors, busts of heroes and mythological figures and animals ornamenting every available surface, the whole dominated by a clock tower affording a view of rivers and distant hills, City Hall reminded Sally of government buildings she'd seen in Paris. It belonged in Europe, not the new world.

City Hall's proper maintenance was beyond the city's budget. The granite exterior was grimy, the tiles in the corridor walls needed re-grouting, the public restrooms were better avoided. Louis XIV or Napoleon would have approved of the ornate Mayor's reception room and City Council chambers, although they would have ordered that the brass and crystal chandeliers, the wall sconces and reading lamps, be re-gilded. The haughtiest barrister would have felt at home in the walnut—walled courtrooms, while regretting the worn carpets and dirty windows.

Sooner or later everyone came to City Hall, for a permit, certificate or license, to probate a will or register a deed, to pay a tax or fee or fine, to petition a politician, to appear in court as a party, witness, or juror. No one thought the old pile, seedy but grand, was a temple of justice, least of all the judges with bags under their eyes, frayed robes, and forty cases on their daily list, or the grizzled tipstaves, or the sad-eyed sheriff's deputies escorting hand-cuffed prisoners to a van in the courtyard. Life plays some rotten tricks. Get on with it. Daumier and Dickens were there. And Sally wanted to be.

Chief Judge Green had received Sally's explanation of why she had applied to him for a clerkship with a long look and no comment. He heaved himself from his desk, and, turning his back to Sally, looked out the window down to the traffic swirling below. After some time, during which Sally reflected on the inadequacy of her answer about thinking state law more important than federal, the judge resumed his seat, folded his hands, and, looking at Sally with a look almost tender and deeply serious, said: "Well, Miss Link, if I were your father or law school adviser, I suspect I would advise you that by applying to me you were making a mistake. You surely could obtain a clerkship more distinguished than I can offer. However, I am not your father or advisor. I have neither standing nor desire to criticize your decision. Besides, I wish that I'd been a rebel when I was young. So, I should be delighted to have you as my clerk. If you like, I'll introduce you to my secretary, Mrs. B, who knows how everything works around here. She'll give you the forms you'll need to sign. You may start whenever you like. May I suggest, however, that you take a break after the bar exam and start right after Labor Day."

Sally had been a wonderful clerk. As her law school record promised, she was a strong legal analyst and a powerful researcher. Since Judge Green was neither, she complemented his strength, which was a stubborn sense of fairness, nourished by having seen a great variety of cases over a good many years as an assistant district attorney and trial and appellate judge. The judge's happiest work hours were when he discussed with Sally the cases he had just heard argued and explained the basis of the votes he had noted in his journal. These discussions were, to an extent rare between judge and clerk, discussions between equals, for each knew and respected the other's strengths. Sally's technical ability, her probing of the judge's reasoning, enabled his largely intuitive conclusions to be cast in formally persuasive opinions—indeed, the bar noticed a considerable improvement over the opinions it had been accustomed to the judge filing. Sometimes Sally's questioning led the judge to change his mind. He had told her at the outset that she was not to draft an opinion to say what she thought he wanted her to say but what she thought the law required.

If, as they worked together, the judge learned technique from Sally, Sally began to understand Holmes's dictum, that the life of the law is not logic but experience, that a gut judgment of what is fair may be the key to deciding a case. At law school, Sally had been taught to start by asking, What do the cases say? Sometimes, she learned, a better first question was, What should they say? And another question Sally began to ask, which she hadn't asked at law school, was whether the lawyers had presented the facts of the case. When a case reached the Supreme Court, the record was complete. No more witnesses could testify, no more exhibits could be offered. When she reviewed a record with Judge Green, Sally often worried that not all the facts had been presented. If that were true, how could one decide what judgment would be fair? Would the Supreme Court's decision ratify a result that was unfair and should never have been reached?

Sally was not only bright and curious but good company. She was lovely to look at, tall and slender, with golden hair, which she wore rolled up in a bun, sapphire blue eyes, high cheek bones and tipped up nose, and delightful to be with, sunny, flippy, helpful, never a mean word.

Judge Green had, of course, noticed how attractive Sally was—and how the other law clerks, all young men, found frequent reason to stop by his chambers—but he had never acted on his admiration. His relationship with Sally had been affectionate but formal. Beyond shaking her hand, when she had said she would like to be his clerk and would start after Labor Day, the judge had never touched Sally. Her sudden embrace on the deck of *Emily* not only surprised but overwhelmed him. It was as though a dam had broken, flooding him with memories and emotions he had suppressed, or didn't know he had.

As his arms tightened around Sally's bare back, Judge Green thought how much he would miss her, miss their discussions of his cases, miss her gaiety and sweetness. He admired the spunk and resourcefulness she had shown in helping him rescue the boy—a side of Sally he hadn't seen before. But most of all, the judge felt that Sally's embrace had somehow changed him. Unknown to Sally, or to Emily, Judge Green expected soon to be exposed as a fraud and to be required to resign from the bench. On the advice of his lawyer, Roger Littleton, he had so far discussed this expectation with no one, but sooner or later he would have to tell Emily. The judge didn't fear the effect exposure would have on him—in fact he stoically considered it would be merited punishment—but when he thought how hurt Emily would be, his heart broke. And so, it was a desperate man Sally suddenly embraced, and, although she didn't know it, comforted. Feeling his arms tighten around her, Sally laid her head against the judge's cheek and moved in against him. He felt the length of her body, the fullness of her breasts, her nipples. It was life he was holding, he thought. Sunshine. Joy. He mustn't give up hope that somehow everything would work out all right.

Emily rolled sharply in the Coast Guard cutter's wake, as though protesting her aimless drift. Suddenly self-conscious, Judge Green released Sally from his grip and took *Emily's* wheel. "Now you're shivering," he said. "I'm going to run for the cove. There's no point in our following them in. I'll drop you off at the dock, and while I put the boat away, you go up to the house and get a hot shower and into some dry clothes. There's some brandy in the corner cupboard in the dining room. A spot of that should help."

Chapter 3

Judge Green reread Sally's letter, put down his cup of coffee, which had gotten cold, and slumped back in the old wicker rocker: a big man, on the sunny end of the porch, looking out at his rose garden.

"Morning, Judge. Another beautiful day."

"Sure is, Bill. You off to the harbor?"

"Yep. Got to hit the grocery store. First I'll hit some golf balls."

"Well, good luck. Stay out of the blueberry bushes."

"I'll try, anyway."

We don't really see, do we? Sometimes we can't. People put up too many screens. Chat easily. Agree with what we say. Change the subject. Divert our attention when we get too close. The judge's screens were up. Bill, on his way to the harbor, didn't know it, but Emily did, and she was afraid. Since they had arrived on Squirrel, except once, when she had stayed home to make that rhubarb pie, she hadn't let her husband out of her presence. She had never known him to draw so deep within himself as he'd done the last few days. Fighting down her dread, she had decided her wisest course was to wait, until, by a look, or squeeze of her hand, by some sign, he signaled that he was ready to open up.

Heaving himself out of the rocker, Judge Green opened the screen door and went through the living room into the kitchen, where Emily was making a fish chowder. He showed Emily Sally's letter, and while Emily read it, poured himself another cup of coffee. "Think I should answer. Guess I better do it today. She seems to be on a pretty tight time table. Don't know what to say, though. Anyway, I'll be in the living room." "I'll finish making this chowder. We can have lunch whenever you want."

Judge Green was a nominal Unitarian but didn't attend church. Emily belonged to the Episcopal church near their home and sometimes, particularly on Easter and at Christmas, she asked him to keep her company, which he always did because he loved her. While he enjoyed the music and flowers, and said so, he was careful not to show his irritation at the sermon, lest he make Emily feel she'd imposed on him.

Judge Green drew a distinction between teaching and preaching. He had taught many boys to play baseball. He knew the mechanics of throwing the ball, swinging the bat, getting in position to field a grounder. He could both tell and show his players what to do, and he had seen them learn and improve. He saw no reason to think, however, that the minister was qualified to teach him how to be good, as he was qualified to teach someone to throw a curve, and he saw no evidence that preaching produced better people, as good coaching produced better teams. He would agree that some church goers did kind and generous things, like operating a soup kitchen for homeless people, but, for him, religion was unacceptable because of its exclusivity. When a minister said that to be saved, one had to subscribe to certain beliefs, the judge cringed, and wanted to argue back.

Emily, sensing his discomfort with a sermon, had once gently pointed out that he didn't really believe that morality couldn't be taught. He himself, she observed, was a stern teacher of sportsmanship. If, for example, one of his players cursed an opponent or the umpire, he was sent to the bench—no matter whether he was a star and the game was on the line. And what was the law, after all, except a statement of the community's morality? But she didn't press the point. She shared the judge's distrust of organized religion, and she recognized that his irritation with preaching was a manifestation of his humility and gentleness, for which she loved him. Unwilling to try to impose on another person views he himself doubted, he regarded preachers' assurance as cockiness, as at bottom a conviction that some people were better, more deserving, than others, and they knew why. The judge was convinced that Emily was as good as anyone could be. He refused to deduce from that conviction that he had the ability to tell others how they should live.

Reading Sally's letter for the third time, Judge Green remarked to himself that he had no idea why "in the last few months" Sally had "begun to wonder" whether to be a lawyer. Nothing she had said in their discussions of his cases had alerted him that she had begun to question what she should do after her clerkship. She couldn't have lost confidence in her ability as a legal analyst. She must have known that her performance as a law clerk had been outstanding. In any case, he wasn't going to advise her that she should, or shouldn't, be a lawyer. That would be preaching, which would be bad enough in any case but especially in the case of Sally. "Love, Sally," she had written. She'd learn soon enough, when he was exposed as a fraud, that he didn't deserve her admiration and trust.

Meanwhile, though—today—he had to answer Sally's letter. The way to answer, the judge finally decided, was simply to be honest—to tell Sally about the doubts he himself had suffered, and still suffered, about becoming a lawyer. He hadn't wanted to go to law school. He had never learned how to try a case. As for learning to be a judge, Holmes, he once read, told Learned Hand that judging was a "job." Well, he didn't know how to do his job. Whatever Sally's doubts were about becoming a lawyer, maybe, if she compared them with his, she would be helped a little to decide what to do.

"My dear Sally . . . ." he began.

*　　*　　*

Jimmy Green was the best pitcher the city high school league had ever seen. He led his team to three successive championships, along the way throwing two no-hitters. "Big strong kid," a major league scout jotted in his notebook. "Mostly counts on his fast ball but has a pretty good curve. Good control. Should watch him." The city university gave Jimmy an athletic scholarship, and he pitched the university's team to a championship. The major league scout had been watching, and one day he and Jimmy's coach asked Jimmy whether he'd ever thought about playing pro-ball. Jimmy said he hadn't, and wasn't interested. He knew he wasn't any student—his grades were C or worse—but he wanted to finish college, maybe get a phys ed degree, and be a coach, preferably of city kids. He'd worked a couple of summers at one of the city playgrounds, and done a little coaching. He loved it.

Coaching was not what Jimmy's father had in mind for his son. Jimmy's father, Michael Green, was a general contractor. Michael's father had emigrated from Ireland as a boy and become a bricklayer. From the time he was ten, Michael worked as his father's helper. When his father was killed in a fall from a scaffold, Michael quit school and went to work for the contractor who had employed his father. Soon he owned the business. By the time Jimmy started college, Michael Green—at least according to other contractors—owned the town. His company had been awarded the contracts for the city hospital, the new football stadium, the gas works. Whatever job Michael Green bid, he got. Jimmy, he decided, was to go to law school.

Jimmy protested that he didn't want to be a lawyer and wouldn't be a good one, citing his poor college grades. Michael Green was chair of the executive committee of the university's board of trustees. In support of the university's last capital fund drive he had endowed a chair at the law school. Jimmy's grades wouldn't be a problem. "Time to give up games," his father said. "At law school you'll learn how things work. Hell, sometimes I think lawyers run the world. If you decide you don't want to be a lawyer, you can go into something else. Politics. Business. Sports, even. I'm told the hot new course at the law school is Sports Law. Maybe you'll be an agent." Obediently, Jimmy applied for admission. He was accepted.

With no reason to go to law school except to obey his father, Jimmy looked for a reason in his studies. Jimmy recognized that lawyers possessed specialized knowledge that others didn't have but needed—how to fill out tax returns, for example, and he knew that his father's business had to comply with many different sorts of regulations, which required legal advice. Law school, he supposed, was where one acquired such knowledge. His professors, however, told him that there was a much more important reason than that to go to law school. Specialized knowledge, like tax law, was subject to change. Most of the law lawyers needed now, they said, didn't even exist years ago. The principal reason to go to law school was to "learn to think like a lawyer."

This admonition struck Jimmy as both thrilling and ominous. It seemed to promise access to unbounded power, while offering no guidance on how to exercise that power. "Let us teach you to become wizards," the professors seemed to say. But what magic did lawyers work?

To the extent that Jimmy had thought about the matter at all before, he had a vaguely benign view of the law, which he supposed to be a set of rules to achieve justice. "To think like a lawyer," however, as far as he could tell, had nothing to do with thinking about how to achieve justice. What a lawyer thought about, it seemed, was how to win. If a statute forbade certain conduct, could you think of a way to interpret it to permit that conduct? If the opinion of a court said that an injured party could recover damages only upon proof that the defendant caused the damages, but you couldn't prove causation, could you think of a way to explain away the court's statement and recover damages anyway? Every rule seemed to have an opposite. When the words of a statute are plain, the court will give the words their plain meaning; but if that meaning leads to a result that is absurd or unreasonable, the court will ask what was the legislature's purpose in enacting the statute and construe the statute to serve that purpose. The rule of stare decisis—that a court will follow its earlier decisions—assures that the law is predictable and that everyone will be treated equally; but stare decisis may deaden the law by preventing it from responding to change. "Think like a lawyer" seemed to mean, "If a rule doesn't help you, invoke its opposite."

Now, Jimmy liked to win as much as anyone. He'd stared down the most dangerous hitters, had found strength he didn't know he had. But in baseball the rules were clear. You could argue that a pitch should have been called a strike, but there was no doubt about the definition of "strike," and no one even thought about arguing that for some reason different rules should be applied. ("The game will be evener and therefore more exciting if Ted Williams is allowed only two strikes".) As Jimmy compared the way he had played baseball with the way his classmates tried to win arguments, it seemed to him that "thinking like a lawyer" was somehow immoral, an attempt to evade the rules—to win by cheating.

This conclusion curdled Jimmy's usually clear, sunny disposition. No matter how late he worked, how often he read the assignment, he couldn't match his nimble classmates. Whatever arguments he made, in class or study sessions or at moot court, they turned the arguments around against him. They didn't mean to be cruel—for them it was all a game—but the implied taunt hurt. Jimmy became withdrawn, sarcastic, defensive. He fell silent in class and dropped out of his study group.

The standard practice of the professor who taught the course on evidence was to devote the last class to a review of the cases that had been discussed in earlier classes, as a framework, he explained, for preparing for the final exam. Jimmy would never forget the conclusion of this professor's last lecture. "When you have completed your review of the cases we have studied together," the professor had said, "I hope you will have discovered someone you will think of as a hero. The law is often cruel or oppressive. Many of the cases we have studied are, I think, plainly wrong, not just because they're illogical but, which is much worse, because they're plainly unfair. It is disappointing that the judges who decided those cases didn't see how unfair they were being. It is also disappointing—to me as a teacher even more disappointing—that the lawyers who tried and argued those cases may have contributed to the unfairness. You will find, when you practice, that some judges are unfair. They may be prejudiced, or callous, or too lazy to read your briefs. You will also find lawyers, many lawyers, I'm afraid, who are unscrupulous and untrustworthy and greedy. I beg you," and here the professor had stopped, as though surprised at himself, and indeed he had never before spoken to them this way, but then he resumed—"I beg you, do not be discouraged, do not lower your own standards because there are lazy judges and bad lawyers. There are also great judges and good, very good, lawyers. Only a great judge could have written *Zackowitz*, and many a mediocre judge has come out right because of a good lawyer's guidance. So when you get discouraged—and you will, I promise you—think of a lawyer you admire, someone, not necessarily someone famous or rich but someone who used a lawyer's skills, the skills I hope you're learning here, to protect the weak and despised. Or take down your old case book and reread one of the decisions that have made the law a little less cruel, a little more understanding and fair, a decision like *Zackowitz*. Well, class! So endeth the lesson. Good luck on your exam."

That night, in his apartment, Jimmy had reread *People v. Zackowitz*— the full name of the case his professor had cited. In their casebook, *Zackowitz* was the first case on circumstantial proof, under the subheading, Evidence Of Other Crimes. It had been decided by the New York Court of Appeals by a four to three vote, with the Chief Judge, Benjamin N. Cardozo, writing the majority opinion. The dissenting opinion summarized the rule on when evidence of other crimes could be admitted, and Jimmy, when he first read the case, had underlined the rule. It was a complicated rule, and hard to memorize: the state may not prove that on another occasion the defendant committed a crime other than the crime charged in the indictment unless such proof tends to establish (1) motive, (2) intent, (3) absence of mistake or accident, (4) a common scheme to commit two or more crimes so related to each other that proof of one tends to establish the other, and (5) the identity of the person named as the defendant in the indictment. Trying to recite the rule to himself, Jimmy found he had forgotten some of the exceptions.

For Jimmy, *Zackowitz* exemplified everything he had found confusing, frustrating and humiliating in studying law. Why had his professor cited it as written by a heroic judge; as a source of inspiration, a decision that had made the law a little less cruel? What was there about the case that caused this usually austere, formal teacher, who never addressed his students by first name or engaged in small talk, to burst out as he had? Jimmy determined to find out. He would try to read the case as, apparently, his professor did—as a case in which kindness had won.

As he started to read, Jimmy noticed the stakes in *Zackowitz*—something he hadn't paid attention to before. The defendant had been convicted of first degree murder and sentenced to death; Zackowitz's lawyer was trying to save his client's life; the judges had to decide whether Zackowitz should die. Jimmy also for the first time paid close attention to the facts of the case. He noticed how meticulous, even fussy, Cardozo was in stating the facts. Zackowitz was "an optician regularly employed," Cardozo wrote, "without criminal record or criminal associates." Late one night, he and his wife were walking home from a dance, Zackowitz had been drinking and "was heated with liquor." (Jimmy was uncertain what to make of this stilted language until he noticed that Cardozo had carefully refused to say just how "heated" Zackowitz had been. Jimmy knew that in stating the facts, a judge should stick to the record. Perhaps, he thought, the record didn't show how much Zackowitz had been drinking.) Four young men, one of them named Frank Coppola, were repairing an automobile in the street across from the apartment house where Zackowitz and his wife lived. Zackowitz dropped behind a moment to buy a newspaper. When he caught up with his wife, she was in tears and told him that one of the men had insulted her. Enraged, Zackowitz went across the street, and, among other things, told the men that "if they did not get out of there in five minutes, he would come back and bump them all off." When they were back in their apartment, Zackowitz's wife told him that one of the men had offered her two dollars to have sex with him. His rage aroused again, Zackowitz put a pistol in his pocket, selecting it from his gun collection, which included three other pistols and a tear-gas gun, and returned to the scene. He kicked Coppola in the stomach; Coppola went for him with a wrench; "[t]he pistol, Cardozo wrote, "came from the pocket, and from the pistol a single shot, which did its deadly work." (again Jimmy remarked to himself on the stilted language); Zackowitz and his wife fled the scene; on the way he threw the pistol into the river; when he was arrested, the three pistols and tear gas gun were found in his apartment,

Having thus stated the case, Cardozo noted that "[a]t the trial the vital question was the defendant's state of mind" at the moment of the homicide. "Did he shoot with a deliberate and premeditated design to kill? Was he so inflamed by drink or by anger or by both combined that, though he knew the nature of his act, he was the prey to sudden impulse, the fury of the fleeting moment?" (Jimmy now understood Cardozo's stilted description of the shooting: it implied nothing about the shooter's state of mind.) Cardozo noted that the evidence looked both ways. The evidence that Zackowitz had selected a pistol in the apartment and returned to the scene pointed to premeditation; but the evidence that he did not shoot at once but rather drew the pistol "later," Cardozo noted, "in the heat and rage of an affray," pointed to sudden impulse. Given the evidence, determining what had been Zackowitz's intent when he shot Coppola was an inquiry "[d]elicate enough and subtle . . . even in the most favorable conditions, with every warping influence excluded. There must be no blurring of the issues by evidence illegally admitted." Zackowitz's possession of the three pistols and tear-gas gun in his apartment was a crime—illegal possession of firearms. As Jimmy's underlining indicated, the general rule was that evidence of a crime couldn't be admitted in a case where the defendant was charged with committing some other crime. Zackowitz was charged with murder, not illegal possession. How come, then, that the trial judge had admitted evidence that he had illegally possessed firearms?

Jimmy re-read the rule he had underlined and was reminded that the rule was not a flat prohibition against evidence of a crime other than the crime charged. It had five exceptions. The right question to ask, therefore, was: Did the evidence that Zackowitz had illegally possessed firearms fit within any of these exceptions?

Jimmy, when he had first read *Zackowitz* hadn't asked this question. He had only underlined the rule, and tried to memorize, not apply, it. Now, when he did try to apply the rule, he got a surprise.

On Zackowitz's appeal from his death sentence, the Court of Appeals, by a four to three vote, with Cardozo writing the majority opinion, vacated the sentence and ordered a new trial on the ground that the evidence of Zackowitz's illegal possession of firearms did not fit within any of the exceptions to the rule that evidence of a crime other than the crime charged should not be admitted. The three dissenting judges, however, said the evidence was properly admitted, and they voted to affirm the death sentence. But—and here was a surprise—those judges *agreed* that the evidence didn't fit within any of the exceptions to the rule of forbidding evidence of another crime. By what reasoning, then, did they nevertheless conclude that the evidence was admissible?

Feeling queasy and tense—the way he had so often felt when he argued with the others in his study group—Jimmy re-read the dissenting opinion. If, the dissenting judges said, Zackowitz "had been arrested at the time of the killing and these weapons had been found on his person, the People would not have been barred from proving the fact, and the further fact that they were nearby in his apartment should not preclude the proof as bearing on the entire deed of which the act charged forms a part." After reading this sentence three times Jimmy's tension exploded. This was nonsense! In the first place, Zackowitz had *not* been arrested at the time of the killing with "these weapons" "on his person." "And what," Jimmy wondered, was this reference to "the further fact" that the guns were found in Zackowitz's nearby apartment? "Further fact" suggested there was some *other* fact—and there wasn't. The gun had *not* been "found on [Zackowitz's] person" when he was arrested. In other words, Jimmy thought, the *only* "fact" the dissenting judges cited as supporting the admission of evidence that Zackowitz had committed a crime other than the one he was charged with was the evidence of the crime itself—the illegal possession of firearms in the apartment. Jimmy's head ached, as he felt himself losing his bearings. Wasn't the question whether the evidence of Zackowitz's other crime—illegal possession—was admissible as within an exception to the rule forbidding evidence of other crimes? And if that was the question, what exception did the dissenting judges say applied? Hadn't they admitted that none did apply?

For the fourth time, Jimmy re-read the dissenting opinion, this time focusing on the statement that evidence of the guns in Zackowitz's apartment—that is, evidence of the other crime—was "proof . . . bearing on the entire deed of which the act charged [murder] forms a part." Apparently, the dissenting judges believed that evidence of another crime that "formed a part" of the crime charged was admissible. Jimmy re-read the rule as he had underlined it, and as the dissenting judges had stated it. There wasn't any "formed a part of the entire deed" exception. Jimmy felt sure that something was wrong with the dissenting judges' argument, but he couldn't say exactly what it was. He turned to Cardozo's opinion.

Many years later Jimmy read that Cardozo had been an accomplished appellate lawyer, whose arguments always went for the jugular. Cardozo's opinion went for the jugular. The evidence of Zackowitz's gun collection *couldn't* be proof of "part of" the murder, Cardozo said: the guns "were left in his apartment where they were incapable of harm" And then Cardozo did what Jimmy's professors had repeatedly told their students they should do: he considered the reason for the rule at issue. Why, Cardozo asked, should there be a rule forbidding evidence of a crime other than the crime charged? Because, Cardozo explained, of the presumption of innocence. Everyone accused of a crime is entitled to be presumed innocent. But, if the jury learns that the accused had committed a crime other than the crime charged, the jurors will likely think of the accused as a criminal, a bad man, instead of thinking of him as presumably innocent, that is, as innocent unless the district attorney, beyond a reasonable doubt, proves he is guilty. The district attorney, Cardozo noted, had told the trial judge that he was not trying to prove that Zackowitz was a bad man. And the trial judge, and the dissenting judges, took his word. Not Cardozo. He didn't describe the district attorney's statement as disingenuous, if not plain false. He simply quoted the district attorney's brief, which argued that Zackowitz's possession of the weapons showed that he was "a desperate type of criminal," a "person criminally inclined." Thus Cardozo proved that the evidence of Zackowitz's gun collection had been offered for the precise purpose that the rule against evidence of other crimes forbid such evidence: to prejudice the jury against Zackowitz as a bad man, and undermine the presumption that until proved guilty, he was innocent. Accordingly, Cardozo, with three other judges joining him, vacated Zackowitz's sentence to death and ordered a new trial.

By the time Jimmy had worked his way back and forth through the opinions in *Zackowitz*, to the point where he not only understood why the dissenting opinion was illogical, but appreciated why Cardozo's opinion was consistent with the reason for the rule excluding evidence of other crimes, it was two o'clock in the morning. Jimmy had been working at his desk with his back to the window. Now he flipped off his desk lamp, rose, turned and looked outside. A full moon floated above the city. Beneath it lay a jumble of silver roofs and black shadows. A police car cruised slowly down the middle of the street in front of Jimmy's apartment building, indolently turned the corner, and disappeared. The sidewalks were empty, the street was empty, the buildings were dark. Leaning his forehead against the window pane, Jimmy tried to summarize, to organize, to come to some conclusion that would resolve the tension he had felt steadily increasing inside him. He was exhausted, but if he could just hang on, keep pushing, a little longer, he thought, the pieces would fall into place.

Until now, Jimmy hadn't thought it important to evaluate the reasoning of differing opinions. Rather, he simply asked what rule the case stood for, and underlined where the rule was stated. That was the important point, wasn't it? To learn the rule. Why try to get a grip on the slippery differences between the reasoning of the majority and dissenting judges? Because getting a grip might save a man's life. Jimmy understood, as he hadn't before, why his professor regarded Cardozo as a hero of the law, and *Zackowitz* as an opinion that had made the law less cruel. Cardozo's vision of law enforced by reason untainted by prejudice was a noble vision, and the elegant savagery with which Cardozo destroyed the reasoning of the dissenting judges was evidence that that vision might be realized.

Instead of inspiring Jimmy, however, the power of Cardozo's opinion in *Zackowitz* deepened and confirmed the doubt and depression that had been building up within him since he'd entered law school. Looking out over the silent moonlit city, Jimmy felt as though he were standing on the edge of an abyss. Despite the frustration and humiliation he had suffered because of his inability to do well in his studies, he'd never given up believing that the law was a set of rules that, if correctly applied, would lead to justice. Now, with his new-found understanding of *Zackowitz*, he didn't believe that any more. The district attorney must have known that the rule precluding evidence of other crimes precluded the evidence of the guns in Zackowitz's apartment. Instead of accepting the rule, however, he tried to think of an argument that would get around the rule. "That's what 'thinking like a lawyer' means," Jimmy thought. The argument the district attorney thought of required him to lie to the court—to say that he wasn't trying to prove that Zackowitz was a bad man when in fact that was exactly what he was trying to prove, as later slipped out in his brief to the Court of Appeals. "How could the district attorney do that?" Jimmy asked himself. It was all very well for his law school classmates to come up with clever though fallacious arguments in an effort to win a moot court case. Nothing, except a good mark, or bragging rights, was at stake. The district attorney, however, conceived and made his argument to persuade the jury to convict Zackowitz of murder: he was trying to have Zackowitz strapped into an electric chair and killed. "Why!? Why!?" Jimmy asked himself "Because he wanted to show how tough he was on crime? Because he wanted to be re-elected? Is that what learning to think like a lawyer does to you? Teaches you to be so clever you think you can use the law to get whatever you want? And what about the three dissenting judges? They weren't under any pressure to 'win' the case. Why didn't they see through the district attorney's argument? If at first they were fooled by it, as apparently the trial judge was fooled, how could they continue to accept the argument after Cardozo had destroyed it?" Jimmy knew that if he had been Zackowitz's lawyer, he wouldn't have been able to expose the fallacy in the district attorney's argument. He just wasn't sharp enough. Was justice, then, only an accident? You got it if you had a good lawyer and if there happened to be a Cardozo on the bench? How many good lawyers were there? How many Cardozos?

Many years later Jimmy would learn that Cardozo himself had wondered what justice was and how a judge could provide it. Legal rules, Cardozo recognized, were not like pieces of a jigsaw puzzle, which, if your eyes were sharp enough, could be neatly fitted together. Sometimes they could be, but often their edges didn't quite match. Judges had to choose among rules that contradicted each other. The choice, as Cardozo had said in *Zackowitz*, was one "not of logic, but of policy," and in choosing a policy, judges sometimes disagreed. In *Zackowitz*, for Cardozo the controlling policy was that a defendant accused of crime should be presumed innocent. While the dissenting judges did not directly challenge that policy, they were willing to undercut it more than Cardozo was. When confronted with such a disagreement, how should a judge decide which choice of policy was better? Reflecting on this question and on his struggle to answer it, Cardozo had written, "How trackless was the ocean on which I had embarked," adding, "as the years have gone by, I have become reconciled to the uncertainty, because I have grown to see it as inevitable."

Jimmy Green, third year law student, knew nothing of Cardozo's meditations, but after his study of *People v. Zackowitz*, he sensed the futility of all the work he'd done, underlining and memorizing rules. Perhaps his professor was justified in his apparent belief that in the long run the law would become more just, that reason, exemplified by Cardozo, would defeat, at least would blunt, prejudice and passion. Jimmy himself wasn't so sure of that, and at the moment he didn't care. He didn't want to think like a lawyer, to fight with words, to feel lost and helpless as clouds of shifting rules swirled about his head. He turned his back on the moon, which was starting to fade as dawn approached, and threw himself onto his bed. "First thing Monday, I'll see the dean and tell him I'm withdrawing."

If, when Jimmy made this resolution, it had been early Sunday morning, perhaps he would have withdrawn from the law school, but, as it happened, it was early Saturday morning. By Monday, Jimmy's resolve had weakened. He had only one more semester to go. Having gotten so far, he didn't want to drop out ("quit" would no doubt have been his father's word). Besides (as his father had said), he didn't have to be a lawyer. Maybe, after he graduated, he could get a job in sports, even be an agent, or (he thought defiantly) a coach.

And so, Jimmy soldiered on. His grades didn't improve, for he never regained the intensity of his examination of *People v. Zackowitz*.

Instead, he reverted to his old habits, which had more or less served him, of underlining and memorizing rules. He managed to graduate—just. Under the law school's rules, a student who failed more than two courses was not permitted to graduate, and but for the dean's intervention, Jimmy would have failed taxation, which would have been his third failure. As the dean explained to the young untenured assistant professor in taxation, however, in rather blunt language, failing young Green might be of marginal benefit to the legal profession, but would surely discourage any further gifts from Michael Green to the law school's endowment. "Graduating him isn't doing him any favor, you know," the young professor had argued. The dean was unmoved. "That may, or may not, be so. Who knows? He's a nice kid."

*   *   *

Jimmy Green's first job after graduating from law school was as an assistant district attorney. He got the job without having to look for it—which was just as well, considering that his resume described his athletic accomplishments in considerably more detail than his accomplishments as a student. The district attorney himself telephoned Jimmy, to say that he'd heard that Jimmy had recently graduated from law school. Would Jimmy be interested in becoming an assistant district attorney? The district attorney had heard about Jimmy's graduation from Jimmy's father. Michael Green was a major contributor—six figures—to the district attorney's party. The district attorney planned to run for governor. He had no difficulty finding a slot for a new assistant.

After a six month assignment to arraignments and preliminary hearings, Assistant District Attorney James Green tried his first case—a routine charge of possession of a controlled substance—before a judge sitting without a jury. With no apparent effort, a veteran criminal defense lawyer chewed him up in little pieces, suggesting by his questions that the arresting officer had planted the evidence on a young man who had run from the officer for fear of being beaten, and that the police laboratory technician was not only incompetent but had likely tested material taken from another suspect. On defense counsel's motion, the judge dismissed the case without hearing any defense witnesses and without leaving the bench.

The nature of the trial process continued to elude the young prosecutor. He had supposed that a trial was to determine the truth. He knew that his law school professor of evidence had said that the rules of evidence were not designed to determine the truth, but he had regarded this statement as an exaggeration, uttered to make the point that the rules had purposes beyond, or in addition to, determining the truth. Someone who knew the truth, a priest, for example, or a lawyer, might be forbidden to speak it because of the importance of protecting the penitent's or client's confidences. Surely, however, these were exceptional situations. His professor had said that a trial was designed to achieve a fair settlement of a dispute—as far as human frailty permitted. But if the dispute was whether A hit B, wasn't the fairest way to settle that dispute to determine whether in fact—in truth—A did hit B? Not, Jimmy learned, in the opinion of defense counsel, who showed remarkably little interest in determining the truth. In their view, a trial wasn't a search for truth or justice. It was a fight, with a specific objective: dismissal of the charges, acquittal, or at least a mistrial.

Jimmy had been assured in law school that the truth would emerge from a fight: the lawyers would search out and marshal all the evidence favorable to their respective clients, and by cross-examination and argument would expose the weaknesses of their adversaries' evidence. From the outset, Jimmy had questioned this theory. Fighting, he thought, was more likely to defeat than find the truth. Fighting stirred up anger and fear, which were likely to lead to hiding or denying or even falsifying the facts. In any case, fights were won by those who were the strongest—sometimes by those who were the dirtiest fighters.

Perhaps because he didn't like to fight, Jimmy wasn't good at it. Jimmy soon realized that the criminal defense bar regarded him as an easy mark, unable, for example, to protect himself against leading questions, or cross-examination that suggested possibilities with no support in the evidence, or to prevent a witness from blurting out inadmissible evidence. "Mr. Green," one trial judge had admonished him, "if you think defense counsel is offering inadmissible evidence, you should object before the witness answers. Then I will rule on your objection." The idea that the judge was a passive spectator, unable to intervene unless invited to, not only puzzled but angered Jimmy. Why should he be the one admonished? He'd done nothing wrong—unless being slow was some how wrong. It was defense counsel who was fighting dirty. Why didn't the judge admonish him? Of course there had to be rules, but they should favor the weak, not the crafty and strong.

Jimmy's hurt feelings, his confusion and anger, elicited no sympathy from the other assistant district attorneys, who seemed to Jimmy like a kennel of pit bulls, yapping about their latest victories. Once the district attorney suggested to his assistants that they watch "two great trial lawyers" try a case that the media were greedily covering, "to learn how it should be done." What Jimmy learned—or at least decided—was that he'd never be a great, or even competent, trial lawyer. The lawyers' polished manners, the clarity of their questions, the easy quickness with which they anticipated and responded to each other's moves, were, he was sure, beyond him. He felt like a boy told by the coach, "Look, kid. I appreciate your interest, and I know you've practiced hard. But you're just not fast enough."

After reviewing his new assistant's performance, the district attorney also decided that Jimmy would never be a trial lawyer. Unwilling to fire Jimmy, and then face Michael Green, the district attorney reassigned him to preliminary hearings, where the prosecutor could hardly go wrong. All the prosecutor had to do was to make out a prima facie case, which could usually be done by calling the arresting officer and perhaps also the victim, who were rarely cross-examined, defense counsel preferring not to reveal how they planned to attack the witnesses at the trial. The other assistant district attorneys saw Jimmy's reassignment as a demotion: back to kindergarten. Jimmy, however, found his bearings, and became a star.

Courtroom B, where preliminary hearings were held, had once been a storage room. The floors were linoleum, not marble, the walls, fiberboard, not walnut. The judge sat at the far end behind a table on a raised platform. To one side stood an American flag, beside that, a chair for the witness. In front of this "bench" were two tables, which had been taken from a cafeteria, one table for the prosecutor, the other for defense counsel, and several rows of folding metal chairs, the front rows for police officers and witnesses, the rest for persons with some interest in an accused—a mother or wife or girlfriend, sometimes some children, restless but subdued. The room stank of misery, bitterness, poverty, and failure. Occasionally private counsel appeared, assured, good suit, leather briefcase, but most of the accused were represented by the public defender, usually an earnest young man or woman, sometimes a veteran filling in because staff was short, with too many files to fit into a brief case and too little time to have done much more than glance at them. Anyway, the accused was almost always guilty. The only question was, guilty of what? Homicide? Rape? Robbery? Most of the cases were drug cases or involved some sort of assault, and most of these, Jimmy soon learned, weren't what they seemed The district attorney's settled policy was to overcharge. Possession of two joints was possession with intent to sell, a school recess fistfight was assault with intent to kill. This policy, the district attorney believed, demonstrated his outrage and righteous determination to punish those who preyed on law-abiding citizens. Jimmy, however, had no interest in impressing anyone. He accepted the fact that in some cases punishment, as retribution or deterrence, was inevitable, even appropriate, but he had no ambition to be its instrument. His hope was to help to heal or repair the injury done.

We are regularly admonished that our actions may have unintended consequences. An unintended consequence of the district attorney's policy of overcharging—at least it seems safe to assume that it was unintended—was to afford Jimmy the frequent opportunity to modify the rigors of the criminal law, to bring into one courtroom a sense of proportion, a recognition that a misstep may ruin a life. If satisfied that the accused was a shoplifter, not a burglar, a user, not a seller, a joyrider, not a kidnapper, Jimmy had no hesitancy in making a deal with the public defender. "If your client will agree to plead guilty to possession, and promise to enter and complete a program for drug addiction, I'll move to dismiss the charge of possession with intent to sell and recommend probation, to be revoked if he doesn't complete the program." Or the condition might be to pay for the stolen goods, or for repairs to the car, to work with the contractor who was renovating the crack house, to paint over the graffiti—with probation or parole to be revoked and prison to follow if the promise wasn't kept.

Before long, Jimmy had won the confidence of everyone in the courtroom. He played fair. He showed the public defender his file, and, if a deal wasn't reached, he kept his word not to disclose what the public defender had said in the negotiations. The deals Jimmy made were reasonable. His summers on the city playgrounds had given him a good eye for estimating the likelihood of a defendant keeping his promise. The police respected Jimmy. To them he was "Big Jim," who did a lot of coaching for the Police Athletic League. Victims understood that Jimmy wasn't coddling some one who had hurt them but had their interests at heart in a situation that permitted no good solution. Witnesses were grateful for Jimmy's efforts to minimize the inconvenience to them, such as putting them on telephone call. At first doubtful, the judge assigned to Courtroom B came to trust the new assistant district attorney's appraisal of the true gravity of a case. A typical daily list in Courtroom B was thirty-five to forty cases. Before long, the judge was able to report that at the daily call of the list, between ten and twenty cases were disposed of by negotiated pleas. In due course, the district attorney noticed that thanks to the number of cases disposed of in Courtroom B before trial, the backlog of untried cases had fallen. In his annual report, the district attorney observed that as a result of combining vigorous law enforcement with imaginative and sensitive management of the trial calendars, his office had reduced the backlog of untried cases by twenty per cent. He assured the public that he would continue his efforts, and looked forward to further reduction.

And so, Jimmy Green became a fixture in Courtroom B, a cog that kept the wheels of justice grinding up their human debris. As the months wore on, Jimmy's loping stride as he entered court lost its spring, his "Good morning, Your Honor," its ring of conviction that the morning was good, that misery was not beyond relief. Hope finds fragile shelter in the law. Plea agreements that Jimmy had negotiated failed: "defendant did not complete treatment program;" "did not attend vocational training course;" "was dismissed for repeated failure to report for work on time." Programs, jobs, housing were scarce. Once Jimmy almost wept in open court, as he watched the sheriff's deputy lead away, in handcuffs, parole revoked, the former second baseman of one of the teams he'd coached. "I'm sorry, Big Jim. I just couldn't stay away from the stuff." Jimmy felt the hemlock of failure turning him numb. He wasn't a lawyer who could be trusted to try a case. He was an ineffectual social worker, his dreams naive, stupid.

Emily Summers was a librarian in a branch of the Public Library, next to a playground where Jimmy Green coached third and fourth graders from the nearby public school. Some of the children Jimmy coached belonged to Emily's after-school and summer reading clubs. They liked the gentle librarian and begged her to watch them play baseball. She did, and also watched their coach.

Emily's mother worried about Emily. "I do wish she'd wear some lipstick. And do something about her hair, which is really quite nice." (It was light brown. Emily wore it in a page boy cut.) Emily's clothes had no style, in her mother's opinion, and working in a library wasn't any way to meet a nice young man. Emily's mother had a point—Emily had a lot of girl friends, whose weddings she attended, but no man seemed to have noticed her. The boys in Emily's reading club were more perceptive. They saw that she cared about them, wanted them to learn, was sure they could learn. When she read them *Charlotte's Web*, they sensed her tenderness. When she showed them N.C. Wyeth's illustrations of *Treasure Island*, they saw the sparkle in her eyes and knew that she, like them, had a sneaky admiration for Long John Silver. Sitting in a semicircle, looking up at Emily, the members of the reading club felt respected and loved, they glimpsed new worlds, they knew life could be an adventure.

Late one afternoon Jimmy watched as some of Emily's boys tumbled down the library steps and onto the playground, laughing and pulling her along by her hand. Jimmy, who recognized fitness when he saw it, noticed Emily's athlete's figure and how easily she skipped along with the boys. (He wasn't deceived. Emily had recently biked fifty miles to raise money for breast cancer research, and she regularly rowed on the river with three girl friends in a quad.) When, after the baseball game, Emily told the boys how well they'd played—Jimmy had been about to tell them they could do much better—Jimmy reacted as the boys did when she read them stories: he wanted to see her again.

Many years later, sitting on the high point of Squirrel Island's south shore and looking across the strait to Damariscove, Jimmy told Emily that from the moment he met her, the clouds began to lift. "You have been the light of my life." One time in particular, he said, he would always remember. After the sheriff's deputy led away Jimmy's former star second baseman, Jimmy had called Emily at the library. Would she meet him after work at D'Angelo's? There, sitting in their favorite booth, from which they could watch old men playing bocce and skateboarders with their caps on backward jumping the curbs, Jimmy told Emily about the second baseman's parole being revoked. "He's not a bad kid. Now, what little chance he had to make it is gone. He's facing five years. He'll come out tough, hopeless, no skills. End up dead in some alley." The tears he'd held back in court ran down his cheeks. And that hadn't been the only parole revocation, he continued. Within the past month, three other plea agreements hadn't been kept. "I'm just a failure." Emily pushed aside the bread basket and bottle of Chianti, reached across the table, and put her hand on top of Jimmy's. "Jimmy, you are not a failure. No one can do everything. You are the kindest, bravest man I've ever known. No matter what the odds are, you never give up. And you never stop caring." Emily's mother was quite mistaken in thinking Emily plain because of her clothes. She was in fact a vibrant young woman, whose heart was in her eyes, which were as blue as a summer sky and clear as a mountain stream. Emily lifted her chin, looked straight at Jimmy, pressed down his hand. She flushed. "You are gentle, and strong, and good, and I love you."

They were married in front of the fountain in the botanical garden. Counting families and friends, perhaps twenty persons attended. "Mother, we just don't want a big wedding. Of course I love you and Daddy. It's only that we'd feel we were showing off. We'd like it to be quiet and simple, with only those we love most." They found a Father-Son-and-Holy Ghost row house on a cobble stone alley in the old part of the city. Emily had a direct subway line to her branch library, Jimmy could walk to City Hall. At Emily's suggestion and with her help, Jimmy reorganized his plea agreement program. He started keeping records, to learn which treatment programs and courses got the best results; he visited the programs and courses to see for himself how they were conducted; and he monitored the performance of the defendants who had promised to participate. He formed an advisory council of volunteers, who helped find new programs. He persuaded the probation department to assign a counselor to Courtroom B, and the dean of the university's school of social work to assign interns to work with him and the public defender in negotiating plea agreements. Emily taught him to write grant applications, and in response to one of these a local charitable foundation agreed to support a joint program by the district attorney and public library to provide literacy and computer courses to selected defendants.

Failures continued, of course, but Jimmy knew, he could prove, that the Courtroom B plea agreements made a difference. The district attorney's annual report came to include a separate section describing the "model program," with photographs and brief accounts of defendants who had broken an addiction, gotten a job, were supporting themselves and their children. The foundation renewed its support, and renewed again. After awhile, the American Bar Association's Section on Criminal Law learned of the program. The district attorney was invited to the Bar Association's mid-year meeting in Atlanta to receive a special award. Not entirely blinded by ambition, he took Jimmy along and introduced him as the "architect of the program." Jimmy received a nicely printed citation, which Emily had framed and hung in their bedroom.

Although they tried, Jimmy and Emily had no children—except that Emily expanded her reading club to include the fifth grade, and Jimmy continued to coach and umpire baseball and basketball. Two gentle persons, living gentle lives.

*   *   *

"I understand you're in line for one of those new judgeships, Jimmy," said Michael Green, at Sunday dinner. His understanding had a solid foundation. After some years of nagging by the bar association, the district attorney, the public defender, the chamber of commerce, and the media, the legislature had created positions for three additional trial judges in the city. In response to Michael Green's inquiries—delicately stated but unambiguous—the district attorney, the chairman of the Democratic Party City Committee, and counsel to the governor had each expressed his fervent support of Jimmy's nomination to one of the positions. "Oh, I don't think so, Father. I"m sure persons more experienced than I am will be appointed." "Well, we'll see. Don't sell yourself short. The work you've done rehabilitating minor offenders has gotten a lot of favorable attention."

Jimmy's nomination to be a trial judge caught the bar by surprise. Despite some jaundiced comment in City Hall corridors, however ("In this town, money counts." "So what else is new?"), the nomination was generally well received. Two highly regarded trial lawyers were nominated to the two other new positions, and this combination of experience with Jimmy's comparative youth and record of social service was said to "strike a good balance."

The accomplished trial judge rules by courteous terror, which is invisible to everyone except counsel. Before the trial starts, the judge invites counsel into chambers. There counsel are told "how we try cases in this court." Counsel will address only the court, never each other. Counsel will state the ground for an objection, without any argument. If the court wishes to hear argument before it rules on the objection, the court will say so. There will, of course, be no leading questions on a material issue. If any question suggests that something may have happened, or that some one said or will say something, there had better be evidence offered later that supports the suggestion. If, during the trial, counsel violates one of these rules, the jury is invited "to stretch your legs a bit while counsel and I have a brief discussion." In the ensuing recess, offending counsel is asked to explain the violation, to state for the record any objection to the cautionary instruction the court proposes to give the jury upon its return, and, on occasion, to explain why the court should not hold counsel in contempt and impose an appropriate sanction. In most cases, from there on the trial clicks along very smoothly, a light clearing of the judicial throat or a lift of the eyebrow being sufficient to keep counsel within their allotted bounds. In the rare case where counsel, either careless or reckless, exceeds those bounds, retribution is swift and merciless. Counsel had better settle, or notify his malpractice carrier. Juries vote for the lawyer they trust as much as they vote on the evidence. A lawyer excoriated by the judge enjoys little trust.

Judge Green's courtroom did not operate along these lines. The judge lacked the necessary confidence to rule without hearing argument. When he heard argument, he wavered, equivocated, sometimes changed his mind, which resulted in having to tell the jury it should forget evidence it had heard (don't think about a purple elephant). Counsel crossed every line, confident they could talk their way out of any rebuke or sanction ("My opponent opened the door, Your Honor;" "I certainly did not mean to suggest . . . ."; "As I understood Your Honor's ruling, I was permitted to . . . .") "It's a zoo in there," one veteran lawyer was heard to remark in the corridor. A senior lawyer was heard advising a junior not to bother with any more objections. "There's so much error on this record already we can win an appeal five different ways."

Roger Littleton, senior partner and senior litigator of Littleton Jones, LL.P, saw something others missed. Speaking at the firm's litigation department's monthly luncheon, he said: "Judge Green either doesn't understand, or he doesn't like, the adversarial system. He thinks the trial judge should actively seek a fair result. He constantly interrupts counsel to question a witness. The other day I heard him ask counsel, in open court, whether a person named by a witness would be called. Counsel, who was Bill Brantly of the Auerbach office, lost his cool and replied that the court was interfering with counsel's presentation of his client's case. Well! Judge Green apologized profusely—he really seemed to mean it—and then he said something like, 'I was only trying to find out what happened, Mr. Brantly. After all, in the end the jury will have to decide where the truth lies.' I don't know how the case came out, but Brantly's blood was certainly all over the floor. My advice is this: If you're assigned to Judge Green's courtroom, give up any idea that you're going to be able to try your case as you had planned. Try to preempt any trial at all by asking the judge to discuss with you and opposing counsel the possibility of settlement. If the judge agrees, put all your cards on the table, and make, not your lowest and not your best, but a good faith, obviously reasonable offer. Of course, you need your client's permission first, but I suggest you really twist the client's arm to get it. Because once the trial starts, about all you can be sure of is that whatever the result, it will end up on appeal—and predicting how appeals will come out is not the best way to serve our clients."

A few weeks later, Roger Littleton followed his own advice. His client was a large pharmaceutical company (the juiciest of juicy targets, in the eyes of plaintiffs' counsel). The claim was that one of its products, Dylox, had caused cancer in some six or seven thousand persons, all of them plaintiffs as members of a class. At a pretrial conference, Littleton summarized the expected expert testimony for both sides—so impartially that plaintiffs' counsel, when asked by Littleton whether he accepted the summary as fair, replied, suppressing his surprise, that he did. Littleton then gave the judge (and, of course, plaintiffs' counsel) a list of five names, each of an undeniably distinguished expert, and said that if the judge appointed one, more, or all of these experts, defendant, Littleton's client, would agree to accept their opinion on whether its product had caused plaintiffs' cancers. If they said it had, the trial would then be limited to deciding plaintiffs' damages.

Judge Green was enchanted. "What could be fairer than that, Mr. Picone?" he asked plaintiffs' counsel, quite forgetting that plaintiffs' counsel was not concerned with fairness but with how the jury would decide—and he was sure the jury would decide to accept his experts' opinion, not the opinion of the trained seals, as counsel planned to describe them, hired by the billion-dollar-in-assets pharmaceutical company. Roger Littleton agreed with this appraisal. He was equally sure that Judge Green would not understand, or at least would shrink from, his duty to decide preliminarily for himself whether an expert's proposed testimony was scientifically acceptable, and if it wasn't, to rule that the jury wouldn't be permitted to consider it. He expected that in the end Judge Green would say something like: "Well, Mr. Littleton, I do see your point that the Supreme Court does seem to have said that before permitting an expert to testify I must decide whether the expert's opinion is scientifically acceptable. But I'm certainly no scientist. I never even studied biology or statistics when I was at school. I know you think plaintiffs' experts are charlatans—I think that was your word—and perhaps the jury will agree with you. In any case, I've decided to let the jury decide which experts' opinion to accept. If they accept plaintiffs', you may of course move for a new trial or judgment notwithstanding the verdict, and then I can consider the issue again." It was the prospect—the virtual certainty, as he saw it—of such a ruling that Roger Littleton had invoked when he had persuaded his client to authorize him to make his pre-trial offer. "The jury will return a verdict of millions—with an additional award of punitive damages of hundreds of millions. Green won't disturb it. Maybe, on appeal, the Supreme Court will give you a new trial. But maybe not. At least three judges on that court never saw a plaintiff's claim they didn't like. I'm sure the impartial experts will come out our way. Plaintiffs' experts really are a couple of charlatans. And whatever else you can say about him, Green never hides his opinion of what is fair. I'm sure he'll tell the jury that on my motion he appointed the impartial experts and that unlike the other experts, they have no possible interest in the case. I think the jury will follow the impartials. More to the point, Al Picone will think so, too. I know Picone well. He's probably the best plaintiff's lawyer in the city today, and he didn't get rich by being greedy. If the impartial's report is that Dylox had nothing to do with plaintiffs' cancers, we'll be able to settle, for not too much." And so it turned out.

"The Littleton gambit," as the trial bar came to call it, became Judge Green's favorite opening. Shortly after the Dylox case settled, the judge issued an order that before being scheduled for trial, every case on his list would be reviewed at a pre-trial conference. Many of these conferences proved to be protracted affairs. The rules of evidence were foreign to them. The judge wanted to discuss everything—not only the expected testimony and the expert witnesses' reports, but hearsay, speculation, why the parties hated each other. "Like a god damned beagle after a rabbit," one veteran grumbled. (The image came naturally. He lived in a suburb where, after a hunt breakfast and mint julep, they still rode to the hounds or climbed over walls and through brambles after a pack of baying beagles.) Slowly, however, a wary bar came to trust Judge Green. He never violated or exploited anything counsel disclosed ex parte in confidence—for example, that counsel was afraid his client might refuse to testify because she had recently been diagnosed as having cancer and was depressed. He proved to have an accurate eye for the value of a case. He was also inventive in suggesting solutions that a trial couldn't produce, for example, in a will contest, declaring the testator competent, with the family agreeing to a distribution to the disinherited son.

Jimmy Green and Emily Summers didn't watch TV much. Emily read, everything, especially biographies and books her childrens' summer reading club might like. Jimmy watched baseball, and sometimes football. One program they regularly watched, though, was "Rumpole of Old Bailey." They delighted in the grouchy old barrister's puncturing Queen's counsel's silky arguments while fending off the haughty judge who had apparently drunk vinegar at lunch. One evening, after watching Rumpole triumph yet again, Jimmy turned to Emily. "You know," he said, "sometimes I wish I was a judge." "What do you mean by that? You *are* a judge." "Not really, my love. I haven't tried a case for three years—three and a half. What I am is a glorified mediator. I'm a good mediator—pretty good anyway. A mediator, though, isn't a judge. A mediator persuades. A judge enforces the law."

"Are you saying that force is better than persuasion, that you'd rather be an enforcer than a persuader?" Jimmy was startled by Emily's statement of the issue. What *was* he saying? he wondered to himself. Had Emily identified the reason his old sense of failure had seeped back, like dirty rainwater flooding the cellar? He'd felt it lapping around him before, when he was re-assigned to Courtroom B; but then, he met Emily, she helped him organize and strengthen his plea negotiation program, and the dirty water receded. Now it was back. His list of undisposed of cases was growing longer, settlement conferences seemed endless, counsel postured, maneuvered, dissembled, solemnly insisted they'd made their best offer, only to make a better one the next day. They were respectful, but not really. Really they were mocking, covertly defiant. No one was afraid of what he might do if counsel persisted in refusing to make a good faith effort to settle. No one thought he drank vinegar. Not that all counsel were crafty and obdurate, and even those who were usually ended up settling when, after playing their game, they acknowledged to themselves the expense and uncertain result of going to trial— especially before Judge Green and his unpredictable rulings. Even so, Jimmy Green was no fool. He knew counsel were playing him like a fish. Oh, they liked him, but they rather pitied him. A well-meaning, enthusiastic kid among the pros. The easy mark at the regular Saturday night poker game. He also knew what he should do. Order all discovery completed in two weeks. Exclude the expert's testimony for failure to disclose his report timely. Enter judgment imposing liability for failure to submit to depositions and list the case for trial on damages only. "Your objection is noted. Perhaps the Supreme Court will share your view that I've committed error. Meanwhile, we will proceed." But he didn't have the heart. Or the steel in his spine. Apparently, to be a good, or anyway, an effective trial judge, a judge who was respected, you had to be a son of a bitch.

He returned to Emily's question. "I'm not saying that force is better than persuasion. But let's face it, the law depends on force, not persuasion. Do you know what Oliver Wendell Holmes said the law was? It's power. It's what a bad man thinks the court will do to him if he does what he's thinking about."

"Is that what you think, sweetheart? That the law is power? Power to do what? Anything the law says you can do? I've been reading about slavery. One of the children in my reading club told me his great grandmother was a slave who escaped by the underground railway. That started my reading. I have learned there are houses in this city that were on the underground railway. I'm going to take my children to visit some of those houses. If I can persuade a foundation to give me traveling money, we'll visit Cambridge, Maryland, where Harriet Tubman escaped. Now, then, let me ask you this. You're the judge."

Jimmy noticed that Emily's cheeks had flushed. She hadn't raised her voice, but there was a definite tremor in it.

"The underground railway was illegal. Under the law, the owner of an escaped slave could follow the slave and take her back, or him, by force, back to slavery. And that meant, back to an elaborate system which had been set up by lawyers and was enforced by judges. Did you know that in 1723 a statute in Virginia provided that if the testimony of a slave was shown to be false, the court was to order one of the slave's ears nailed to the pillory for an hour, then the ear was to be cut off and the other ear nailed for an hour and cut off, and then the slave was to be sent to the whipping post and given thirty-nine lashes on his or her bare back? Did you know that?"

Emily continued, a little breathlessly. "By the time we fought the Revolution, because, we said, all men were equal, slavery was illegal in England. According to Blackstone, every person was formed by God. Not in Virginia. Under Virginia law, slaves weren't persons. They were property, things, no different than furniture and animals. And they could never escape. The children of a slave were like the offspring of an animal—the property of the owner. Now, then, I ask you, how can I explain this to my children? Don't I have to tell them the law was wrong? That the lawyers who wrote the statutes making slavery legal, and the judges who enforced those statutes, were wrong? That the slaves who escaped were brave and the people who hid them in their cellars and secret rooms were heroes? What would your Oliver Wendell Holmes have said? That the law is power? Power said slavery was legal. So, Judge Green, do you enforce the law?"

Judge Green sat before the darkened television screen, stunned. He remembered when, at law school, after studying the majority and dissenting opinions in *People v. Zackowitz,* he'd looked out of his apartment window over the silent moonlit city. He remembered the despair he'd felt as he contemplated the law as a tangle of rules to be manipulated by the clever, the ambitious, the unscrupulous, how he'd seemed to be standing on the edge of an abyss. And now, Emily's question had pushed him over the edge. Cardozo had untangled the rules of evidence, to expose the deceit underlying the district attorney's argument. Having untangled the rules, Cardozo then enforced them. But Emily's question went deeper. Assume the rules *were* untangled. What Emily was asking was, "Why *should* a judge enforce them? Just because they *are* rules?"

It seemed to Jimmy that Emily had taken his words out of context. When he said the law depended on power, he certainly didn't mean to say that the law depended on judges always enforcing its rules, even if those rules required cutting off someone's ears. What, then, did he mean to say? Cardozo surely hadn't enforced the rule against evidence of other crimes only because it was a rule—a command a judge must obey. He enforced it to protect the presumption of innocence, to ensure that Zackowitz would get a fair trial, to achieve justice, in other words. Did that mean that Cardozo was somehow above, or beyond, the rules? In a way, yes, Jimmy thought. Rules don't just float above us, like the moon over the city, like some sort of god. Rules are passed to accomplish a particular end. The rules of evidence were passed to ensure a fair trial. What Cardozo did was to decide what sort of trial would be fair, and then define the rules to provide that sort of trial—which didn't explain where he got his idea of fairness, or why the dissenters' idea was different.

Emily was stricken by Jimmy's prolonged silence, and by the stunned expression on his face. She had never attacked him before, and hadn't meant to now. "Come," she said, and pulled him onto the sofa, to sit next to her. "I only meant that I think persuading people is better than forcing them to do something. I think a judge who persuades people to settle their differences is a better judge than one who enforces the law." Jimmy put his arms around Emily and squeezed her against him. "I don't know how to answer your questions. I don't think the law can depend on persuasion. Some people can't be persuaded. And some people have to be punished. Murderers, rapists, for instance. A judge's duty is to enforce the law. I hope you don't think I would have ordered the slave's ears cut off. But darling, where does a judge draw the line? George Washington and Thomas Jefferson didn't find anything wrong with the law that slaves were property. I'm not so sure I would have either."

With this, Emily put her head on Jimmy's chest and burst into sobs. After awhile, the sobs subsided, she pushed herself away and wiped her eyes. "My darling husband, please forgive me. I never thought you'd order the slave's ears cut off, and I never meant to suggest you might. I remember your father once said, 'Don't sell yourself short, Jimmy.' And he was right. You mustn't think that some how you're a failure because you can't persuade some lawyers to make a reasonable settlement. They're the failures, not you. And you mustn't think that somehow you're stupid because you can't say just what you would have done if you'd been a judge in a slave state. I guess I spoke the way I did because reading about slavery made me realize the terrible things that have been done in the name of the law. And are still being done. Given a choice, I'd choose kindness before I'd choose the law. But that's easy for me to say. I'm not a judge sworn to enforce the law. You must trust yourself, darling. No matter what situation you find yourself in, you will never do terrible things. You won't abuse your power in any way. You wouldn't know how. Do you remember the first time I said I loved you? I said you were the kindest, bravest man I knew. Well, you still are, and I love you now more than ever."

*   *   *

Having decided, after ten years of careful spadework, to run for governor, the district attorney asked Michael Green to be the chair of his campaign finance committee. "I need your support. I don't want to announce my candidacy unless I have it." Michael Green said he'd be delighted to serve. His committee raised some twenty-five million dollars, which paid for every bell and whistle any candidate could want, including an unstaunchable flood of TV spots effectively depicting the district attorney's opponent as at once inexperienced and the long-time spokesman for big businesses that had their headquarters out of state. The district attorney carried every county except three, where he hadn't bothered to campaign because "there are more bears there than people." Victory was particularly sweet because it was a presidential election year. The district attorney's coat tails swept in the electoral votes that gave his party the presidency. Michael Green had a lot of chips.

"The Governor tells me he's going to appoint you to the vacancy caused by Judge Magruder's resignation." "But Father, I don't want to be on the Supreme Court. My settlement program is really rolling. I've finally learned how to knock some heads together. Judges on the Supreme Court sit in chambers all day and read briefs and records. They never even see the lawyers except at oral arguments. They can't work anything out. All they can do is vote to affirm or reverse."

Michael Green pushed the cribbage board to one side, picked up his brandy snifter, leaned back in his leather chair, and studied his son, who was sitting across the game table in a matching leather chair. Behind his son a sofa faced a fire place in which some well-seasoned birch logs were burning in the even, steady way birch logs do. On either side of the fire place a french door opened out onto a terrace. All around the room were shelves of books, from floor to ceiling. Michael Green didn't pretend to be an intellectual. He was as he seemed, a gregarious, hard-bitten, hard-living, hard-driving man. As he had no pretensions, neither did he have any interest in appearances. There were no matched sets with uncut pages on his shelves. These books had been read, and their titles reflected back their owner. Biographies, mostly of political and military leaders. Franklin D. Roosevelt and Eleanor, Theodore Roosevelt, Truman, Lyndon Johnson, Benjamin Franklin, John Adams, MacArthur, Patton, Sherman, Jeb Stuart among them. History, mostly Europe and England (all of Winston Churchill's and Barbara Tuchman's books), a separate shelf on Ireland and Irish immigration to America, the American Revolution, the opening of the west, three shelves on the Civil War. Several atlases, a globe on a wheeled stand, books on trout fishing, and, on the coffee table in front of the fireplace, a book of colored photographs of castles and country houses in Scotland and Ireland (he was negotiating to buy one of the houses). Michael Green sipped his brandy, rolled it on his tongue, swallowed. "There's something I don't understand, Jimmy. I'm a pretty good cribbage player, but most of the time, you clobber me. Like now." He gestured at the board. "When you pitched ball, you were a killer. No one wanted to win more than you did. Last summer, for the I don't know how many times in a row, your team won the city title for juniors. Why don't you want to be on the Supreme Court? Isn't that the top of the tree? Don't you want to win?"

Jimmy Green sat quiet for a long time. "Well, Father, when you put it that way, maybe I don't. I do like winning games. But law isn't a game, or at least I don't think it should be. When you play a game, you know the rules. My kids won the title because, within the rules, they were the better players. They threw more strikes and made more double plays. That's not the way it works in the law. Oh, it does sometimes, of course. But in the big cases, the ones where there's a lot at stake, which usually means a lot of money, the lawyers try to change the rules. If a rule says they can't use certain evidence, they find a rule, or make one up, that says they can."

"That sure as hell is what I'd want my lawyer to do. Anyway, isn't it the judge's job to decide what the rules are?"

"Yes, Father, it is. And I'm not very good at it. I am good at bringing people together, pointing out to each side where a case is weak and where it's strong, and suggesting a fair settlement. And as I said, I've gotten pretty good at knocking heads together to get to a fair settlement. There are a lot of different ways a judge can get across to a pigheaded lawyer or litigant that if he doesn't see things the judge's way, maybe the trial won't go so well. But when it comes to deciding what the rules are, that's a different game. When I was at law school, one of our teachers told us to pay particular attention to the opinions of Benjamin Cardozo. He was a judge on the New York Court of Appeals, which is New York's Supreme Court. Anyway, Cardozo was a master at defining the rules. I'm no Cardozo. Never will be. In baseball terms, he's Hall of Fame, I'm a minor leaguer."

Michael Green got up, slowly, a bit heavily, walked across his library to the coffee table in front of the fire place, and opened the humidor on the table. He selected a cigar, smelled it appreciatively, lit it with a chrome-plated lighter, returned to his chair, and blew out a puff of smoke. "I just read a story about an old Irish revolutionary whose son wouldn't help him. I guess I'm not the first father not to understand his son. And won't be the last. Probably I shouldn't have pushed you to go to law school. Would I be right, Jimmy, that you don't much like the law?"

"About law school, Father: forget it. I know you love me and were only trying to help. If I didn't want to go to law school, I could have said no. About the law: I like it some of the time. I like it when I can work something out because I'm a judge. Mostly, people in court are desperate or frightened or angry. Lots of times I've been able to make their lives a little better, a little happier. I like that. What I don't like about the law is, often it's cruel, or greedy. The bullies win."

"Hell's bells, Jimmy! Nothing works all the time. Look how that fathead got himself elected Senator. And Reagan was elected twice! Seems to me the law works pretty well most of the time. Anyway, can't a Supreme Court judge make it work better?"

"Maybe. My problem is this, Father. I want to help as many people as I can. I'd like to make half as much difference as Emily makes in the lives of 'her children,' as she calls them. I'm just not sure the Supreme Court is where I can do that."

"Jimmy, I'll say my piece and then I'll be done. You're right. I do love you. And I love Emily. And I admire what you both do. But you and Emily and I don't see the world the same way, or maybe I should say, we don't want the same things. I don't think the peacemakers of the world win. I think the ones who win are the ones who make the rules. And Jimmy, I like to win. Now, if you don't want to be on the Supreme Court, you'll have to tell the governor. Before you do, though, you should talk to your mother. She's excited about your appointment. She told me she thought it was wonderful news but that she wouldn't congratulate you until it had happened. Well, it's getting late. I don't really want to finish this cribbage game. Do you?"

Jimmy did not talk to the governor. A week later, the governor nominated him to fill the vacancy on the Supreme Court. The nomination was approved by voice vote. After three years on the court, he was elected by the other judges to be Chief Judge, not because of their regard for him but because they so disliked each other they couldn't agree on any one else.

* * *

The longer Chief Judge Green thought about how to answer Sally Link's letter, the more he doubted that he was entitled to advise her on whether she should become a lawyer. He didn't deserve any of the positions he'd held. He felt as though he'd won a game where the umpire had been bribed. He would never have been appointed an assistant district attorney, or a trial judge, or to the Supreme Court except for his father's political clout. He was proud of some of the things he'd done along the way, but he knew they weren't why he had climbed so high. He had to abandon his settlement program—his effort to be a peacemaker, as his father had put it—when he accepted appointment to the Supreme Court, and he didn't feel he had accomplished anything worthwhile as a Supreme Court judge. He knew the bar and the law schools regarded the court as mediocre, at best, and he hadn't done anything to change that perception.

Judge Green's sense that he was not entitled to advise his recent law clerk arose, however, from a source much deeper than his estimation of himself as some one who owed his career not to his own efforts but to his father's political influence.

Three days before the judge and his wife, Emily, were scheduled to go to Maine for a long Memorial Day weekend, with the judge's departing law clerk, Sally Link, as their guest, the judge's secretary gently tapped his inner chambers door. "Yes, Mrs. B?" "There's a Mr. Albert Johnson to see you. He says he knows he doesn't have an appointment but that it's urgent." "Show him in."

Judge Green knew Albert Johnson as the Executive Director of the Commission on Judicial Discipline. Decisions of the Commission were appealable to the Supreme Court, and on three or four occasions Johnson had appeared before the court to argue an appeal as counsel for the commission—a workmanlike, unimaginative public servant, with an edge of prosecutorial zeal. The last case he had argued before the court had attracted considerable attention. The commission had ordered a trial judge suspended for six months without pay because the judge, who was married, had had an open affair with another man's wife. In his argument Johnson cited the judicial canons that a judge's conduct must never undermine but should preserve and promote public confidence in the integrity of the judiciary. According to Johnson, and the commission, the public, especially in cases involving divorce and child custody, could have no confidence in the integrity of a judge who had shown no respect either for his own or another man's marriage. By a four to three vote, the Supreme Court reversed the commission and ordered the judge reinstated. Chief Judge Green had written the dissenting opinion, but the majority had scornfully rejected his arguments, which were the commission's, too, as holier-than-thou. The law making adultery a crime, the majority said, had long ago been repealed. No doubt some members of the public wouldn't trust an adulterer, but others would be more understanding. Certainly, the majority said, it would not forget the injunction on how to live in glass houses. The commission, the majority concluded, had to prove that the judge's affair had affected his decision in a specific case, and it hadn't done that. There was some rude speculation in the media about the possible significance of the majority's reference to glass houses, but the commission's petition for reconsideration had been summarily dismissed.

"Good morning, Al, what can I do for you?" Judge Green stood up behind his desk and by a gesture invited Johnson to sit down.

"Good morning, Your Honor." Albert Johnson sat down, without taking off his coat, his hat on his lap. "I'll only stay a minute." He was a picture of discomfort, back stiff, hands clenched, lips tight. "First, Your Honor, it's my duty to advise you of your right to be silent. I must say, Your Honor, this is a most painful occasion, but I don't see any way to avoid it. The commission has received information that you have never passed the bar examination. According to our informant, after you failed the examination two times, you paid him $5,000 to take it for you, which he did. The date he says he took the examination corresponds with the date in the notice you were sent by the State Board of Law Examiners advising you that you had passed the bar examination. As you know, ordinarily the commission initiates proceedings by filing a written complaint. In this case, because of the extraordinary nature of the complaint, and because of my personal regard for you, and out of respect for your office, I decided that I would notify you informally of the information we have received. Again, Your Honor, may I urge you not to say anything but to consult your personal counsel. If your counsel will call me, he and I can decide how to proceed. I hope he will call me promptly. You may tell him that no formal complaint will be filed before twenty days from today. Again, Your Honor, may I say how painful this has been. Good morning, Your Honor." Johnson stood up and almost bolted out.

It was just as well that the judge's secretary did not enter the judge's chambers as Johnson left them. She would have cried out, "Judge! Are you all right?" The judge's usual ruddy cheeks were as gray as his hair, his usual sparkling, somewhat quizzical blue eyes were glassy, like a blind man's. And indeed the judge would not have seen her. He was back in a bar, twenty five years ago.

Jimmy Green had just left the last session of the cram course for the bar examination. It was late in the afternoon of a miserable February day, raw and drizzly. If the temperature dropped, as was predicted, the sidewalks and streets would become a sheet of ice. People would slip and break their legs, automobiles would bang into each other Hunched under his jacket's hood, Jimmy hurried along towards his apartment. On the way he came to Duffy's Bar and Grill. He went in, partly to get warm, partly with the vague idea of getting something to eat, but mostly for the same reason other lonely, unhappy men go into a bar—to escape the world for a little while. He ordered a beer and whiskey chaser.

"Jimmy Green! What are you doing here? I haven't seen you for, what, two, three, years? How's everything?" Jimmy looked up from his beer and chaser to the man who had climbed onto the bar stool next to his. Genik Kwiecinski. Kwiecinski had been in law school two years ahead of Jimmy. They had gotten to know each other in the trial practice course, where Kwiecinski had been a star—the star, really. A handsome man, dark hair, dark eyes, the build of a linebacker, which he'd been, with an assured, swash buckling manner, he had shown a precocious ability in cross-examination. After graduating from law school, Kwiecinski became an associate of Robert Carroll, who, until he hired Kwiecinski, had been a sole practitioner and was widely regarded as the dean of the criminal bar. Two years later Carroll had a stroke and Kwiecinski, with Carroll's tutelage, took over Carroll's practice. He was an instant success, in his first trial getting a hung jury in a case described by the district attorney as a slam dunk, and in the second persuading the jury to acquit a defendant who was charged with extortion and was reputed to be the most powerful mob boss in the state—the boss of bosses.

"Not all that great, to tell the truth, Genik. I've got to take the bar exam this weekend. Ducked in here to build up my confidence."

"How come you didn't take it in July, after you graduated?"

"I did. Flunked. Took it again in October. Flunked again. If I flunk this time, I'm done. Three strikes and you're out."

Genik Kwiecinski's dark olive eyes narrowed. Perhaps, he thought, he saw an opportunity. Genik Kwiecinski was in physical danger—not death, he didn't think, although he wasn't sure and was deeply frightened. But the opportunity he thought he saw to avoid that danger might put him in prison. It was necessary to proceed very cautiously.

Kwiecinski's sudden ascent to the status of celebrated criminal lawyer had gone to his head. A week before he met Jimmy Green at Duffy's Bar and Grill, he had used a five thousand dollar retainer to make the down payment on a nifty red Jaguar convertible, which made quite an impression on his current girl friend. Then he had a nasty quarrel with the client who had paid him the retainer. The client, offended by Kwiecinski's perhaps too bluntly expressed appraisal, "If you testify, you'll really fuck yourself;" had fired Kwiecinski on the spot, and had demanded the immediate return of the retainer. Kwiecinski protested that a lawyer was under no obligation to return a retainer when the only reason he was fired was because the client rejected his advice. The client—former client, rather—replied that he wasn't interested in smart talk, he wanted his money back, now. When Kwiecinski said that he couldn't pay it back just then, he had invested it, he was informed that he had better have it by the end of the week. "You know what happens to wise guys who get out of line." Kwiecinski did know. He had been retained to defend his former client on a charge of ordering the murder of a man discovered to be an informer.

"Jim, how about joining me in the corner booth over there. I have an idea you might be interested in. Come on, drink up." Kwiecinski turned to the bartender. "We're going to that booth over there. Bring my friend another of the same. My tab." Once in the booth, Kwiecinski probed for the roots of Jimmy Green's melancholy, allowing time for the whiskey chasers to have their effect. "We'll each have another, thanks." He learned that Jimmy had hated law school and just scraped through; that the only reason he'd gone to law school was his father's insistence; that the old man couldn't understand how in hell he'd flunked the bar twice; and that if he flunked again—as he was sure he would—he simply didn't think he could face his father. He supposed he would . . . .

Well, he didn't know what he would do. Go live somewhere else, he guessed. Maybe abroad. There must be something he could do somewhere.

"Jim, some people just aren't any good taking tests. They know the stuff all right but they tighten up. In my opinion, the bar exam is very unfair. In real life you don't make multiple choice decisions. But that's the way the exam is set up. I myself found it easy. I thought law school was easy. It was just a game. I never could take it seriously. I quit the law review. Too stuffy. Not enough action. Anyway, with multiple choice questions all you do is narrow the five choices down to two, and then you make your best guess. I got a ninety three on the bar exam when I took it. Now, here's my idea. How about if I take the exam for you? I'm sure I'll pass."

Jimmy straightened up from his slump. "Well, I mean . . . ." His words were a little blurred. "I don't see how that would work. I mean, I appreciate your generosity. But that would be cheating, and I've never cheated before. And anyway, you'd be sure to be caught and then we'd both be in trouble. Big trouble."

"Well, it's your call. I don't think I'd be caught, though. Do you have your I.D. sticker from the Board of Law Examiners?" Jimmy nodded. "When I took the exam, all they wanted to see was my I.D. sticker. I just handed it over, they checked off my name, and in I went. No photograph, driver's license, nothing. I'd just hand over your sticker as though I were you. No one would know I wasn't. Anyway, Jim, I'd get there a little early. If I saw that they were requiring further identification, I just wouldn't go through with it. Trust me, I'm not going to forge your name or do anything like that. So far as they would know, you just didn't show up. Not showing up is a lot different from flunking. You could tell them you'd gotten sick, or had an accident, or something. I'm sure they'd let you take the exam again. You might have to pay a fine, or something, but I doubt it. So what's to lose?"

"You'd be really, really careful?"

"You can count on it. But Jim, let me put all the cards on the table. That's the only way I like to do business, especially with a friend. I *would* be taking some risk, and in fairness, I think I should be compensated for that."

"Compensation? What does that mean?"

"Well, Jim, I think about $5,000 would be fair. Of course, if I don't take the exam, I'll give it back. And if I don't pass, though that's not very likely, I'll give it back. And if I do pass, you'll get your license to practice law, which is certainly worth a lot more than $5,000."

"Still seems like I'd be cheating."

"I can understand why you say that, Jim, and I respect your feelings. In fact, I was sure that you being who you are, you'd feel that way, which is why I hesitated to suggest that I take the exam. But I look at it a little differently. You're in a jam, and I think that's not fair. You worked hard and got through law school. A stupid multi-choice exam shouldn't keep you from being a lawyer. Besides, Jim, no one will ever know. Certainly you're not going to tell anyone. And you can be sure I never will. Why should I ever say I took the exam for you? How dumb could I get? Lose my license, go to jail, for $5,000? Tell you what. I know you're under a lot of pressure. Why don't you meet me here same time tomorrow? If you decide to let me take the exam, be sure to have your I.D. and $5,000, in cash, Jim, twenties and fifties. If on the other hand you've decided to take the exam yourself, well, that's okay. Just tell me, I'll wish you luck and say good-bye. I can go either way. I'd like to help, but as I said, it's your call. I need to know soon, though. Today's Tuesday. The exam is Saturday, and if I'm going to take, it, I'll have to clear my calendar. So. See you here, same time tomorrow."

Jimmy got the money, on his credit card, and gave it to Kwiecinski the next day, with his I.D. Four weeks later he received a letter from the State Board of Law Examiners congratulating him on having passed the bar examination. Two weeks after that he was sworn in as an assistant district attorney. Meanwhile, Genik Kwiecinski returned the $5,000 retainer. His former client did testify and was sent to prison for thirty years. The judgment of court watchers was that if he'd kept his mouth shut he would have walked. Kwiecinski's practice flourished. The court house parking attendant always saved a place for the red Jaguar.

After Albert Johnson bolted from chambers, Chief Judge Green sat motionless behind his broad, polished desk, paralyzed by bitterness, shame, sorrow, and dread. Why had Kwiecinski reported him now, after so many years? What a coward he had been! He knew Kwiecinski's proposition was wrong. Suppose he *had* flunked the exam. What could Father really have done about it? "Anyway, thank God he and Mother aren't still alive. But Emily is. It's always the good and innocent who are hurt the most. I just don't see how I can tell Emily. She's always been so proud of me. She'll be shattered. I can't do that to her. It might be better if . . . ." Sensing that his thoughts were veering out of control and into a darkness he'd never explored, the judge forced himself to stand up, to walk to the window, to look down at the teeming, colorful life below, the white and red buses, the yellow taxis, the jostling automobiles, the dawdling, hurrying, straggling pedestrians. Then he called Roger Littleton. Alerted by the strain in the judge's voice, Littleton said he'd come at once, and within fifteen minutes Mrs. B announced, "Mr. Littleton is here to see you, Judge."

Roger Littleton looked like someone in a Masterpiece Theater production. "Imperially slim," he wore a dark three-piece suit, a gold watch chain across his vest. He wasn't wearing spats but if he had been, they wouldn't have looked out of place. Thin gray hair, carefully brushed, a rather gaunt, deeply lined face, and bushy white eyebrows, beneath which smoldered eyes dark brown or black, depending on the light. Steel rimmed half-glasses on a black ribbon. Roger Littleton was seventy-five years old. Some fifty years ago, with a classmate, he had founded the firm of Littleton Jones, which had become one of the ten largest in the country, with offices from coast to coast, in most of the capitals of Europe, and in Tokyo and Hong Kong. His partners had long ago voted to waive the firm's rule of mandatory retirement at sixty-five. "The old man" (an appellation never used to his face) was too valuable. Major clients, many of whom he had brought to the firm, regularly asked, "Have you run this by Mr. Littleton?" It was understood that he would argue any case before the United States Supreme Court, where the Chief Justice greeted him with a cordial, "Good morning, Mr. Littleton. It's good to see you again." He regularly surprised his partners with his audacity and self-confidence. On appeal, he would waive every issue except the one or two he considered most persuasive; and no one else in the firm would have dared to "bet the entire case, for God's sake" on the opinion of a panel of impartial experts, as Littleton had done before Judge Green. Clients regarded him with awe. More than one general counsel had been overruled by the C.E.O., with a remark to the effect that "we didn't hire Mr. Littleton just to tell us the law but to advise us on what he thought we should do." While Judge Green knew almost nothing in detail about Roger Littleton, he believed he knew the measure of the man. He had never forgotten Littleton's appearance before him when he was the trial judge in the Dylox case. Littleton had also often argued before the Supreme Court. In one case, in five minutes, he had explained to the court why the law ineluctably led to a result that both supported his client and was as fair as possible. Once, sailing in Maine, Judge Green had capsized. As he sank into the icy water and the world turned black he had wondered whether he would see the light again. That was how he felt as Roger Littleton entered chambers. He didn't want to know the law. He wanted advice on what he should do.

"Good morning, Judge."

"Good morning, Roger. I appreciate your coming over so promptly."

"Not at all."

Judge Green told Littleton what Albert Johnson had said, and described in detail what had happened between him and Genik Kwiecinski at Duffy's Bar and Grill. "So, there you have it, Roger. Emily and I were planning to go to Maine for the Memorial Day weekend. We were taking my law clerk with us. We thought we might stay for an extra week. But of course I'll have to cancel that now. It seems to me I should resign. The sooner the better, though I guess I should finish up my cases, but that won't take long. I could say it was for personal reasons. Maybe then Johnson would agree not to file a complaint. Of course, I'd still have to tell Emily why I was resigning." Judge Green's eyes filled. "To be frank, Roger, I'm not sure I can do that. It would break her heart. I'm willing to take my medicine. I know what I did was wrong. But hurting Emily . . . ." His voice trailed off.

Roger Littleton had listened to the judge's narration with the immovable patience and intensity of a great blue heron poised on a rock. And indeed he rather resembled some great bird of prey. His knife edged trousers were crossed, black shoes glistened, fingers were tented beneath his chin, hooded eyes focused on the judge's face. As Judge Green struggled to regain his composure, Littleton struck, with a combination of courtliness and force well known to judges and opposing counsel. "Judge, it will be a particular privilege to represent you. I am deeply honored by your decision to consult me on a matter of such importance to you and your family, and to the entire legal system. May I offer three suggestions. First: Don't cancel your trip to Maine. By all means take your law clerk with you. Sally Link, I believe. Our firm's Hiring Committee, I understand, is about to make her an offer. She was a summer intern while she was at law school and worked on one of my cases. A lovely and exceptionally able young woman. Her company will do you good. Second: Don't resign. And third: Don't discuss with Emily or anyone else either what Albert Johnson told you or what you've told me. While you're in Maine I'll have a chance to talk to Johnson and learn what he's got. Also, I'll put one of our best young associates on researching the law. As soon as you get back from Maine you and I can meet again and decide on our best course of action."

"But Roger, you already know what Johnson's got. As I told you, I did pay Kwiecinski to take the bar exam for me."

"I understand, judge. I do know the facts. You've told them to me. But I don't know whether Johnson can prove them. I believe, but I've got to make sure, that when the commission files a complaint, it has the burden of proving the allegations by competent evidence. I also want to explore some policy considerations. If you were to be removed, would that invalidate every decision in which you wrote the opinion or were a deciding vote? Shouldn't there be some sort of statute of limitations? I'll feel much more able to advise you when I know the answers to questions like that, and I'm sure I'll have the answers by the time you return."

Chief Judge Green sat quietly, for a long time. Finally he said: "Roger, it seems to me you're trying to get me off on some sort of technicality. I'm not sure that's right. I'm not worthy to be a judge. I'm a fraud."

Roger Littleton's gaunt face seemed to soften, his firm tone became almost gentle, even, some one listening might have thought, tender. "Judge, I've knocked around the courts for some fifty years. I've seen more judges and more lawyers, more bullies and scoundrels, than I could ever name. When you were an assistant district attorney, I was chairman of the board of the Public Defender and so I knew about your negotiated plea program. I made it my business to spend two days in Courtroom B, watching you conduct it. Judge, that courtroom was an oasis of kindness, understanding, respect. I only appeared before you once when you were a trial judge, but as chairman of the firm's Litigation Department I was intimately familiar with the way you conducted pretrial settlement conferences. We regularly had cases on your list. Over and over again you felt your way between the quarreling parties to a reasonable and fair solution. To be candid, judge, I'm not sure the appellate bench is the best place for your talents. But I am sure that you are a good man who cares, and cares deeply, about making life a little fairer. Judge, I'm your lawyer, and as such I must abide by your decision. But I'm also an officer of the court, and as an officer of the court, I don't want you to leave the bench. I beg you, don't resign, and don't talk to Emily, not yet anyway. Give me a little time. Go to Maine and call me when you get back. I know it will be hard, very hard, to keep everything to yourself. But it will only be for ten days or a little more. Then you can decide, on better information than we have now, what you should do."

Like most of Roger Littleton's clients, Chief Judge Green followed instructions. He and Emily went to Maine, with Sally Link. While in Maine he said nothing to anyone about Albert Johnson or Genik Kwiecinski or possible resignation from the bench.

Chapter 4

The City Garden was Sally Link's favorite restaurant. The restaurant was on the first floor of one of a row of four or five story brick town houses that had been built in the early nineteenth century and fronted on a street still cobblestoned. The block was mostly residential, although several of the houses displayed a polished brass plate identifying a doctor's or lawyer's offices. Four marble steps, which were worn down in the center by long use and scrubbed as white as a bar of Ivory soap, led to a massive varnished oak door. Inside, in what must have been the parlor, a tuxedoed receptionist took guests' coats and escorted them past a small bar to their table. The dining room was a long narrow room that extended the depth of the old house, but it didn't look narrow because both walls were mirrored. The tables each had a bouquet of fresh flowers and were set with crystal glasses carefully arranged on starched white linen. Glints of light from crystal chandeliers ricocheted between the mirrored walls. At the far end of the dining room were French doors that opened onto a large enclosed courtyard garden with espaliered wisteria and grape vines. When Sally and her companion, George Thacher Putnam IV, arrived for dinner, the french doors were closed. It was March 21st, Sally's birthday, and, as Sally's parents had often happily remarked, the first day of Spring, but still too cool for outdoor dining.

Sally Link and George Thacher Putnam were a head-turning couple. Sally wore a "basic little black dress"—certainly little, and in its subtly cut but unambiguous revelation of Sally's figure, an open appeal to basic instincts. Her companion, though, was equally striking. George

Thacher Putnam IV was never addressed as George, except by telephone salesmen. Since he had been a little boy he had been called "Thacher," but more often, "Thatch," a nickname reinforced by his thatch of orange red heir. Trim, with an easy, confident air, perhaps five feet ten or eleven, he had the white white skin so many red heads have, a sprinkling of freckles on his cheeks, and eyes as blue as cornflowers. He wore tan slacks, the standard-issue Brooks Brothers blue jacket, with brass buttons, and a white dress shirt open at the throat.

Thatch Putnam's great great great grandfather had fought under George Washington. His rifle was mounted over the fireplace of his house, which was now the Putnams' weekend retreat. Thatch's grandfather had been a United States Senator. His father was President of the only bank in the city that hadn't been gobbled up in a merger. Since Thatch had been three years old—or, not to exaggerate, say, four—he had been told that the family's honor required that he excel in whatever he did. And in fact he had excelled in a quite remarkable number of activities. In his bedroom at home—his father forbid display anywhere else—were several shelves of silver cups, goblets, and plates attesting to tennis and squash championships and victories in sail boat races. There were also blue ribbons won at various horse shows. Thatch's Phi Beta Kappa key was framed with his summa cum laude college diploma. He had a nice light tenor voice and regularly sang with a men's chorus founded a long time ago, which twice a year presented a concert of quite inconsequential music, sung, however, very well. In addition, Thatch had often sung the romantic lead in Gilbert and Sullivan operettas, and his bedroom shelves held several pictures of him in dashing costume.

Sally had met Thatch at law school when she was elected to the law review. He was two years ahead of her, and was editor-in-chief of the review. Sally still had her own apartment, but since becoming Chief Judge Green's law clerk she had lived most of the time with Thatch. Her friends referred to Thatch as "Sally's hunk" and expected that when she finished her clerkship and got a job, they would be married. A casual observer, glancing occasionally at Sally and Thatch as they sat at their table in the City Garden, would not have been surprised at this expectation. A closer observer, however, might have had some doubts. Thatch, talking with vigorous motions of his hands, was dominating the couple's conversation. As he went on, Sally gradually stiffened. She drew back in her chair, her expression became not quite hostile but wary, with a suggestion of impatience and skepticism.

Thatch was an associate at Littleton Jones, where he was regarded as a rising star, clearly on track for early election to partnership. He was telling Sally—in her view, was boasting—about his most recent success. On his motion, summary judgment had been entered in his client's favor because the plaintiff, who was suing Thatch's client for breach of contract, had refused to testify at his deposition. Thatch's client had told him that the plaintiff was suffering from depression and might not be able to withstand the pressure of a deposition, and indeed midway through the deposition the plaintiff had burst out, "I don't see why this is necessary. It's all in the books. You're simply trying to trick me by asking me to remember things that are written down." When Thatch persisted, the plaintiff refused to answer any more questions, adding that he didn't care what the questions were about.

"Was the information you wanted in the books?" Sally asked. "It probably was." "When you moved for summary judgment, did his lawyer say anything about the his client suffering from depression—by filing a doctor's statement, for instance." "No, he didn't. My guess is the plaintiff is one of those people who are ashamed to admit to mental illness." "I can understand why the judge held that you were entitled to the plaintiff's own sworn statements, but, since the information you wanted was in his records, and since you knew about his mental condition, why didn't you just serve him with written interrogatories? Did you want to break him? Is that why you took his deposition?" "For crying out loud, Sally, my job isn't to be the plaintiff's physician! My job is to win the case." "I see."

Sally's reaction to his victory hadn't been what Thatch had expected, and a longish silence followed as they ate their salad. "Well," Sally said after their waiter removed the salad plates, "since it is my birthday, which you haven't mentioned, by the way, perhaps you'd be interested in hearing what happened to me this morning?" "I'm sorry, Sally. I did know it was your birthday. That's why I suggested we come here. I guess I was too excited about the summary judgment. It's the first case I've won on my own, though you don't seem to think it's all that great. Anyway, many happy returns. Tell me, what did happen to you this morning?" "I was offered a job, starting salary $ 150,000." "What?!" Sally suddenly had Thatcher's undivided attention. His own salary, as a third year associate, was $ 135,000, and he knew that the current top rate for new associates, offered only by the major firms, was $ 100,000. "Who made the offer?" "Arthur Black, of Arthur Black & Associates."

*   *   *

Sally had been interviewed several times before, for one sort of job or another, but never had she had an experience comparable to her interview with Arthur Black. A week before her birthday dinner with Thatch Putnam, she had received, on heavy, cream colored bond paper, a letter advising her that Mr. Arthur Black would appreciate the opportunity to discuss the possibility of her joining his firm, and asking whether perhaps March 21st at 10:00 a.m. at the firm's offices would be convenient. Sally telephoned the designated number to say that that time would be convenient. She looked up Arthur Black & Associates in Martindale-Hubbell, which stated that the firm specialized in class action litigation, was wholly owned by Black, and employed some twenty lawyers.

Arthur Black & Associates owned its own building, in center city. Designed and built to the firm's specifications, the building was a slender ten story circular column sheathed in pink marble, each floor marked by an unbroken ribbon of green tinted glass windows. The city newspaper's architect columnist had hailed the building, on its completion two years ago, as a "graceful ornament, lending some distinction to an otherwise bland row of unimaginative gray high-rises." The building directory stated that Arthur Black's office was on the tenth floor. As Sally stepped from the elevator, at the appointed time, she entered directly into the waiting room. The polished parquet floor was mostly covered with oriental rugs that looked, to Sally's admittedly non-expert eyes, very old. The walls were of some dark wood, black walnut, Sally guessed. On one wall hung a Braque still life, on the other, a Picasso drawing of a rooster. A small, marble fountain bubbled quietly in a corner of the room. It was of classical design, a nymph rising from a bowl that overflowed into a circular pool. A few dark red leather chairs were scattered about in a casual arrangement. As Sally stood looking about, a receptionist rose from behind a desk across from the elevator. "Good morning. You must be Miss Link. Mr. Black is expecting you. Please, let me have your coat, and then I'll show you to his office."

Sally handed over her coat, waited a moment as it was spirited away, and obediently followed the receptionist across the Oriental rugs. The receptionist was a woman of perhaps thirty—thirty-five?—forty?— of generous proportions. Her blouse had a hint of decolletage, her long skirt was slit to above the knee, her manner was an elusive combination of hard-boiled competence and worldly understanding. Watching the gently undulating form leading her, Sally wondered whether the receptionist's services sometimes extended beyond making and announcing appointments.

"Oh, Miss Link! So good of you to come!" Arthur Black hurried forward from behind an enormous rosewood table inlaid with mother of pearl. The table was set in front of a semi-circular wall of windows looking out over the river. Two tankers were anchored in the river, awaiting their turn to go beneath the suspension bridge upstream. A gleaming brass telescope enabled one to inspect the river traffic and waterfront. Another Braque. Another large very old Oriental rug. Two more red leather chairs. "Won't you sit here?" Sally settled into one chair, as Arthur Black settled into the other, turning it a little so that he was looking squarely at Sally.

Arthur Black was a dark, trim, compact man, perhaps a head shorter than Sally. Thick black hair, pencil thin black mustache, jet black eyes, watchful and inquiring, with no hint of the thoughts behind them. Polonius would have approved of Black's appearance—dark suit, rich but not gaudy, white and gray striped silk necktie, gold cuff links suggestive of a panther's head and vaguely Aztec or Mexican, mirror bright black shoes.

"First of all, please let me explain why I asked you to stop by. I expect that over the next year or so, this firm will grow from about twenty lawyers to twenty-five or so lawyers. In a moment I'll explain why I think we'll be doing that. A few weeks ago one of the judges on your court, with whom I have an occasional social contact, told me that in his opinion you were by far the ablest law clerk the court has ever had. I've spoken to several of your professors at the law school, and if your ears weren't ringing they should have been. One superlative after another. Now, then," Black paused for a prolonged moment, re-crossed his legs, shot his french cuffs, and then continued. "Before I say anything else, it's important, at least it's important to me as an officer of your court, to make something clear. I assume that you are aware of the fact that this firm has a case pending before your court. *The Lead Paint Case.* It has been briefed and argued and the parties are awaiting the court's decision. Please understand, Miss Link, that I did not ask you here because of that case. That would be most inappropriate, and could only cause you embarrassment. I don't know whether you have worked on the case, and I don't want to know. I don't want to know, and I'm not going to ask, anything about the court's deliberations on the case. From our point of view, the case is over. We're simply awaiting the court's decision, as I said. Nothing I will say to you is in any way intended to have any effect on that decision, whatever it may turn out to be. I am going to express my earnest hope that some day you will decide to join this firm, but I am not going to make you an offer. That would be premature, and, I think, out of order. When you finish your clerkship, then you will decide where your future lies. I hope that in making that decision, you will consider applying to this firm. Please, Miss Link, do you have any questions about what I've said? Are you willing that I continue?" Opaque black eyes searched her face.

Listening to Black, Sally had been at once skeptical and a bit intimidated. Talk about an iron hand in a velvet glove! She would not want this man taking her deposition! She did know about *The Lead Paint Case*, where the Black firm had won a jury verdict of $ 50 million dollars compensatory damages, plus $ 500 million punitive damages—the largest verdict in the state's history. Judge Ericson had circulated an opinion to affirm, and Sally had drafted Chief Judge Green's proposed dissent. Which opinion would prevail had not been decided, for the other judges had not yet voted. Was Arthur Black as entirely ignorant of the status of the court's deliberations as he said he was? Should she have told Judge Green about Black's invitation to an interview before she accepted it? Clearly, Black was ten steps ahead of her. His precisely worded disclaimer of any knowledge of the court's deliberations, his unequivocal disavowal of any intent to influence those deliberations, were, so far as anything she knew, impregnable. At the same time, in a cordial and apparently open manner, he had boxed her in. If she had any questions, she could ask them. If she had any doubts, or second thoughts, she could tell him to say nothing more, and leave. "Does he think he is impressing me?" Sally asked herself, with an inner smile, and replied, "Well, if he does, he is certainly correct!" "No, Mr. Black. You've been very clear. I accept your statements and on that understanding, I'd be interested in hearing what you would like to tell me." Was she mistaken, or did she detect an appreciative glint in Black's inscrutable eyes, an adversary's acknowledgment of a skillful parry?

"Very well, then. It would help me, Miss Link, if I knew more about you. I know from your teachers that you were a brilliant student, but that's really all I know. Perhaps you might tell me why you went to law school and what sort of lawyer you'd like to be. Then I could tell you about this firm and how I see the next ten years of the firm's practice."

"I didn't decide to go to law school until my senior year at Bryn Mawr College. My father is a doctor and he despises lawyers. I think he regards them in the way Plato regarded the Sophists—as tricky and dishonest, and willing to take any side for money. He hoped I would be a doctor, and I went to Bryn Mawr because it has a very strong pre-med program. I majored in pre-med, and I enjoyed it. But I also took some courses in American History and I liked those even better. One of the courses was on John Marshall's great decisions and I was fascinated with how Marshall by sheer force of logic defeated Jefferson and laid the foundations of our government. I love my father very much. I decided, however, that he was mistaken in one respect. The logic of science is not the only valid logic. The logic of the law, at least as exemplified by Marshall's decisions, is also valid in the sense that it can help people live together and respect each other.

"This was a very important discovery for me. My brother Karl, who is three years older than I am, and I went to a Quaker school. I was attracted to the Quaker belief that differences between people should not, and cannot, be resolved by force, or violence, but only by working together until a mutual agreement, or what the Quakers call a consensus, is achieved. My brother thought this was sentimental nonsense, and he and I used to argue about it a lot. He would say, "Sally, there are bad people in the world who don't respect you and will kill you before they agree to a peaceful solution." I am very proud of Karl. He's now a Marine lieutenant, and flies helicopters. Last week

CHOICE OF LAW · 71

he was married, and I'm sure that every girl, or woman, who was there felt her heart go flip-flop. No country could have a more honorable or better protector. Even so, I think we resort to force too quickly and too often. So, to answer your question—and I apologize for being so long-winded—the reason I went to law school instead of medical school was because I wanted to learn about the law as a way to reconcile our differences while respecting each other. I can't answer your other question—what sort of lawyer do I want to be? Or let me change that. I think I do know what sort of lawyer I want to be but I don't know whether that's possible. It may be that I'm naive, or simply confused. I've enjoyed being Chief Judge Green's law clerk. I admire the judge and have learned a lot. But I realize that clerking and practicing law are different worlds."

"Did any of your professors at law school teach, or suggest, what sort of lawyer you, or their other students, should be?"

"Well, lots of them, especially in our first year, told us we should 'think like lawyers,' but that doesn't get you very far. In fact, some students took it to mean that a lawyer should be tricky. Then there was the trial practice course, where we were taught that a lawyer's job is to present the client's case as persuasively as possible. That did begin to make you think about a lawyer's role because questions were raised about whether a lawyer could ask misleading questions or offer perjured testimony, and so on. But the course that really made you think about what sort of lawyer you wanted to be was Professor Wordsworth's course on Professional Responsibility."

"Professor Wordsworth was one of the teachers I spoke to. He told me that your final examination paper was the finest he has ever received. I'd be interested in knowing what he asked you and how you answered."

"He did give me a very good mark, which surprised me. I thought I'd written a sour, negative exam. It was a single question exam. Our first assignment had been the statement Lord Brougham made as counsel for Queen Caroline at the proceeding to dissolve her marriage to King George and remove her as Queen." Arthur Black held up his hand. "Please, Miss Link, let me interrupt you. That statement is my credo. I know it by heart. Lord Brougham said that a lawyer's duty was to save the client 'by all means and expedients, and at all hazards and costs' without regard to 'the alarm, the torments, the destruction which he may bring upon others,' even though it should 'involve his country in confusion.'" "Yes. Well, . . . Professor Wordsworth's question was, Having read the course materials, to what extent did we agree with Lord Brougham's statement of a lawyer's duty?" "Oh, and what did you say?" Sally flushed deep red. "I said I didn't agree, that I didn't think a lawyer should be the client's slave"—another deep flush; nothing like a green lawyer telling seasoned counsel that his credo made him a slave—"that while a lawyer should of course help the client achieve the client's objective, so long as it was legal, the lawyer should never do anything that offended the lawyer's own conscience." Arthur Black said nothing, only lifted an eyebrow. Sally rushed on. "I also said that I thought that the Rules of Professional Conduct were hypocritical, that while they pretended to disagree with Lord Brougham, they really didn't, at least not significantly."

"Well, you did lay about you, didn't you? Why do you think the rules are hypocritical?"

"According to the preamble to the rules, a lawyer has three duties: to act as the client's advocate, as an officer of the legal system, and as a public citizen having a special responsibility for the quality of justice. The rules impose some limitations that Lord Broughman might not have accepted, but as I explained in my answer, I thought he probably would have been willing to accept most of them. He might not agree with a few—for example, the provision that in certain circumstances a lawyer must tell the judge the client has lied—but as a practical matter those hardly ever come up. Where the rules are hypocritical, in my opinion, is in saying that the lawyer is not only an advocate but an officer of the legal system and a citizen with a special responsibility for the quality of justice. Sometimes those three roles will conflict. For example, the client may want the lawyer to do something that is perfectly legal but will degrade the quality of justice—a rich defendant tells the lawyer to bleed a poor plaintiff to death by filing all sorts of motions, technically permissible motions but not really necessary. In such a case the lawyer must make a choice between being an advocate or an officer of the legal system and a good citizen. Nothing in the rules, nothing, tells the lawyer how to make that choice. So far as the rules are concerned, a lawyer can tell the client, 'I'll be as tough as Lord Broughman was,' and at the same time brag to the public about being some one who especially cares about the quality of justice. That's hypocrisy."

"Having destroyed Lord Brougham and the rules, Miss Link, how did you end your paper?"

"Not with a bang but a whimper, I'm afraid. I said I didn't want to be the sort of lawyer Lord Brougham was but that I was afraid I'd have to be, to be a successful practitioner, and if that proved to be the case, I didn't know what I'd do—whether I'd knuckle under or do something else, like going to med school, for instance."

"Miss Link, a quality I value very highly is honesty. There was no need for you to blush when you said that Lord Brougham thought a lawyer should be a client's slave. I've been called much worse than the client's slave. I asked you what you said on your exam about Lord Brougham, and you told me. I certainly don't mean to argue with you. To the contrary, I respect your position. But since I've said that Lord Brougham's statement is my credo, perhaps I should explain my own position. I agree with you, the Rules of Professional Conduct are hypocritical. I'm careful to comply with them, of course. Not to is asking to be disciplined or sued for malpractice. But, as you said in your exam, the rules reflect no coherent philosophy of what it is to be a good lawyer. In my opinion, the rules are a typical ABA exercise in cosmetics. I agree with Lord Brougham because, like him, I think the best way to justice, if we can ever get justice, is through a fight. In my experience, Miss Link, there are two kinds of fights. One kind is about what happened, where two lawyers argue about what the evidence shows. The other kind is, for me at least, more interesting. It's where two lawyers argue about what the law is, or should be. One lawyer is satisfied with the law as it is because it favors that lawyer's client. The other lawyer wants the law changed. And that's the way the law grows, from two lawyers arguing, reasoning, about what the law should be. That's the way the law becomes more just."

"Maybe the law doesn't grow. Maybe it contracts and becomes less just."

Arthur Black sat very still in his red leather chair, as still and quiet as a stone, his black eyes locked into Sally's blue eyes. Finally he said, "Miss Link, you are an extraordinarily thoughtful person. If you decide to become a lawyer, you will be a great lawyer. It may be, however, that you should choose another career. I myself couldn't practice law if I didn't love a fight and believe that some good will come of it. It may be that I delude myself. In any case, I would never presume to advise you. Whatever your choice of career may be, I wish you great happiness. With your permission, I should like to tell you about the fight I foresee this firm undertaking for the next five to ten years."

This little speech caused Sally some considerable inner turmoil. No sooner had she blurted out her remark about the law perhaps not growing than she had caught her breath. "How rude of me! How argumentative and conceited!" she thought. Arthur Black's deeply serious and courteous response, his wish for her happiness, had caught her by surprise, as did his willingness to defer to her decision whether to continue the interview. Was there a layer of irony beneath this unfathomable man's offer to continue? For still another time, Sally felt her face flush. "Please do, Mr. Black."

"Very well, then. As you may know, this firm specializes in securities litigation. We have engaged in other class actions. *The Lead Paint Case* is one. But today most of our work is in the field of securities law, and, while I don't wish to sound immodest, in that field we are the leading firm in the country. No other firm has so often been designated lead counsel in multi-district litigation, and we've won more seven and eight figure verdicts than any one else has. Two weeks ago a California jury returned verdicts for our clients totaling one billion dollars. There will be others. Securities law, in my judgment, is on the edge of a revolution. The seeds of the revolution were planted during President Reagan's administration."

Arthur Black paused. "'Seeds' is not a good metaphor. It would be better to say, 'The eggs that were fertilized have hatched, and the poisonous snakes are wriggling out.'" Sally grimaced a bit. "That's ugly, isn't it? And I meant it to be. Permit me to explain." He paused, shot his cuffs, and resumed. "The driving force of the capitalist system is greed. And the fatal weakness of the capitalist system is greed. Because greed is insatiable. We always want more, and more, and more. Who ever heard of a capitalist who didn't want more profits, and who wouldn't destroy anyone who stood in his way? There is no such phenomenon as a free market, and there never has been. Left to themselves, capitalists will grab everything they can. That's why we have anti-trust laws, and laws regulating the banking and securities businesses, and federal agencies like the SEC. The point of Teddy

Roosevelt's campaign against 'the malefactors of great wealth,' as he called them, and the point of FDR's New Deal, was to save capitalism from the capitalists. TR and FDR both knew that if we were to enjoy the benefits of capitalism, the government would have to ensure that in their greed for ever greater profits, the capitalists didn't destroy the system. But Ronald Reagan didn't know that. For him, greed was good and government regulation was bad."

Arthur Black lifted one hand as though to ward off disagreement. "Please, Miss Link, I'm not discussing politics. I have no interest in politics. My only interest is in the facts. And the facts are that President Reagan's economic philosophy, if that's the right term, has become a political religion, or should I say, a dogma. Those charged by law with regulating business and finance don't regulate. Some of them don't believe in regulation—foxes appointed to guard the chicken coop. Others think there are two classes in the United States: their buddies, who belong to the same secret societies and country clubs they do, and the rest of us. The law doesn't apply to their buddies. And others are prostitutes, who sell themselves for goodies like all-expense paid trips to exclusive resorts where they moderate panels on the moral virtues of free enterprise. Meanwhile, the agencies' staffs still go through the motions, collecting data, making studies, but no one pays any attention to their recommendations, so, they do what civil servants always do, they keep their noses clean until their pensions vest."

Arthur Black smiled. Not a pleasant smile, Sally thought. A bitter one, curved by contempt. He seemed to hesitate, as though wondering whether he should qualify his description. Then he continued. "Of course, I paint with a rather broad brush. There are honest, conscientious regulators, who try to enforce the law. And there are honest capitalists—capitalists who make a better product, for a better price, which attracts more customers, which produces bigger profits, which increases the value of the company, which causes the market value of the company's stock to rise, which means that a lot of people get rich. The CEO earns a handsome salary, and the shareholders can sell their shares at a handsome gain. And that's good. That's the American way. That's the sort of capitalism FDR wanted to preserve. But, Miss Link, making a better product for a better price isn't the way to get really, really rich, rich beyond John Rockefeller's or Andrew

Carnegie's wildest dreams, rich beyond decency, swiney rich. The way to do that is, first, lie, and then, steal."

Sally wondered if she had just heard a phrase from Arthur Black's address to that California jury. "Miss Link, I'm sure you've read about the companies that went bankrupt after being looted by their officers. Believe me, there are plenty more cases like them, perhaps not quite as brazen but bad enough, as I know from cases we are developing right now in this firm. I spoke a moment ago of poisonous snakes hatching. I think I did because I hate snakes. I wanted to suggest how I feel about what crooked capitalists and their lackeys have done. But it still wasn't really a good figure of speech. Snakes at least don't kill at random. These men—and so far they do all seem to have been men, Miss Link. I've just about decided that feminists are right, that men are more dangerous, are given to greater excess, than women. In any case, these men are cruel beyond any cobra or rattlesnake. So that they could wallow in luxury, they ruined hundreds and hundreds of thousands of innocent people."

Arthur Black got up from his red leather chair, walked to the window and looked out over the river. After a moment he turned back to Sally. "Miss Link, have you visited the university's arboretum recently, to see the restored fernery? You really must go. It's a delightfully ornate Victorian greenhouse with an arched and pointed glass roof. It's heated by steam pipes. You'll feel as though you've entered a sauna. A little stream trickles through it. And ferns are everywhere! Growing out of the walls, curving over the stream, hanging from dead branches and a rotting stump. Pale green, deep green, delicate and pointed, huge and heavy. You half expect you'll suddenly see Rousseau's lion push its head through the jungle, to stare at you. Well! As I said, we're working on several cases like the bankruptcies you've read about, and as I think of what I've learned from the evidence we've analyzed so far, I'm reminded of the fernery. What a variety of lies! Delicate lies, artistically crafted. Huge, crude lies. These liars, Miss Link, were artists. Their purpose was to persuade their shareholders and employees that the company's stock, which was really worthless, was not only valuable but was going to get even more valuable. Was the company saddled with debt? Create another company, have it 'buy' the debt, with its own worthless stock, and record the purchase price as an 'asset.' Were profits non-existent? Pretend you've won a contract, estimate what the profits on that contract will be, and enter those profits as 'earned income.' And shareholders and employees were deceived. They bought more or the company's stock, and as the company's annual reports continued to describe its strong financial position and to boast about its glowing future, they bought still more, driving the price of the stock still higher, and higher.

"And now comes the time to steal. Imagine, Miss Link, that you're a member of this gang. When you became CEO or CFO you negotiated stock option agreements. While you've been inflating the value of the company, you've acquired thousands of shares of the company stock, for nothing. But now you know the game is almost over. The company didn't win the new contract. There are no profits. The huge debt has got to be paid. So, you exercise your stock options, and sell your shares, at the top of the market—which nets you a modest profit, commensurate with the services you have performed, say, eighty million dollars. The next week, when the company's true financial position is finally revealed, the company goes belly up, and files for bankruptcy. The employees lose their jobs, and the company's stock is worthless, wiping out the employees' 401(k)'s and the individual shareholders' accounts. Hundreds of thousands or persons are ruined.

"One more point, Miss Link. You didn't accomplish all this by yourself. You had help, highly sophisticated, professional help. Investment bankers structured a leveraged buyout. Accountants audited the company's financial statements. Lawyers prepared the company's SEC filings. Brokers pushed the company's stock. All of these professional advisers made lots and lots of money in fees and commissions. Many of them accepted without question the false figures and phoney explanations you provided. No one from the SEC asked any tough questions. Neither did any member of the board of directors, including the independent directors and the members of the auditing committee. You were given a free hand. And you made the most of it. Never give a sucker an even break, right? I've got mine, Jack. Vacation homes, flat in London for the mistress, private plane, yacht, a tub of caviar. The good life.

"Miss Link, I said a moment ago that there were two kinds of fight, one to prove the facts, the other to define the law. I don't anticipate much of either kind of fight so far as concerns the CEO's and CFO's who inflated the value of their stock and then cashed in. Mostly it's clear what they did, and that what they did was criminal. It should be possible to make them pay back what they stole. But that won't be enough to make my clients whole. The question, therefore, will be whether my clients, the shareholders and former employees, can recover their losses from the bankers, accountants, lawyers, and brokers who advised the crooked CEO's and CFO's. And on that question I expect one of the biggest, bloodiest fights in the history of American law. And I expect this firm to be leading the fight."

Arthur Black could barely contain his excitement. It was a though he were opening to a jury. He rose from his red leather chair and stood behind his rosewood table. "First, I'll prove what these professional advisers knew. What documents did they see? What were they told? What questions did they ask? What advice did they give? And then I'll argue the law." He sat down and folded his hands in front of him. "Miss Link, are you familiar with Cardozo's lectures, *The Nature of the Judicial Process*. No? It is the most dog-eared book in my library. Cardozo argued that judges don't find the law, they make it. And the principal way they make it is to follow what he called 'the directive force of a principle.' That's what I'm going to do. Now, then, these financial advisors, accountants and lawyers, these directors, who guided and were responsible for supervising the officers who looted the companies my clients invested in and worked for, were all professionals. What would you say is the directive force of the principle of professionalism?"

Arthur Black laughed, a delighted, spontaneous laugh that seemed to surprise him, and certainly surprised Sally. "Miss Link, I'm about to sound more like Sally Link, who wants lawyers to act as their conscience dictates, than like that fierce old client's slave, Henry Brougham. I think the directive force of professionalism is the obligation to give the client independent advice. Be sure you know the facts. Then tell the client what, in your best judgment, those facts require. Now, lots of professionals do just that. But some don't. Some don't want to know the facts, because they're afraid that if they do know they'll have to blow the whistle and then they won't be able to collect their fat commissions or charge their three figure hourly rates. And some want to work both sides of the street—accountants, for example, who charge consulting fees on how to cook the company's books and auditing fees for certifying the company's reports. I want the courts to rule that professionals have an independent duty to get the facts. Is there a document that would make a prudent person ask, 'What's going on here?' The professional has to check it out. Does the CEO's story sound too good to be true? Check it out. Even if no alarm bells are ringing, check it out. I want the courts to require professionals to question their clients as they would an adversary, and seek corroboration of the answers they get. You call yourselves experts in finance, who understand how a sound economy works? Then serve the economy, not those who would loot and abuse it. You call yourself officers of the legal system? Then serve the legal system, not those who would manipulate it for their gain. I will quote you in my briefs, Miss Link. I will argue that a professional is not a slave to his client, that a professional has duties beyond the client. I will also quote Alexis de Tocqueville. When Tocqueville visited the United States, more than a century and a half ago, he found a society without the institutions to resolve disputes and maintain order that other societies had—a dominant religion or class structure, for example. In America, Tocqueville said, this gap was filled by lawyers. As he put it, lawyers taught society the spirit of the law. If I can persuade the courts to return to that ideal, to hold that professionals should once again become the supporters of the rule of law, for the benefit of society, then I will be able to ask juries of ordinary, decent citizens to hold responsible for my client's losses, and to punish, not just the crooked CEO's and CFO's but the professional lapdogs who made their frauds possible. And when I can do that, the practice of finance, accounting, and law will change. The only way to defeat greed, Miss Link, is with fear. And when the lapdogs know that they will have to pay for losses they make possible, they will be afraid. Then they will do what professionals should do: get the facts, and tell their clients what the facts require."

Arthur Black stopped abruptly. His tone changed, from intense to conversational, almost diffident. "Well, there you have my dream, Miss Link. I have dedicated the remaining years of my practice to achieving it. I'm not sure I can. The legal profession is very smug, very self-protective. It will be difficult to persuade the courts to admit that the professions' standards have been low. In addition, my opponents are wealthy, they are entrenched, and they will be fighting for their lives. They can afford, and they will engage, the ablest counsel to defend them. But there is only one man I fear. You know him, Miss Link. You worked for his firm one summer while you were at law school. He is Roger Littleton. His strategy will be to keep me from addressing a jury, for he knows that there I'll prevail. He will try to define the issues as issues of law only, to be decided by the courts, which in the end will mean the United States Supreme Court, for there he is without peer. Nevertheless, I am confident in the justice of my client's claims, and, as I said, Miss Link, my faith as a lawyer is that in struggle, the law works itself clean and justice prevails."

Sally recognized—how could she not?—the challenge in this peroration. She could almost hear Arthur Black's gauntlet slap the top of his rosewood desk, in challenge to her own expression of skepticism that perhaps the law didn't always grow more just. While she wondered how, or whether, she should respond, Arthur Black continued. "Some day, I hope, I will have the opportunity to introduce you to the persons who constitute this firm. The top five floors of this building are for our lawyers. Happily, we allowed for some growth when we designed the building, and your office, if you come with us, would be on one of those floors. Two of the other five floors are for computers and document storage. In our litigation, any given law suit may require the analysis of as many as a million documents. The remaining three floors are administrative and specialized personnel— secretaries, paralegals, and various experts, particularly in economics and the securities market. I expect we will be hiring additional experts in accounting and finance. Our library, which is extensive, is spread throughout the building, but the librarians and most of the library are on the same floors as our experts.

"Well, you must be tired of listening to me. Please forgive me. As you can see, I care deeply about the firm and its work, and I sometimes get carried away. To repeat what I said at the beginning, I know it would be premature to ask you now to join the firm, and I'm not doing that. I do hope that when, after your clerkship, you think about your future, you will consider applying for a position as an associate with the firm. I expect that a new associate's salary will be $ 150,000, with, of course, full medical benefits and a 401(k), to which the firm would make a matching contribution. I will be glad to answer any questions you may have, to the best of my ability, and I will certainly understand that in asking them, you are not in any way committing yourself."

Far from being tired of listening to Arthur Black, Sally had been fascinated, half enthralled and swept off her feet, half the admiring critic. It had been a magnificent performance, she had thought to herself, its pace ebbing and flowing, drawing the audience in, then pushing out, hot anger mixed with cool argument, all culminating in a quiet, humble expression of faith in justice. Sally thought she could tell when a seduction had been attempted. Not sexual seduction. At no point had Arthur Black indicated any sexual interest in her. But seduction nevertheless. He had flattered her by respecting her as a professional equal. He had led her to heights from which she could contemplate exhilarating litigation of transformative significance. He had promised her riches. Most tempting, he had turned their apparent disagreement about the proper role of a lawyer completely around, depicting his goal as persuading the courts to adopt Sally's view of a lawyer's responsibilities as transcending the lawyer—client relationship.

And Sally was tempted. But she wasn't seduced. She would ask no questions, and make no comment, she decided. Engaging in any further dialogue would be like playing with a tiger. A relaxed, contented tiger, sunning itself outside its lair, but a tiger nevertheless. Could so ferocious a man contain and channel his ferocity? He had admitted that not all corporate officers and directors were driven by greed to corruption, not every banker, accountant, lawyer, broker was a blind or willing instrument of fraud. But could he distinguish, would he slaughter the innocent? Others had been swept by idealism into bloodshed. Sally distrusted messianic visions. In any case, were class actions really the way to remake society? While Sally was no expert in class actions, she had some sense of how some one as skillful as Arthur Black could use them as a bludgeon. Assert a meretricious claim on behalf of thousands of claimants. Find an expert willing to support the claim. (Not hard to do, for a suitable fee.) Sue everyone in sight— the manufacturer of a medication, say, the doctors who prescribed it, the hospital on whose staff the doctors practiced, the pharmacists. What are defendants' counsel likely to advise their clients? To settle the case. That is, to pay money, a lot of money. Will the trial judge refuse to let your charlatan expert testify? Maybe, but maybe not. Will the appellate court set aside the jury's infuriated verdict? Maybe, but maybe not. And if the defendants lose they're in bankruptcy. And so, the defendants settle, for the best price they can negotiate, and plaintiffs' counsel, some one like Arthur Black, pockets a fat contingent fee, with which to underwrite another meretricious but threatening claim. According to Thatch Putnam, this sort of maneuver was common in class action litigation. Sally suspected he was exaggerating, but she didn't really know, and it seemed plausible. What was meretricious to a manufacturer might seem arguable to aggressive counsel who saw a chance for a million dollar fee. Was Arthur Black immune from such temptation? Sally wondered. What was he willing to do to own two Braques and a Picasso? And then, there was the temptation of power. To Sally, Black seemed fearless, exulting in the prospect of bringing low the mighty. He didn't shrink, he wanted to be hated and feared. "Thank you, Mr. Black. I don't think I have any questions, at least not just now. You've given me a lot to think about. I appreciate the time you've spent with me and the chance to meet you." "I assure you, Miss Link, the pleasure was mine." He rose, made a small, formal bow, "I hope we may meet again."

* * *

On hearing Sally say that it was Arthur Black who had offered her a position as an associate at the magnificent starting salary of $ 150,000, Thatcher Putnam snorted. "Oh! Well, that makes it easy. He's a real sleazebag."

"Have you met him?"

"No, but I know the sort of cases he brings. In fact, the firm's defending one now, so I've read some of his briefs. The man has no respect for the facts or the law. He'll do anything to win."

"Just like you, is that right?"

"Whoa! What does that mean, Sally?"

"Well, didn't you just tell me you thought it was all right to break that man on his deposition—that you weren't his physician, your job was to win?"

"Sally, that's not fair . . . ."

"Tell me, Thatch, Do you think all class actions are wrong? Haven't there been cases where class actions are the best way to provide relief? What about the tobacco litigation? Don't corporations sometimes really do wicked things, like making an addictive product they know causes cancer, or an automobile that's likely to explode when hit from the rear?"

"O.K. I will tell you. I think class actions are wrong and should be abolished. I understand why they were created. If Mrs. Jones buys a $ 27 toaster from GE, which won't pop the toast, she's stuck. It would cost more than the toaster is worth to sue GE, and no lawyer would take the case. So, it seemed to make sense to provide that one thousand Mrs. Joneses could get together and form a class and sue GE, or ten thousand Mrs. Joneses. Plenty of lawyers will prosecute a claim for $ 27,000, or $ 270,000. The lawyer will take a quarter of the recovery as his fee, and from what's left, each Mrs. Jones will receive at least part of her $ 27. But it hasn't worked out that way. Lawyers like Arthur Black don't file class actions for persons who have $ 27 claims. They file actions for a class of persons who have claims of $ 100,000, $ 500,000, or more—for having gotten cancer or given birth to a defective child. Some other catastrophe. That means the action is for millions of dollars, maybe hundreds of millions. And that kind of money breeds corruption the way a swamp breeds mosquitoes. False claims, perjured testimony, crackpot experts, prejudiced juries. So, if I had my way, I'd abolish class actions. If Mrs. Jones claims a GE product gave her cancer, she can sue GE, But she shouldn't be able to sue as a member of a class of a thousand other Mrs. Joneses. As for corporations doing wicked things, I admit, sometimes they do. You won't find me defending the tobacco companies' morals. I just don't think class actions are a good way to protect consumers. I'd leave that to government regulators."

"And suppose the regulators don't regulate?"

"Well! Mr. Black really did propagandize you, didn't he?"

Sally flushed red. "Do you call that an answer to my question?"

"Sally! Why are you so angry?"

"Because I'm hurt and disappointed, that's why. I looked forward all afternoon to telling you about my interview with Arthur Black. He's a fascinating, and scary, man, and he said some very provocative things. But oh no, you're not interested. All you're interested in is the summary judgment you got. So far as you're concerned, Arthur Black is a sleazebag, and you know all the answers. Including the answer to whether I should accept his offer, which you informed me I shouldn't do, since I clearly don't have the ability to decide that for myself."

Sally's lower lip visibly trembled. Fighting back tears, she tossed her head, lifted her chin, and continued. "Thatch, when we were on the law review together, I loved working with you, and being with you. You were fun. I don't mean just making love"—another flush—"but in every way. You didn't say mean things. You were sweet, and gentle. Studying was a game, life was a game, which you played for the pleasure of it. You've changed, Thatch. Now you play to win, even if that means unnecessarily hurting some one. Now you've chosen sides. Your opponents are sleazebags. Ideas are good or bad according to whether they'll help your clients. And"—despite her best efforts, Sally's voice broke—"you don't respect me. You think I'm a dope to clerk for a state court judge. You think I'm too soft-hearted to do what lawyers have to do. You think I'm too gullible and impressionable to be able to evaluate Arthur Black's offer. So, Thatch, I think we'd better call it quits. You go your way. You'll make partner in record time. I'll go mine, I'm not sure where, but I'll find that out. Tomorrow after work I'll get my things and move back to my apartment."

Chapter 5

"Good morning, Mr. Littleton. I have your usual table. Please follow me." Roger Littleton gently nudged Professor Emerson to go ahead of him, as the tall, lean tuxedoed maitre d' led them to a table for two by the window, looking out onto the parkway and a fountain's surging column of water and falling spray. "Coffee? Orange juice? Your waiter will be with you in a moment, gentlemen."

"Thank you for seeing me, Mr. Littleton. And this is certainly a pleasant place to do business." Dwight Emerson was a young Associate Professor of Philosophy at the university, who looked like a graduate student: slight build, corduroy jacket with leather patches on the elbows, shaggy dark hair, steel rimmed glasses; an inhabitant of the library. "My pleasure. Now tell me about this presentation you're to make to the Supreme Court."

"Two weeks ago the Chief Judge of the court telephoned me. He said that the court was going to have its usual annual retreat soon and asked if I would be willing to make a presentation. When I asked what he had in mind, he explained that he had read an article I recently wrote on law and literature in which I argued that lawyers could learn from literature about the nature of justice. I illustrated my argument with references to various works of literature, among them *Billy Budd* and *The Merchant of Venice*. Would I be willing to discuss those two works at the annual retreat. Probably foolishly, I said I'd like that, and so two weeks from now I'll be meeting with the judges, and their law clerks, I understand, and we'll talk about the summary court martial and execution of Billy Budd and Portia's treatment of Shylock's action on

Antonio's bond. As I thought about what I'd say, I realized I knew nothing about the judges I'd be meeting with. I looked them up in the manual of state officials, which has a thumb nail biography of each judge, and that was some help. I learned, for example, that four of the judges had been district attorneys. Still, I had very little sense of what sort of audience the judges would be. A friend of mine at the law school suggested I talk to you. She told me that you have often argued before the court. I do appreciate your willingness to see me."

"I *have* often argued before the court, and believe me, it's an ordeal. I expect you will find the judges a very difficult audience. Suppose I say a little about how the practicing bar regards the judges as a court, and then we'll talk a little about the judges as individuals." Roger Littleton smiled an encouraging smile. "Don't worry. It will be good for them. Stretch their little gray cells. You'll do fine. Afterwards we must have breakfast again and you can tell me how it went.

"Well, then. The court is really two different courts. On criminal cases, it's very conservative, as you would expect, with so many former prosecutors on the court, although I should add that the Chief Judge is a former prosecutor and he and one other judge sometimes dissent, but that's rare. It's a law and order court. On civil cases, on the other hand, the court is deeply divided. Four of the judges are pro-plaintiff, and three are pro-defendant. From the point of view of the corporate defense bar, which is my practice, this makes for a very difficult situation. The two blocs seem intransigent. In fact, as nearly as I can tell from oral argument, the judges don't seem to like each other very much. They tend to interrupt each other as often as they interrupt the lawyers who are arguing."

Roger Littleton sighed. "If I may say so, professor, it's quite an arrogant court. Sometimes when I've argued, or have listened to other lawyers argue while I waited my turn, I've had the feeling they've already made up their minds, even though their questions suggest they haven't read the briefs And as I think your law school friend will tell you, their opinions are rarely scholarly. Are you going to assign reading?"

"There are good inexpensive paper back editions of *Billy Budd* and *The Merchant.* I've suggested to the Chief Judge that the court buy enough of them for the judges and their clerks each to have a set. He said he'd see to it."

"The clerks will have read them. I'd be surprised if the judges will have. You may wish to be prepared to summarize the stories."

"I'm sure you're right. I also plan to use videotaped excerpts from movies of *Billy Budd* and *The Merchant.* Laurence Olivier plays Shylock. It's like being hit between the eyes by a two by four."

"I wish I could be there. I'm sure your program will go very well. Now then, let's talk a bit about the individual judges. First, the Chief Judge. An interesting man. He doesn't like conflict, it seems. As an assistant district attorney his main interest was in negotiating plea agreements designed to rehabilitate the defendants. Probation conditioned on giving up drugs and getting a job. That sort of thing. As a trial judge, he didn't much like to try cases. He thought they should be settled, and he was very good at working out settlements. He hasn't been what you would call a distinguished appellate judge, but he's a decent, fair-minded man. Whenever I argue before the Supreme Court, I pitch my argument at him. Judge Ericson—Eric Ericson—is the brightest judge on the court, in my opinion, also the cockiest. He's the leader of the pro-plaintiff bloc, what some defense lawyers rather bitterly call Ericson's Gang of Four. He was a very successful personal injury lawyer, and as an appellate judge he doesn't hesitate to bend the cases to expand liability. He has substantially changed the law of torts in this state. Judge Robert Carlisle is at the opposite end. Old line conservative Episcopalian from the middle of the state. A quintessential WASP. Family business the biggest employer in town. Main street named after his family. If Judge Ericson has never seen a plaintiff who shouldn't be compensated, Judge Carlisle has never a defendant who was at fault."

Roger Littleton smiled a self-deprecating smile. "You will forgive me for exaggerating, I hope. Then there's Judge Llewelyn, Harold Llewelyn. His father emigrated from Wales to work in the anthracite mines, which were then this state's major industry, and as a boy the judge helped his father bring out the coal. My friends who practice criminal law tell me that the judge regards search warrants as a bothersome technicality, and the presumption of innocence as rebutted by a police officer's testimony. He's one of the Gang of Four. I suspect his sympathy for some one who's been hurt is shaped by memories of how the coal operators treated the miners and crushed their union. You'll like him. A gray-haired fire plug of a man, and I'm sure one of the most congenial drinking companions you can imagine. Then there's Judge Weinstein. I said Judge Ericson is the brightest judge on the court. Judge Weinstein is probably just as bright but he's not so fiery. In fact I wonder sometimes whether his health is failing. But if for some reason he rouses himself, you get something really quite good, especially on the criminal side. Some of his opinions, all of them dissents, I should add, are genuinely moving expositions of the principle that the purpose of the constitution is to protect the weak, which is interesting because he wasn't a criminal lawyer. He represented major developers of real estate and I suspect made a good deal of money himself before deciding to be a judge. On the civil side, most of the time, he's with the Gang of Four, but sometimes not. His sympathies are with the injured party, but he's too good a legal craftsman to go along with Judge Ericson's often glib analyses, so sometimes he's the swing vote. Judge Dante Marcone is all heart. A lovely man, really. His father was a stone mason, and if you get a chance to talk with the judge I predict he'll tell you how much he loved and admired his father, how his father saw to it that all of his children went to college, what a beautiful craftsman his father was and how the walls he built still stand. I don't think Judge Marcone ever really practiced law. He was mayor of his town for several terms, and then was elected a state senator something like four times, the last time without any opposition. He's hard to predict in criminal cases, I gather, probably because, as I once heard him say from the bench, he's always for the underdog. He's a regular member of the Gang of Four. The most junior member of the court, and the only woman, is Judge Dorothy Hull-Jackson. Her field of practice was family law, where she made a big name for herself representing the aggrieved woman in some messy celebrity divorce cases. She must have been a tiger—tigress, I guess I should say. Once when I was waiting to argue, a lawyer arguing the case before mine had the misfortune to represent a wealthy man who was in arrears on his alimony payments, which he thought were excessive. On, my! I have never seen a judge tear apart a lawyer the way Judge Hull-Jackson tore apart that lawyer. She hasn't been on the court very long. So far she hasn't joined the Gang of Four. She did join one of Judge Weinstein's dissents in a criminal case. My guess is that she isn't interested in much except family law, and there, I suspect, she's going to ruffle a lot of feathers. Just last month the court heard argument on whether a lesbian who had helped raise a child was entitled to visit the child after she and her lover quarreled and separated. I'm sure the court will split, and it will be interesting to see what position Judge Hull-Jackson takes and how many of the judges join her."

Roger Littleton poured himself another cup of coffee and buttered another croissant. "Well, there you have it. I know I've given you an oversimplified and exaggerated picture. What I've done is to describe each judge as his or her severest critic might. My own view is that there's considerable truth in each description but certainly not the complete truth. In any given case any one of the judges may surprise you. That's what makes arguing before the court such a challenge, and why we so often advise settlement."

"Mr. Littleton, I can't thank you enough. My law school friend told me your perspective would be helpful, and you've certainly proved her right. I must admit, I see what you mean when you say I'll have a difficult audience."

"May I ask you, did the Chief Judge say what he hoped to achieve by asking you to make your presentation?"

"He didn't really—only that he had enjoyed my article and thought the judges would find a discussion of *Billy Budd* and *The Merchant of Venice* challenging."

"Professor, I'm not a philosopher. I hope, however, that I may offer a suggestion."

"Please do, please, by all means."

"Well, I'm not sure that challenging the judges would be the most useful way to proceed. If you will forgive me for saying so, I'm afraid some of them will regard you as a young person from the ivory tower, who doesn't know much about the real world and who knows nothing about the law. Instead of being challenged by your presentation, they'll ignore it, and may be quite rude in the bargain. And yet it seems to me you have a great deal to contribute."

Another cup of coffee, another croissant.

"From the little I know of it, the philosophy of the law has always seemed an elusive and fascinating subject—very difficult to grasp and yet of tremendous importance—a sort of golden fleece or holy grail—a promise that there is a road to justice but with directions so obscure or misleading we can't find the road. I've spoken harshly of the

Supreme Court. I've called it arrogant. I've said it's an ordeal to argue before the court. And I doubt that any of the judges would like or agree with my descriptions of them. So I'd better add a corrective. I think most judges, most of the time, including the judges on the Supreme Court, try to be fair—or do justice, as it is sometimes put. And I think most of the time they do a pretty good job. Sometimes when I think to myself that they're not as competent or diligent or unbiased as I would like, I remind myself that maybe I'm the one who's being arrogant. You don't get on the Supreme Court without a lot of savvy and pretty sharp elbows. Well, I think the Chief Judge is an exception. My impression is that he got on the court because of his father's political clout. But the fact remains that collectively the judges represent a lot of experience and knowledge of people, and they see a tremendous number of cases of all different kinds. So, from an academic point of view, or a practitioner's, they may not be much of a court, certainly not a distinguished one, but from the point of view of the every day citizen, they're not bad. If I may make a respectful suggestion, perhaps you might think of turning your presentation around. Instead of you challenging the judges, you might ask them to take the lead, to tell you, so that you might tell your colleagues and students, how they decide cases. Make them the teachers. As I remember *Billy Budd*, for example, its central theme is whether the law, to be law that must be obeyed, should conform to God's law, what we would call natural law."

"That's right. That is the central theme."

"Suppose, instead of laying out the theme, you were to ask the judges how they would have decided whether to execute Budd. My guess is, you'd get a divided vote. If the judges were then asked to explain how they reached their respective decisions, my guess is that you'd get a spirited debate about what judges think they're swearing to do when they take an oath to uphold the law. I don't know why the Chief Judge asked you to make a presentation. By nature, though, he's a mediator. When he was a trial judge he was happiest when he could work out a win—win settlement. It may be that he thinks of your program as a way to make his fractious colleagues a little less fractious. If you can lead them to appreciate, not by what you say but by what they say to each other, that there are strong arguments for very different approaches to the law, perhaps they will have more respect for each other than their written opinions suggest they have. Well, now! Please forgive me. It's your program and I don't mean to be presumptuous in suggesting how you present it. It's only that I was imagining myself listening to your presentation. However you do it, I'm sure it will be very challenging and worthwhile."

"Mr. Littleton, let me say again, I can't thank you enough. I love your suggestion. It relieves my apprehension about the program. I'll let you know how it goes."

Chapter 6

Mountaintop Lodge was in fact on top of a mountain. Oh, not what anyone from Colorado or Wyoming would call a mountain. A high point, rather, in the old, worn down Alleghenies, but still, elevation over five thousand feet. Surrounded by a lake, gardens, rolling lawns and an emerald golf course, and with an unobstructed view over lines of ridges retreating from green to brown to lavender, the lodge was visible long before one wound up the gently switch-backed drive to the porte cochere and the welcoming green-uniformed doormen. Some of those arriving had come for vacations every year since they were children. Stepping from Mercedes Benz and Lexus sedans, they remembered their fathers' Pierce Arrow and Packard phaetons, with lap rugs and canvas-covered trunks strapped to trunk racks.

The lodge had been built in the 1920's by a syndicate whose members had more money than they knew how to spend. Provided an unlimited budget, the architects and contractors had followed to the letter their instructions to "Build it right!" The lodge was built of stone quarried nearby. In design, it was a sort of combined Scotch castle, English stately home, and king's hunting lodge. One entered an enormous pine-beamed and pillared room. At the far end was a fireplace made of boulders and wide enough to burn five foot timbers, at the other end, the registration desk, and beyond that the pine-beamed and pillared dining room, its walls of windows overlooking gardens. When the judges of the Supreme Court arrived at the lodge for their annual conference it was early April. A fire was contentedly purring in the fireplace, the gardens were golden clouds of forsythia floating above carpets of daffodils, white crocuses and hyacinths.

A meeting room discreetly hidden behind the library had been set aside for the court. The room was equipped with slide and video tape projectors and screen. Waiters in tuxedoes regularly replenished silver urns with coffee or hot water for tea, and set out pitchers of orange juice, cream or milk, and platters of muffins, Danish pastries, and cheeses. In front of the screen stood a podium facing several long tables on which were neatly arranged yellow legal pads, containers of sharpened pencils emblazoned with the lodge's coat of arms, pitchers of ice water, and crystal drinking glasses.

The first two days of the court's annual meeting were devoted to tedious, though no doubt necessary, discussion of the court's budget, proposed new rules of civil procedure, and recent developments in the law. Professor Dwight Emerson's presentation was scheduled for the third, and last, day. Each day's sessions were from 8:30 to 1, after which the judges and their clerks had lunch together and were free to do as they wished—swim in the indoor pool, hike the trials, take a nap.

* * *

Following the Chief Judge's fulsome introduction—"a brilliant young professor of philosophy whose work has attracted national recognition"—Dwight Emerson rose, leaned lightly against the podium, and considered his audience. The clerks looked like any collection of graduate students. The judges were poker faced, as though on the bench awaiting the beginning of argument. Except for the Chief Judge, they radiated, if not exactly hostility, at least skepticism and boredom. While refilling his cup of coffee, Professor Emerson had heard Judge Llewelyn muttering to Judge Ericson something to the effect of "lot of nonsense, can't imagine what Green was thinking of." The professor had had dinner with the judges the night before, to find Roger Littleton's description of them amply confirmed: a savvy group of opinionated, somewhat contentious, individuals, personable enough individually, even delightful, with no noticeable sense of collegiality or respect for each other. It was going to be a difficult audience.

"Good morning. It is a particular pleasure for me to be here. I've been looking forward to it for weeks. Usually my responsibility is to be a teacher but this time I expect to be a student." The young professor paused. "The most powerful person in the world is the President of the United States. But when the United States Supreme Court ordered President Nixon to produce his secret tapes, he obeyed. And when the court ordered President Clinton to submit to being deposed by Paula Jones's lawyer, he obeyed. No one in our country is above the rule of law. The rule of law is the rule of judges. It is your rule. As the Chief Judge said in his too generous introduction, I am a philosopher. The greatest philosopher of the twentieth century, in my opinion, was John Rawls of Harvard. In the 1970's he published his master work, *A Theory of Justice,* in which he described what a society should look like to deserve being called a just society. Every year, in universities throughout the world, philosophers discuss Rawls's theory. I myself teach a course on Rawls at least every other year, and some day I would love to tell you about his theory. But today, I thought, we might do something much more worthwhile than listening to me talk about the theory of justice. Instead, I propose that we discuss the practice of justice. For you are practitioners of justice. My role, as I see it, will be to ask you, How do you do it? When you decide a case, what factors do you consider? How do you weigh those factors? How do you harmonize them? University faculties have found that an occasional comprehensive review of their field of study is enjoyable and helpful— a reminder of the past and a guide for the future. I hope that you will find that so of a review of your field, the practice of justice."

Dwight Emerson stepped away from the podium and turned to the Chief Judge. "Chief Judge Green, would this way of proceeding meet what you had in mind?" "Sounds fine to me, Professor. I look forward to the discussion. I'm sure we all do."

Emerson resumed. "I've noticed that practitioners of other professions—medical doctors, for example—often discuss their work by describing particularly difficult cases they have had. I thought you might enjoy doing that, and so I've picked two cases that seem to me particularly difficult. I didn't pick them from law books, for example, from the reports of your decisions, but from literature, and I did that for two reasons. In the first place, I thought you might find it a pleasant change of pace, and in the second place, literature is a repository of cases that describe the human condition as nothing else does. We see ourselves most clearly, we feel our strengths and weaknesses, our pains and pleasures most keenly, in literature. The first case I've picked is from Herman Melville's novel, *Billy Budd*, the second, from Shakespeare's play, *The Merchant of Venice*. As it happens, an excellent movie has been made of each of these works, and the way I propose we proceed is this: First I'll play an excerpt from the videotape of the movie of *Billy Budd*, depicting the summary court martial of Budd, and I'll ask you to discuss how, if you had been the members of the court martial, you would have decided whether Budd should be hanged. Then I'll play an excerpt from the videotape of the movie of *The Merchant of Venice*, depicting how Portia decided whether Shylock should recover on Antonio's bond, and I'll ask you to discuss how you would have decided Shylock's claim. I know that the Chief Judge has arranged for each of you to receive paperback copies of *Billy Budd* and *The Merchant of Venice* but I also know that you are very busy people. If you haven't had the time to read the paperbacks, I'm sure you'll find that the videotapes will tell you all you need to know. I expect we'll spend about an hour discussing *Billy Budd*. Then we'll take a coffee break, and after that we'll discuss *The Merchant of Venice*. If someone will dim the lights . . . . Thank you. Now let's hope I can operate this VCR."

*   *   *

Dwight Emerson settled himself behind the table on which the VCR was mounted. "Before we start, perhaps I should set the scene for those who haven't been able to read, or re-read, *Billy Budd*. The time is the period between the French Revolution, in 1789, and Napoleon's rise to power. Great Britain and France are at war. Billy Budd is a young seaman who has been impressed onto a British man-of-war under the command of Captain Vere. John Claggart, the master-at-arms, has accused Budd of plotting a mutiny. Captain Vere doesn't believe Claggart and requires him to accuse Budd to his face. Budd is outraged by the accusation, which is false, but is unable to do more than stammer a denial because he has a speech defect. Frustrated and furious, he strikes Claggart, only one blow, but it kills Claggart. What we're going to watch in the movie is Budd's court martial. As you will see, the three members of the court want to acquit Budd but

Captain Vere persuades them that under the law it is their duty to sentence him to be hanged."

After the videotape had been run, Emerson returned to the podium. "I understand that immediately after you have heard oral argument, you meet and take a preliminary vote, after which the Chief Judge asks one of you to prepare and circulate an opinion. May I ask, how many judges would vote that Budd should be hanged?" Five hands were raised. "Everyone except Judge Ericson and the Chief Judge. How would you vote, Judge Ericson? Please excuse me if I'm out of order. I assume the Chief Judge votes last?" "That's right. I wouldn't have to vote because, if I'd been Captain Vere, I wouldn't have convened a court martial." "Oh. And you, Chief Judge Green?" "I would vote that he was guilty and should be hanged but I would order the execution stayed until the ship had returned to port and the Admiralty, or whoever the proper authority was, had reviewed the sentence."

"Would some of the judges in the majority be willing to explain the basis of his or her decision? Yes, Judge Llewelyn?"

"I don't see any reason to stay execution. It's a perfectly clear case. In your introduction you said we should tell how we decided a case. Well, first we—let me speak for myself—first I look at the facts. Sometimes the facts are in dispute, and then it may be necessary to choose among different versions, and there are special rules about how to do that. But here, we don't have to concern ourselves about that. Here, the facts are undisputed. Budd admits them. He struck and killed Claggart. After I'm satisfied about the facts, I look at the law, and here, the law is also undisputed. The Mutiny Act provides— as I understand it from the movie anyway, I haven't read the Act, of course—that striking one's superior is a capital offense. Claggart was Budd's superior. Budd struck him."

"Do any of the other judges in the majority wish to add to Judge Llewelyn's statement? Judge Carlisle?"

"I would add a brief discussion of the concept of fairness. You've asked us to say how we decide a case. Well, one thing we don't do is decide what is fair. I myself think it isn't fair to hang Budd. His reaction was not only natural but commendable. Any self-respecting person would be outraged by such a false accusation. And while he did kill Claggart, he didn't intend to. Of the two men, Claggart is the evil one. But what I think is or isn't fair is irrelevant. I'm not some sort of expert whose idea of fairness is somehow superior to some one else's idea. My job as a judge isn't to say what I think is fair but to enforce the law, and as Harold—Judge Llewelyn—has said, the law is clear."

"Judge Marcone?"

"I agree with Judge Llewelyn and Judge Carlisle that the law is clear, but I disagree with Judge Carlisle that in deciding a case we don't think about what is fair. At least, I know I think about it. I can't help it. If I felt as Judge Carlisle does, that it was unfair to execute Budd, I'd have a very hard time voting guilty. I might end up doing it anyway, because, as Judge Carlisle said, as judges we have to enforce the law But the law would have to be very, very clear—which here it is."

"Judge Hull-Jackson?"

"I agree that the law is clear but I disagree with Judge Carlisle, as I understand him, that it was unfair to convict Budd. I don't think it was unfair. One factor that always has to be considered in deciding a case is context. In what circumstances did the case arise? In this case, Great Britain and France are at war. Billy Budd is a seaman on a man-of-war. It doesn't seem to me unfair to require, on pain of death, the strictest obedience. Your superior may be a real stinker—even, as Judge Carlisle said, an evil man. But you mustn't ever strike back because then disorder may break out—and just at that moment a French ship may start attacking your ship. I admit, I've never fought in a war, so I can't speak from experience. But I understand that those who have fought agree that the very nature of battle requires the individual to subordinate himself or herself completely to the group. You're a cog in a machine, and whether the machine works depends on your acting as a cog. So, if I were assigned to write the majority opinion, I'd not only say that the law clearly required conviction, but also, that the law made sense."

"Judge Weinstein, you're the only member of the majority who hasn't spoken."

"I've changed my mind. I'm joining the Chief Judge's opinion. I think the law probably is clear enough to require conviction, but I don't see what the rush is about hanging Budd. I'd order him held in irons. The other seamen will certainly get the point, that they'd better not go around striking a superior, even one as odious as Claggart. And when the ship reaches port, Budd can still be hanged if the Admiralty agrees that his conviction was proper."

"Judge Ericson, I'm not sure I understood your vote—or, rather, your statement that you wouldn't have to vote. But if you were a member of the summary court martial, you would have to vote, wouldn't you?"

"Yes, you're right. I suppose my answer was sort of smart-aleck. But I did, and do, want to make a point, which is that it's a travesty that Budd should be charged with any misconduct at all, much less that he should be hanged. I certainly agree with Judge Hull-Jackson that every case should be decided in context. So, let's look at the context. Budd had been impressed. That means Captain Vere had stopped an American vessel and by force of arms had taken Budd to serve as a seaman on his vessel. It's all very well, I submit, to talk about the importance of discipline in wartime. Budd never volunteered to fight in any war. It's hard for me to imagine a greater injustice than executing him for disobeying a military code when he was never properly part of the forces the code was enacted to control. Furthermore, I have fought in a war, and believe me, the other sailors were happy to have Claggart dead. In Vietnam officers like Claggart were murdered by their men. Contrary to Judge Hull-Jackson's suggestion, at least as I understand her suggestion, an effective fighting force is not maintained by protecting officers who falsely accuse their men."

Evidently aware that his voice had been rising, Judge Ericson paused, poured a glass of ice water, took a long drink, and resumed, speaking quietly. "Apparently all of my colleagues agree that under the terms of the Mutiny Act, the mere act of striking a superior—which Budd did do—was a capital offense. I hate that conclusion but I admit, it's probably correct. The language of the Act seems unambiguous. There is no requirement that the person doing the striking have an intent to kill or do substantial bodily harm. The draftsmen of the Mutiny Act could very easily have said that intent was required, and since they didn't, I suppose we must assume that they meant just what they said: the act of striking, by itself, with or without intent, is a capital offense. So, Professor Emerson, as I see it, the question you have asked us is: How do judges decide a case where the law requires a clearly unjust result? And my answer is: They should stand on their hands, if necessary, to avoid the result. That's why I said that if I'd been Captain Vere I wouldn't have convened a court martial. I would simply have told the crew that there had been a regrettable accident in which Claggart had been killed. But since you won't let me off the hook, and I've got to vote, I'll join the Chief Judge and vote that Budd is guilty but his execution should be stayed. Perhaps on review the Admiralty would grant clemency. I must say, though, I feel like a cop-out. I wonder what I would have done if I'd been a German judge when the Nazis took over and passed laws condemning Jews. I hope I would have had the guts not to enforce the law and resign."

"So," Dwight Emerson said, "the vote now stands at four to three. Does any one else wish to change?" "I will," Judge Carlisle said, raising his hand. "Staying execution seems like a reasonable compromise. I think it's better for the court to be unanimous if it can be. If we can all agree, the public will have more confidence that we've correctly stated the law. John Marshall followed that principle, when he was Chief Justice, and Thomas Jefferson was the first to admit that as a result the Supreme Court's decisions, which he hated, were widely accepted." "I'll go along with that," Judge Llewlyn said. "So will I," added Judges Marcone and Hull-Jackson.

Dwight Emerson, who had been standing off to the side while the different judges spoke, returned to the podium. "One of the many interesting things about this program, for me, was your decision to include your law clerks. A good friend of mine was a law clerk and he has told me that he learned more from the experience than he did from college and law school put together. I should like to include the clerks in the discussion we've been having, and since the Chief Judge now has a unanimous court, and, I assume, would write the opinion for the court, may I ask—is it Sally Link?—Miss Link to outline the opinion she would draft for the Chief Judge?" Sally, caught by surprise, turned to Judge Green with a questioning look, but he nodded, at the same time saying, "Sally, please do. Now you will all see how fortunate I am to have Sally as my clerk." Beckoned by Emerson, Sally went to the podium.

"First I'd like to say what a privilege it has been to be the Chief Judge's law clerk. On the first day I started to work for him he told me that when I drafted an opinion for him to review, I should always follow one rule, and that was that I should pretend that I was reading the draft to the losing party. Winners don't care why they've won, but losers should understand that even though they've lost, the court has treated them fairly, which means that it has really thought about their arguments and has explained in plain language why it has rejected them. The reason I should follow this rule, the Chief Judge has taught me, is that respect for the law depends on the loser's respect for the court. Here, of course, Billy Budd is the loser. I'm not sure I could draft an opinion that would persuade him that it was fair to order him hanged, but I'll do my best. It won't be the first time that the Chief Judge has had to change my drafts."

Sally flushed a bit. "Well, here goes! The first section of the draft would state the facts. As Judge Llewlyn has said, the facts are undisputed. The facts I'd emphasize would be: that Billy Budd was an impressed seaman who was innocent of any wrongdoing; that Claggart's accusation was not only false but malicious; that it was natural, especially given Billy's speech defect, that he should sort of explode in rage and strike out at Claggart; and that in striking Claggart, once, he didn't intend to kill Claggart; he may have intended to hurt him, but most likely he didn't have any specific intent, he just lashed out at his tormenter. The next section of the draft would discuss the law. As most of the judges have indicated, when a court must interpret a statute, which it has to do here because the Mutiny Act is a statute, it must follow certain rules, which aren't always consistent with each other."

Sally took a sip of water, and continued. "The first rule is, when the language of a statute is clear, the court must give that language its natural meaning. Here, the Act clearly states that striking a superior is a capital offense. As Judge Ericson said, if the legislature—I guess it was Parliament—had wanted to say that to be a capital offense the striking had to be with the intent to kill, it could easily have said so, and it didn't. The natural meaning of the Act, therefore, seems to be that the act of striking a superior is, by itself, a capital offense. Another important rule is, when construing a statute, the court should consider the reason the legislature enacted the statute. Here, as Judge Hull-Jackson said, the reason for the statute is to maintain military discipline, and making striking a superior a capital offense is consistent with that reason."

Sally took another sip of water. "There's another rule of statutory construction that looks the other way, though. That rule is that the court will assume that the legislature did not intend an absurd result. I don't think all of the judges would agree that that rule is applicable, but as I understand Judge Ericson, he would agree. In any case," Sally hesitated, and then continued, "if I were drafting an opinion for the Chief Judge, I would discuss the rule, for it seems to me that it should at least be considered. If you believe, as Judge Ericson argued, and also Judge Carlisle, that to execute Billy Budd would be unjust, you have to ask yourself whether the drafters of the Mutiny Act really intended to be unjust. I would have to do a lot of research, but I think I would find that a general principle of criminal law is that serious punishment won't be inflicted unless a certain specified intention is proved, such as the intent to kill. If that's right, the question becomes whether the drafters of the Mutiny Act intended to violate that principle. And one way to answer that question is to say that the drafters did not intend to do anything so unusual—that when they said that striking a superior was a capital offense, they assumed that they would be understood as saying that the striking had to be with the intent to kill, or at least to do serious harm—that that was so obvious they didn't have to say so explicitly because it would be understood.

"And that would bring me to the last section of the draft opinion, which would discuss how to decide the case in view of the fact that two rules of statutory construction lead to the conclusion that Billy Budd should be hanged even though he had no intent to kill, or even to do any specific injury, while another rule leads to the conclusion that he should be found not guilty. I would say in the draft that in these circumstances the court should avoid any irrevocable decision. It may be that the stronger argument is that the Mutiny Act should be interpreted to mean that Budd should be hanged, but the argument that he should be found not guilty because he lacked intent is at least a substantial argument. The only way to find out which argument is correct is to give the Admiralty a chance to review the case, which it couldn't do if Budd were hanged. Accordingly, I would conclude, the court should find Budd guilty and order him hanged but stay its order until the Admiralty had reviewed it."

Sally stood by the podium a moment, uncertain what she should do next, then returned to her seat next to Chief Judge Green. "Well, sir," Dwight Emerson asked, as he rose from his chair and turned to the Chief Judge, "would you find such a draft opinion acceptable.?"

"I would indeed, though I'd ask Sally to do some more research, and perhaps to call you for some help, professor. I was struck by Judge Ericson's emphasis on the fact that Billy Budd was an impressed seaman. Frankly, I'd overlooked that fact. I would ask Sally to try to find out whether some principle of international law forbid Captain Vere as a British officer to order the execution of Budd, an American impressed into service against his will. Maybe something like the Geneva Convention. I was also struck by Judge Ericson's reference to judges in Nazi Germany. As judges we've all sworn to uphold the law. But there must be some point at which a law is so unjust that a judge should refuse to enforce it—should rule, in effect, that even though the legislature duly passed a statute, like the Mutiny Act, it really isn't law, and that the case should be decided by other principles. I'm sure philosophers have considered such a case, and that you could suggest some reading material. Of course, if Billy Budd's court martial were an American court, the United States Constitution would apply, and we might decide that to execute Budd would be forbidden by the Eighth Amendment as cruel and unusual punishment. But England doesn't have a written constitution. Even so, my wife, Emily, who has studied the history of slavery, tells me that in the eighteenth century Lord Mansfield held that slavery was forbidden by English law."

The Chief Judge, sensing that he was beginning to ramble, paused. "In any case," he continued, "once Sally had completed her research, a problem would arise that we haven't discussed yet, professor, although Judge Carlisle did touch on it. Whenever a court decides a case it must consider how its decision will affect the growth of the law. In other words, will the decision be useful to future courts? As a general principle, a rule laid down in one case should be followed in later cases, but how well that principle works depends a good deal on how persuasive the first case is. As Judge Carlisle indicated, a well-reasoned case by a unanimous court is more likely to be followed in later cases than is a case where the court is badly divided. And where the dissenting opinion is a strong opinion, instead of stability in the law you're likely to get instability because litigants who don't like the rule laid down by the majority opinion will argue that it should be overruled and the dissenting opinion's rule should be adopted. Now, then, if I were to circulate Sally's draft opinion, I'm pretty sure the court would be divided. The judges who said they thought it was fair to execute Budd,

Judge Hull-Jackson, and also Judge Marcone and I assume Judge Llewelyn, would object to any suggestion in the opinion that construing the Mutiny Act to require execution would assume that the legislature intended an absurd result. Judge Ericson, on the other hand, would probably object to leaving out that discussion, and I expect I would too. I'm not sure how Judge Weinstein would feel. In the end, we might have so many separate opinions that our decision wouldn't stand for any rule. And one other point should be mentioned. We've been pretending we were a summary court martial, which could stay its judgment to give the Admiralty the chance to review it. In real life, however, we are the Supreme Court. Our decisions are final and can't be reviewed by anyone, except, if there a federal question, by a federal court. So, we would have to decide, either that Budd should be hanged or that he should be acquitted. In that case, I'm sure the court would be split, though I'm not sure how. I myself would change my vote and vote for acquittal."

"So would I," interjected Judge Ericson. "I might, too," said Judge Weinstein.

"Well, Professor Emerson," resumed the Chief Judge. "There you have it. Most cases are much easier than Billy Budd's, and in most cases we agree. But as you have seen, in difficult cases, which Budd's certainly is, we may disagree. We may even disagree about why we disagree. Sometimes I think we vote—well, I'll speak only for myself— sometimes I think I vote more according to my feelings than according to the law. One reason I asked you to meet with us was that I hoped we might come to a better understanding of why we disagree—whether it's more about our feelings than about the law. I still hope that."

"Perhaps," Dwight Emerson responded, "this would be a good point at which to take a coffee break. After the break we can discuss *The Merchant of Venice*, which involves not only the Chief Judge's question about what part feelings, or prejudices, one might say, play in determining what the law is, but also examines the relationship between the law, or justice, and mercy."

*   *   *

As the judges and their clerks returned to their tables, some with coffee cups still in hand, Dwight Emerson tapped on a glass. "Before we watch the videotape, let me summarize what has gone before the scene we will be watching—though I suspect all of you will know the story. The place is sixteenth century Venice, the great commercial city of its day. Bassanio wants to court the beautiful and much sought—after Portia, but he doesn't have the money to do it in proper style. He therefore asks his friend Antonio for a loan. Antonio is the merchant of the play's title, *The Merchant of Venice*. Antonio, as it happens, can't make the loan because he is short of funds and his ships are still at sea. He is sure, however, that they will return safely and he very much wants to help Bassanio, and so, he asks Shylock to lend him 3,000 ducats. Shylock doesn't want to because he hates Antonio. Shylock is a Jew and Antonio has often displayed his contempt for Shylock as a Jew. You may remember Shylock's famous reply to Antonio, which ends: 'Fair sir, you spit on me on Wednesday last,/ You spurned me such a day, another time/You called me dog, and for these courtesies/ I'll lend you this much money?' When Antonio replies that Shylock should lend him the money 'as to thine enemy,' Shylock demands that Antonio sign a bond in which he agrees that if he does not repay Shylock on a certain day, Shylock may cut off 'an equal pound/of [Antonio's] fair flesh . . . . In what part of [his] body pleaseth [Shylock].' Antonio signs the bond, his ships don't come in, he can't repay Shylock, and Shylock brings an action to enforce the bond. The parties appear before the Duke of Venice. Meanwhile Bassanio, using the money lent him by Antonio, has wooed and won Portia. Portia knows about Shylock's loan to Antonio and that Antonio is in mortal danger because Shylock's daughter, Jessica, told her she heard Shylock 'swear/ . . . that he would rather have Antonio's flesh/than twenty times' the money he had lent Antonio. Portia disguises herself as a lawyer and pretends she has been sent to preside over Shylock's action against Antonio. As you will see, Portia starts by asking Antonio whether he confesses his bond, and when he says he does Portia says 'Then must the Jew be merciful.' Shylock refuses, saying that he 'crave[s] the law,' and the trial proceeds. First, I'll ask you to comment on Portia's reasoning as she interprets and enforces the law Shylock craves. Then I hope we'll discuss whether Portia is correct, that if the claimant refuses to be merciful, the judge must strictly enforce the law—that mercy and justice are distinct qualities. Before I start the tape perhaps I should say one thing more. The scene we are about to watch is one of the most painful scenes I've ever watched, from any play. Lawrence Olivier plays Shylock, and it's a shattering performance. Buckets of ink have been spilled on whether Shakespeare's depiction of Shylock is or isn't anti-Semitic. Some of the lines Shakespeare gave Shylock may be read as showing sympathy for Shylock. But whatever Shakespeare's personal feelings were, it is clear beyond any question that the law of sixteenth Venice was profoundly anti-Semitic, and that Shylock was punished as severely as he was because he was a Jew."

As Dwight Emerson made his way back to the podium, in the stunned, pained silence that followed the film of Shylock's action on Antonio's bond, Judge Marcone held up his hand. "Yes, Judge Marcone?" "Before we discuss Portia's legal reasoning or justice and mercy, I'd like to ask a question. Did I understand you to say that Portia knew all about the loan before she disguised herself as a lawyer?" "That's right." "Well, then, only one conclusion is possible. She disguised herself and went to the trial for one purpose only: to save Antonio, who had lent money to her lover. That was reprehensible. You've asked us to say how judges decide cases. The first question, the very first question, they must ask is whether they should decide at all, whether, in other words, they can be impartial. With apologies to Judge Hull-Jackson, Portia is a bitch. Did you notice how she had already marked the page of the statute book where it said that the life of an alien who directly or indirectly seeks the life of a citizen of Venice is at the Duke's mercy? From the very beginning, before she heard a word of testimony, she had decided to ruin Shylock, and just how she'd do it."

This outburst provoked Judge Hull-Jackson and Judge Carlisle to say something, which no one could understand because they were both talking at the same time. Dwight Emerson rapped against his glass of water. "Please, ladies and gentlemen! Please! Thank you, Judge Marcone. Portia certainly was a biased judge. Before we jump ahead to the statute about aliens, though, I hope we can discuss how, or whether, her bias affected her legal reasoning. What I particularly have in mind is her reasoning that because Antonio's bond only gave Shylock permission to cut a pound of Antonio's flesh, Shylock could only take flesh. As Portia put it, 'This bond doth give thee here no jot of blood.' Would anyone care to comment on that reasoning?"

"Pretty cute," said Judge Llewelyn. "She may have a point. After all, Shylock wrote the bond and the general rule is that a contract will be construed strictly against the party that wrote it."

"Harold!" Judge Ericson exploded. "Give me a break! If I tell my doctor he can cut my flesh—to take out my appendix, for instance—I've certainly given him permission to take my blood. As for construing a contract against its author, I don't care how strictly you construe the bond, it gave Shylock permission to shed blood. Furthermore, Antonio himself said that Shylock should lend him the money as though to an enemy, which, to my way of thinking, is the same as saying that any ambiguity in the bond should be resolved against him and in favor of Shylock."

"Judge Ericson," Dwight Emerson asked, "are you saying that Portia,—putting aside the issue of whether she is an impartial judge—should rule that under the terms of the bond, Shylock is entitled to take a pound of Antonio's flesh?"

"Yes, that's what the bond says. But that doesn't mean she should let him do it."

"By what reasoning would you forbid him from doing it?"

"Well, it's the same general problem we saw in Billy Budd's case. Sometimes a judge just has to get to the right result, even if his reasoning is maybe not as neat as he'd like it to be. I would simply rule that the bond was invalid and therefore unenforceable."

"Yes, Judge Carlisle?"

"Judge Ericson and I don't always agree, but I don't have any trouble with his reasoning not being neat. I think there are several cases he could cite in support of his ruling that the bond was unenforceable. For example, I'm sure I could find a case holding that a contract by which some one agreed to be a slave was unenforceable. And I think I remember a case holding that a promise to sow a field with salt was unenforceable. A promise to let someone kill you is even worse than a promise to be a slave or to make a farm useless."

"So, I take it, you all agree that even though Portia was obviously biased and her reasoning was tricky and fallacious, she got to the right result when she ruled that Antonio's bond was unenforceable? I wonder if we can look at her next ruling. You'll remember that Bassanio offered to pay Shylock Antonio's debt but Portia wouldn't let him. According to her, Shylock was entitled to merely justice and his bond! Was she right? Judge Hull-Jackson?"

"I strongly disagree with Judge Llewlyn's use of the word 'bitch,' although I equally strongly agree with him that Portia was biased against Shylock. Even so, I think the cases would show she was probably right in ruling that Shylock wasn't entitled to be repaid. I'd have to do research, I'm speaking from memory, but I think the cases say that Shylock had to make an election, either sue on the bond or sue to collect the debt. He elected to sue on the bond. The bond was invalid. So, he's out of luck."

"Do you all agree with Judge Hull-Jackson?" Dwight Emerson asked. "Philosophers get pretty technical sometimes, but that sounds awfully technical. After all, Antonio got the money. Wouldn't it be unfair to let him keep it? Chief Judge Green?"

"Commercial law was never my strong suit. Well, for that matter, neither was any other subject. My guess, though, is that there are cases that hold, as Judge Hull-Jackson said, that Shylock had to make an election, but that other cases, maybe a minority, would hold that Antonio shouldn't get a windfall and should pay the money back. But it seems to me there is another reason why Portia's ruling was correct. If this were an ordinary business loan, it would seem to me unfair to stick Shylock with the loss just because he made a wrong election. But it wasn't a business loan at all. It was a trap, a sort of weapon. Shylock didn't make the loan in the hope or expectation of being repaid. He hoped he wouldn't be repaid—that Antonio's ships wouldn't come in. He wanted to kill Antonio and he conceived of the bond as an instrument by which he could do that. In those circumstances it doesn't seem to me that Portia was all that unfair in refusing to let Bassanio pay Shylock Antonio's debt. Still, her ruling surprises me. It certainly is unusual for a judge to refuse to permit a settlement. I guess Portia would say that permitting Bassanio to pay Shylock would reward a would-be murderer. Maybe she was right."

"And that brings us to the statute Judge Llewelyn referred to at the beginning of our discussion," Dwight Emerson said, "the statute that any alien—and as a Jew, Shylock was an alien—who directly or indirectly seeks the life of any citizen of Venice—and Shylock did seek Antonio's life—forfeits his property and puts his life at the Duke's mercy. Does any one wish to comment on Portia's resort to that statute? Judge Weinstein?"

"I'm the only Jew on this court, and probably that means I shouldn't comment at all because I'm certainly not unbiased. Sometimes, though, silence is misunderstood. Anyway, I'm with colleagues of many years standing and I should participate in their discussion. I'll try to be as objective as I can. Portia may not have been a bitch. I agree with Judge Hull-Jackson, that's an ugly word to apply to anyone. But she certainly was cruel. I could hardly watch the last few minutes of the film, where she threw Shylock to the wolves—or hyenas. And how they picked him clean! Half his property to the state, and half to Antonio, who says he will hold it in trust for Lorenzo—Lorenzo, a Christian, who's run off with Shylock's daughter, Jessica. And then the Duke weighs in. He'll spare Shylock's life, he says, if Shylock becomes a Christian, and if he wills whatever property he has when he dies to Lorenzo and Jessica. Now, let me be clear. I am not defending Shylock. As a Jew I am deeply sympathetic with him for hating Antonio. But that didn't justify his plan to kill Antonio, and his willingness to do it if the court let him. So, declare the bond invalid, and deny him his principal. But take away all his property, take away his religion, make him worship a God he doesn't believe in? There was no reason to do that except to humiliate him, crush him, destroy everything precious to him. And when that's done, Portia asks him whether he's 'contented'! I don't know who the actress was who portrayed Portia but the way she delivered that line made my blood run cold. She sounds as though she's expressing sympathy for Shylock but you know she's gloating. 'I've ruined you, Jew. Have you learned your lesson? Now are you content to keep your proper place?'"

Judge Weinstein paused, obviously to get a grip on his emotions. "For Portia to pretend that Shylock deserved to be humiliated and ruined because he had violated the statute about aliens is monstrous! I must say, sometimes, lots of times, Shakespeare scares me. He sees so deep inside us he knows how we'll act hundreds of years later. The statute made it a crime for a Jew to seek the life of a citizen of Venice. There wasn't any statute that made it a crime for a citizen of Venice to seek the life of a Jew. What does that remind you of? Laws passed in the United States before the Civil War, and afterwards, to keep African-Americans in their place? Laws passed in Nazi Germany to keep Jews in their place? The secret to using the law to oppress someone is to categorize. Categorize the persons you want to oppress as different from you. Of less worth and dignity. The way our Constitution did when it provided that the number of representatives a state should have was to be determined according to the number of free persons plus three fifths of the number of slaves. Or the way we do with animals, when we categorize them as property. Shakespeare understood that that's the way we think, and the way the law works. Portia, Antonio, the Duke could be cruel to Shylock because he was a Jew, and as a Jew, of less worth and dignity than a citizen of Venice. As Antonio said when he spit on him, Shylock wasn't a person, he was a cutthroat dog."

Judge Weinstein stopped abruptly, his voice, despite his best efforts, thick. The law clerks squirmed in their chairs, feeling as though they had somehow intruded on a private moment. The other judges sat stunned. In their experience, Judge Weinstein was laconic and given to slightly sardonic, self-deprecatory comments. They had never heard him make such a long statement, much less one so passionate and revealing, and they sensed that inside their colleague a dam had broken. Indeed, in a few moments they would see the flood burst.

Sensing that as an outsider he was the one to break the silence, Dwight Emerson cleared his throat. "Well, I don't think anything else need be said about Portia's judicial reasoning, so let's go on to the other point I hoped you'd discuss, the relationship between justice and mercy. My guess is that when they were in high school, most of those in this room had to memorize Portia's reply to Shylock when Shylock asked why he should be merciful. I reread it in preparation for meeting with you, and I think I can still recite it.

> The quality of mercy is not strained.
> It droppeth as the gentle rain from heaven
> Upon the place beneath. It is twice blest:
> It blesseth him that gives and him that takes.
> 'Tis mightiest in the mightiest; it becomes the throned monarch
> better than his crown.
> His sceptre shows the force of temporal power,
> The attribute to awe and majesty.
> Wherein doth sit the dread and fear of kings.
> But mercy is above this sceptered sway;
> It is an attribute to God himself;
> And earthly power doth then show likest God's

When mercy seasons justice. Therefore, Jew,
Though justice be thy plea, consider this,
That in the course of justice none of us
Should see salvation. We do pray for mercy,
And that same prayer doth teach us all to render
The deeds of mercy.

I wonder whether you agree with Portia that justice and mercy are distinct, that if some one appearing before you refuses to be merciful— to drop the charges or settle the case—and instead demands his or her legal rights, as Shylock did, you as judges have no alternative: you can't be merciful, you must declare what the parties' legal rights are. Before you comment let me add that some philosophers agree with Portia. For example, two philosophers, in a book entitled *Forgiveness and Mercy*, say this:

> [Society] hire[s] [the judge] to enforce the rule of law . . . .
> We think of this as 'doing justice,' and the doing of this is surely his sworn obligation. What business does he have, then, ignoring his obligations to justice while he pursues some private, idiosyncratic, and not publicly accountable virtue of love or compassion.

According to these philosophers,

> if mercy requires a tempering of justice, then there is a sense in which mercy may require a departure from justice . . . .
> Thus to be merciful is perhaps to be unjust.

Do you agree? Judge Hull-Jackson?"

"No, I don't agree. I think that's just playing with words—with a big fudge factor, I might add. What do they mean by saying 'to be merciful is perhaps to be unjust'? Does 'perhaps' mean that sometimes to be just a judge must be merciful? I think mercy is an ingredient of justice, not separate from justice. Take a criminal case, for example. The judge must decide what sentence to impose. Some judges will always impose the longest possible sentence. They're not just judges. They're called 'hanging' judges. The just judge may be merciful, depending on the evidence. For example, he may impose a short sentence, or even probation, because the defendant's wife is pregnant and has no one to help her. That judge isn't departing from justice."

"That's true enough," Judge Llewelyn said, "but too much mercy is a departure from justice. That's why the legislature passed sentencing guidelines, to limit a judge's discretion. I agree that a hanging judge isn't a just judge. But neither is a soft judge."

"Judge Carlisle?"

"I agree that to be just may require being merciful, but that doesn't quite meet Portia's point, which is, what is a judge supposed to do when one of the parties demands his legal rights, and I think she's right, that the judge has to give him his rights. I'm sure we've all had such cases. How many times have you heard a lawyer say, "It's not the money, it's the principle'? When a lawyer said that to me, when I was a trial judge, I did what Portia did: He wanted the law, I gave him the law, and if it turned out to be against his client, he got no mercy from me."

"Chief Judge Green?"

"I don't quite agree with Judge Carlisle. It seems to me that a judge shouldn't be dictated to by either party. In the end, as Judge Carlisle says, the judge may have to decide the case because the parties won't settle it. But before reaching that point I think the judge should try hard, very hard, to persuade the parties to settle. It's a rare case where there isn't something to be said on both sides. The judge should point that out. If the stronger side recognizes where it is weak and adjusts its demand accordingly, both sides will feel better. The stronger will feel good about its restraint and generosity, and the weaker will feel that it has been treated with respect and its resistance vindicated."

"Do you think you could have settled Shylock's claim against Antonio, Chief?" Judge Ericson asked, not quite mockingly but in a plainly skeptical tone.

"I suppose not. Antonio had given Shylock good cause, over many years, to hate him. But that's really my point. The law is a blunt instrument. Relying on it to settle differences is like a surgeon operating with a dull scalpel. If Antonio could have been persuaded to recognize how narrow minded he'd been and to apologize to Shylock, and if he'd offered to repay his loan—Bassanio apparently could lend him the money to do that, and I'm sure he had other ships that would make other voyages—then Shylock might have withdrawn his claim. And the hatred between the Jews and Christians would have been reduced a little. Who knows, the settlement might even have proved to be the first step in reconciling the two groups."

Judge Ericson started to say something that started with "Give me a . . . ." but was cut off by Judge Weinstein. "Wait, wait a minute! I'm not about to criticize the peacemakers among us. We need more of them. But I respectfully submit, we're missing Shakespeare's point. Ask yourself, why did Shakespeare give those melting lines about mercy to Portia? To reveal her character as that of a gentle, merciful person? Hardly. She was setting Shylock up. She knew he'd refuse to be merciful. By telling him that if he wasn't merciful, she would give him the law she craved, she was excusing herself in advance. She was saying, "Since you refused to show Shylock any mercy, I don't have to show you any. I can be as severe as I like.' She wasn't making a logical argument, that mercy and justice are inherently different, that you have to choose one or the other. In fact, she said that wasn't the case. According to her, earthly power most resembles 'God's when mercy seasons justice.' Well, if God enforces his laws with mercy, why can't a judge do the same? Tell me. I put it to you. How many good, really good, admirable characters did Shakespeare create? Cordelia? Rosalind? A few others. But mostly he created pompous fools, popinjays, hot heads, naive innocents, hypocrites, cowards, villains with hearts so cold they freeze us still. As Hamlet saw, it's a rotten world of madness and murder, which can't be fixed. Prospero knew that everything, including us, is illusion, and that when we die, we leave not a rack behind. So where does Portia fit in? A beautiful woman, adored by Bassanio, with a quick-silver mind, who speaks like an angel, while she slowly strips Shylock of the last shred of his dignity."

"What in the world has gotten into Sidney?" the other judges asked themselves. As if to answer, Judge Weinstein straightened up in his chair, pushing his slender shoulders back, and brushed his rumpled hair out of his eyes. He was not a prepossessing man—not ordinarily, that is, but as he looked at his colleagues across the table, his eyes flashed, he was vibrant with conviction and serious purpose. "I think Shakespeare is using Portia to show that we're incapable of judging one another. Portia could talk about mercy, beautifully, but she couldn't be merciful to Shylock because she was blind. She couldn't see him as a human being, as entitled to mercy as much as Antonio was. Portia would have said that she was simply enforcing the law. In fact, she did say that. If you had a chance to reread the play—as it happens, I did— I'm sure you noticed that when Portia said that if Shylock insisted on the law, then under the law she would have to enter judgment on the bond in his favor, Bassanio beseeched her to '[w]rest once the law to your authority /To do a great right, do a little wrong,' but Portia refused. No, no, she said. If she bent the law in Antonio's favor, her judgment would become a precedent, which would then be followed in other cases. In her words, 'many an error by the same example/ Will rush into the state.'"

Judge Weinstein leaned forward, he turned left, then right, to look directly at each of the other judges. "My dear friends and colleagues, Portia sounds just like us, or we like her. Professor Emerson, I must thank you. When the Chief told us he had invited you, I must say I was very skeptical. But in fact the assigned reading and our discussion this morning have helped me make a decision I've been thinking about making for a long time, without reaching any conclusion. Portia equated law and justice. That's what we do when we speak of the rule of law, as we so endlessly do. There can be no justice, we say, without the rule of law. But as you said at the beginning of our discussion, professor, the rule of law is the rule of judges, and when the judges are blind, the law is unjust. Portia saw herself as a minister of justice. She wasn't. She was a hammer the strong Venetians used to pound down the weak Jews. And so have other judges been hammers. Judges who enforced the law of slavery, in all its exquisite ramifications. Judges who held women unequal to men, judges who described homosexuals as perverts and criminals. The dreadful point Shakespeare makes is this: like Portia, judges don't know when they're blind, when they aren't ministers but hammers.

"It's hard for me to believe I've been on the court for fourteen years, but I have. On June 1st, my term will end. Next week I will write the Governor that I do not wish to be reappointed. Our society is profoundly unjust. Most of its wealth is in the hands of a tiny minority. Its criminal laws are not a system of justice but of cruelty and stupidity, its prisons a separate nation, a lower circle of Hell. I don't want to enforce the law anymore. I don't want to hurt anyone. I want to heal people who've been hurt. Or try to anyway."

As Sally listened to Judge Weinstein's statement she struggled to organize and contain a rush of conflicting emotions. His analysis of Portia as illustrating that the law is inevitably unjust because judges are inevitably ignorant of their prejudice, of their limited understanding of those they judge, caught her by surprise. She hadn't read the play that way. She would need time to think about whether that really was Shakespeare's point. But the judge had given her no time to think. He'd rushed on to illustrate his indictment of the law by reference to ways in which American courts had bungled justice. And then, as she started silently to cheer him on, he turned on himself—a turn she'd never seen coming, nor, apparently, had the other judges. Sally had had almost no contact with Judge Weinstein, whose chambers were in another city. To her, he was a stranger, courteous but impersonal. As she listened to his sudden self-lacerating confession, Sally's impulse was to leave the room to spare him the embarrassment he must be feeling, the way one pretends not to have seen another's accidental exposure. At the same time she felt a surge of sympathy. She wanted to rush to his side to offer comfort. And to seek advice. She wanted to tell him about her break-up with Thatch, her impressions of Arthur Black, to ask him whether she was starting down the same road he had followed. But of course she couldn't do that, she thought. A callow junior doesn't rush to comfort a battered veteran, and what claim did she have on his advice? And so Sally sat in her place, silent, in turmoil, waiting for some one to say something. They couldn't all just sit there, could they? But everyone did.

"Please," Judge Weinstein said, "Please, don't misunderstand me. I'm not saying I think you are hammers pounding the weak, and I'm especially not saying that these wonderful young people who have helped us so much shouldn't be lawyers. I'm only speaking for myself. I used to feel confident about how a case should be decided. I don't any more. I'm like a baseball pitcher who's lost his fast ball, I guess. Time to quit. But that's enough about me. More than enough. I didn't plan to go on the way I have. It was Olivier's portrayal of Shylock that set me off."

"Sidney." It was Chief Judge Green. "Sidney," he said quietly, "I used to be a baseball pitcher, with a pretty fair fastball. Almost became a pro. I'm a coach and manager now, for one of the city league teams. I know pitchers who were harder to hit after they lost their fast ball. They became canny. Nibbled the corners of the plate, slow, low breaking stuff. Then they'd slip in an eighty mile an hour pitch. The batter thought it was going a hundred miles an hour. Judgment, Sidney. Savvy. Pinpoint control. Once Warren Spahn out-pitched a strong-armed kid who wasn't born when Spahn pitched his first game. It was beautiful, Sidney. If you leave the court, we'll miss you, and you'll forever have our admiration and best wishes. But sleep on it, Sidney; you'd be better than ever. It would be a privilege to continue to sit with you."

Sally, to her chagrin, felt her eyes welling up. "Oh for heavens' sake, get a grip," she said to herself. "Do not, repeat, not, reach for the handkerchief."

"Well, Professor Emerson," Chief Judge Green said, "you asked us to tell you how we decided our cases. Have we answered your question?"

Like a cold wet washcloth, the Chief Judge's question abruptly awakened Dwight Emerson from his absorption in Judge Weinstein's statement and the Chief Judge's response. He straightened up as though called to attention and stepped behind the podium, rapping his drinking glass, as much to give himself a little time to collect his thoughts as to refocus the attention of the judges and their law clerks. "Yes, Chief Judge Green, you have. But before I say what I think the answer is, I'd like to thank everyone for one of the most exciting educational experiences I have ever had. I have had some great teachers. As individuals, they were very different, but in two ways they were all alike. They were masters of their subject, and they taught it with passion. And that's the way you've been, as you have taught me how you decide your cases. I can only hope now that you will accept my summary of what you have taught me. Well, then! I think you decide your cases by trying to keep a promise that sometimes can't be kept, and sometimes shouldn't be kept. When you became judges, you swore to uphold the law, and your canons of ethics require you to be faithful to the law. The assumption of the canons is that the law is a set of rules outside of and apart from you. Your promise, and your ethical duty, is to know those rules and to enforce them. Therefore, as you explained, when you must decide a case, first you make sure of the facts, and then you consider what rules of law you should apply to those facts. For appellate judges, at least, making sure of the facts usually presents no major problem. The trouble starts when you consider what rules to apply to the facts. As Portia showed us, some judges may be tricky in choosing the rules to apply. Plato especially despised people who reasoned the way Portia did—the Sophists, who would argue any side of a case, picking their arguments accordingly. Plato believed there were ideal forms, one of which was justice, which you could deduce by honest reasoning. I wish Plato had heard your discussion of *Billy Budd*. As I listened to you, it seemed to me you never did decide what rules you should apply in interpreting the Mutiny Act. If there is an ideal form of justice, you couldn't agree on what it was. Each of you was trying to keep your promise to uphold the law, but you couldn't agree on what the law was. The root of your difficulty, it seemed to me, was the fact that rules are adopted to accomplish a particular purpose. The foundation of every rule is a vision of what is good, an idea of what a just society, a society ruled by law, should look like. But different judges will have different visions, different ideas, of justice, and so, they pick different rules to apply, and come to different results. Some would acquit Billy Budd, some would hang him. And at some point different visions can't be resolved by logic. All you can do is count noses. Four to three, he's hanged. What is the law? Did four uphold it, while three didn't?"

Dwight Emerson paused to take a sip of water. He wasn't expecting an answer to his question—and no one offered any. He wanted to choose his next words as carefully as he could, for he was about to cut close to the bone. "Judges, of course, know all this, even if outsiders like me don't. They've learned to live with uncertainty. But, as spooky Shakespeare showed us, sometimes that uncertainty runs so deep it undermines our own sense of who we are. Portia was not uncertain. She was confident she knew the law. But she was blind. Her vision of justice excluded Jews as persons deserving of the same respect as Christians. It's easy to blame Portia for her blindness, but all of us are blind in some way. And judges know that. They know the history of their profession. They know that their predecessors, under the rubric of upholding the law, have been as blind as Portia was, and so they ask themselves, when they hold someone's life or fortune in their hands, 'Am I, too, blind?' And they can't be sure of the answer."

Dwight Emerson stepped away from the podium. "My time is up. I will forever be indebted to you for your invitation to be with you, and for your candor and generous spirit in our discussions. Thank you."

*   *   *

The shortest way from Mountaintop Lodge to the fitness trail was to cut across the fairway of the third hole, which Sally did. The other law clerks had announced at lunch that they were going rowing on the lake, and they invited Sally to join them. Sally, however, felt the need of a good workout to dispel the confusion of emotions provoked in her by the morning discussion.

Sally had been touched by the Chief Judge's gentle response to Judge Weinstein's announcement that he would not seek reappointment. And she was proud of her boss. She knew he was regarded by some of the judges with condescension, but he was the one who rose to the occasion. The announcement itself Sally had found both sad and unsettling. In her research for the Chief Judge, Sally had come across a good number of opinions by Judge Weinstein, many of them thoughtful and often cited, building blocks of the law. Did the judge take no pride in these? He had compared himself to an over-the-hill pitcher. Did he consider his years on the bench as fleeting and inconsequential as the occasional well-pitched baseball game? He had claimed to be speaking only for himself, but was that a veil courteously drawn to mask what might seem criticism of his colleagues? Was he right in his conclusion that the law hurt people who should instead be healed? But if Sally had been saddened and unsettled by Judge Weinstein's announcement, she had been dismayed by some of the other judges' statements, with their lazy conclusion that the Mutiny Act was crystal clear and their indifference to injustice, or worse, their perception of injustice but unwillingness to do anything about it. And why oh why did so many women judges feel they had to out-macho the men? Judge Ericson, Sally admitted to herself, had surprised her by the passion of his statement that he couldn't imagine a greater injustice than executing Billy Budd. Sally had concluded from reviewing Judge Ericson's opinions, from which the Chief Judge often dissented, that he was self-assured to the point of arrogance. But at least, she decided, he had a heart. In short, it had not been an inspiring morning. Sally wanted to stretch, to run, to sweat—to shake off her doubts and disillusion, and anger, to regain perspective, to see the beauty all around her.

The fitness trail was a path around the lake, wide enough for two persons to run side-by-side. It was smooth and springy, covered with pink and green gravel made from the local sedimentary rock gouged up long ago by a glacier. On one side the trail was lined with white pine, ironwood and rhododendron. On the other side, lapping up to the very edge of the trail, was the lake. Stooping to look down through the clear water, Sally could see fingerling bass flickering in and out of sun and shadow. Every hundred yards or so along the trail was an exercise platform with equipment designed to test different muscles. On one platform were hurdles of graduated height, which one was supposed to jump over, forwards and backwards, back and forth; on others there were parallel bars; a gymnast's horse; rings; chinning bars; and so on.

"Sally, wait up!" Sally, about to start her run, stopped and turned. It was Judge Ericson, dressed to exercise—Nike shoes, tights, loose sweat shirt, visored cap, the whole bit. "May I join you?" "So much for the chance to be alone," Sally thought to herself. But what could she say? "Sure." "O.K., let's go!" The judge set off, not jogging but running, really running, knees high, arms up. Smoothly, as though he were a miler. Sally forgot about contemplation, about letting anger and confusion subside. "So, that's the way you want it!" With an easy burst of speed, she caught up with the judge, to run beside him stride for stride. At the first exercise platform, the judge said, "You go first." Then, and at each subsequent platform, he did exactly twice as much as she did—twice as many jumps, push ups, sit-ups, whatever. After one platform, off they would go, at full run, to the next platform. Finally Sally defeated the judge, which is to say, he could do only as many stair steps as she could. But then came the chinning bars. Sally managed to chin herself eight times. He did eight one arm chin-ups with his left arm, then eight with his right. Sally couldn't help laughing. "All right, all right, you win! I'm impressed!" And she was. Sally regularly went to a health club in the city. Very few young men she saw there were as fit as the judge, who was about forty-five, maybe fifty years old, Sally guessed, gray-blond hair crew cut, sweat running down his cheeks, pale gray eyes laughing back at her, as pleased with himself as a little boy who had just won a race.

Just beyond the chinning exercise platform was a clearing where a few picnic tables were arranged around an open grill for cooking hamburgers and steaks. "Let's sit here for a few minutes," Judge Ericson said. "I can use a breather after those stair steps you put me through. Would you like a bite?" He held out a Granola bar. "No, thank you." On the far side of the lake Sally could see a small fleet of rowboats. The other law clerks, no doubt. It was a typical April day. Sunny and warm, then, when a cloud drifted across the sun, back came winter's bite. A pair of mallards floated near the picnic ground. The judge crumbled the Granola bar and tossed the pieces out onto the water, where the mallards gobbled them up.

"Well, what did you think of the discussion this morning?" "It left me feeling sad," Sally replied. "Oh? Why sad?" "Because of what Judge Weinstein said." "That shouldn't make you sad. A judge who loses his nerve should step down." Perhaps it was the informal, almost intimate, relationship induced by their exercise together. Or it may have been Judge Ericson's casual, dismissive tone. Whatever the reason, Sally's natural reserve snapped. "I disagree. I think the judge who should step down is the one who never loses his nerve." "Ouch! I think that was aimed at me." Sally was chagrined. "Please excuse me. I'm certainly not qualified to argue with a judge about what a judge should do." "No need to apologize. I admit, I do believe that judges should be confident and shouldn't hesitate to do what they think is right. Criticism of judges as 'activist' leaves me cold. Do you think I'm too active, Sally? You agreed with me this morning when I said I wouldn't have ordered Billy Budd hanged." "Judge Ericson, your question makes me uncomfortable. As I said, I'm really not qualified to judge a judge. Anyway, what I think about judicial activism isn't important." "It is to me, Sally." Judge Ericson swivelled side-wise on the picnic table bench, to face Sally squarely. "As you must know, there's very little collegiality on the court. The judges just don't talk to each other. We simply circulate our opinions and take a vote. I'm as bad as anyone else. It's my own fault I get no criticism. But I want criticism, Sally, I want it very much. You were wonderful this morning. Your outline of the draft opinion on whether Billy Budd should be executed made all of us look silly, frankly. You provided a legal framework for what had been a lot of superficial, shoot-from-the-hip comments. So please, Sally, tell me, when you said a judge who never loses his nerve should step down, did you mean me?" Judge Ericson reached out a hand and tipped up Sally's chin.

Sally sat very still, taken aback by the sudden gesture, the gentle firmness with which his fingers held her chin, the naked intensity of his gray eyes. She turned her face away a little, dislodging his fingers from beneath her chin, and tossed her hair. "Well, yes, I was thinking of you. I didn't really agree with you about Billy Budd. I agreed he shouldn't be hanged. But you said you wouldn't have convened a court martial, and I thought that was the wrong way to proceed. It seemed to me you were just doing what you wanted to do, not hang Budd, without bothering to work out a legal basis for your decision, just the way you didn't work out a basis for your decision in *The Lead Paint Case*."

"Sally! That's the most important opinion I've ever written. Let's talk about it. I know from your dissent . . . ." Sally made a face and started to say something. "I know, I know, it's the Chief Judge's dissent. But I also know that you wrote it. First, the facts. You agree, don't you, that the facts are that thousands of kids, some of them now grown, suffered brain damage as the result of ingesting lead paint?" "Yes. I agree with that." "And that the defendant companies made that paint?" "Yes" "And that a jury could find that if the defendants didn't know the paint could cause brain damage, they should have known?" "Yes, again." "Well, then, why shouldn't a court order the defendants to compensate their victims, which is what my opinion did?" "Because, as the Chief Judge's dissent said, the plaintiffs couldn't prove which company's paint had caused their injuries." "Of course they couldn't! Those kids came from poor families. They lived in crummy apartments, which the landlords didn't maintain decently. So the paint crumbled and chipped off, and the kids got it on their fingers and ate it. They—their parents—don't know what company made the paint the landlord's contractor used, and there's no way now to find out." "Just the same, the court has said over and over again—you yourself said it only two years ago—that to be entitled to damages, the plaintiff must prove that the defendant caused the plaintiff's injuries. In *The Lead Paint Case,* twenty paint manufacturers are defendants. So far as anyone can tell, all of plaintiffs' injuries were caused by paint manufactured by maybe only two of the defendants. Why should the other eighteen have to pay damages for injuries their paint didn't cause? Besides, you say, and I agree, that it might be proved that the defendants knew their paint was poisonous. But it wasn't poisonous if it didn't get into the body. Painted on a wall or table, it was perfectly safe. Maybe the landlords should be held responsible for letting their properties run down, but why should the paint manufacturers?" "Well, to answer your second question first. The paint manufacturers certainly knew that the wall or table might not be properly painted or maintained so that the paint might chip off, and a child eat it. As for the eighteen manufacturers, if they can prove that the paint that caused the children's brain damage wasn't made by them, then they won't have to pay damages. I admit, that may be hard to do, but someone's got to bear the loss, either the children or the manufacturers, and it seems to me a lot fairer to put it on the manufacturers." "But that's the problem. You're just doing what seems fair to you. That's not a reason to change the law. You never explain why you're not following the cases that say that plaintiffs have to prove who hurt them." "That's what courts do, Sally. Change the law. There's no statute here. This is tort law. Court-made law. Why isn't it a good enough reason to say, 'The old law is unfair. We'll change it?' You say—the Chief's opinion says—if the law is to be changed, the legislature must do it. Well, let me tell you something. I used to be a legislator. Legislators aren't interested in being fair. All they care about is being reelected. Look at the two bills they just passed last week. Every school child has to recite the pledge of allegiance, and public schools should teach creationism. If it were up to the legislature we'd still have Jim Crow laws and segregated schools."

Sally fell silent in face of Judge Ericson's outburst. After a moment she resumed. "Judge, I don't think I should be arguing with you. I feel disrespectful. I appreciate your saying you care about my opinion, although I don't know why you should. The case is over. The majority and dissenting opinions were filed last week. Three judges agreed with you and so the law has been changed the way you think it should be. I would like to reply to your last point though, about segregated schools, and then maybe we should talk about something else. I agree that sometimes the courts should change the law, and I certainly agree that the United States Supreme Court was right when it overruled the old law and held that segregated schools were unconstitutional. But most people accepted that change in the law as a principled change, principled because most people no longer believed that blacks and whites are fundamentally different but instead that they're fundamentally the same, and so they should be treated the same. The change you made—that plaintiffs don't have to prove who hurt them—didn't seem to Chief Judge Green, and I agree with him, to be a principled change. You just made it, without explaining what other change justifies it. You may be right that the legislature wouldn't make it, but that doesn't mean the court should. At least"—Sally lifted her chin, tossed her head, and looked straight at Judge Ericson—"since you asked me, that's what I think."

Sally stood up from the picnic table and turned as though to go back to the lodge. As she did Judge Ericson also stood up. Stepping between Sally and the way to the lodge, he put his hands on Sally's shoulders. "So, Sally, what's the verdict?" "The verdict?" "What do you think of me?" "Think of you? You mean as a man?" "Yes." "Judge, what a question! I hardly know you. I mean, you're physically very fit, but we really haven't done anything together, except some exercises and talking about the law a little. I can't say what sort of man you are." "But you can say what sort of judge I am." Gently, but firmly, Sally took Judge Ericson's hands off her shoulders. What did he expect her to say? Why did he care? Why does any man care what a beautiful woman thinks of him? So that he can preen? Reassure himself that despite the undeniable fact he's older, he's still attractive, indeed, with age has become more attractive? Sally knew she was beautiful, and she knew the morning exercises had showed off her beauty—her trim legs, flat stomach, full breasts swelling beneath her sweat shirt. She sensed that the combination of her beauty with the thrust and parry of their discussion of *The Lead Paint Case* had aroused the judge. Well, she would tell him what sort of judge she thought he was, tell him straight, let him take it or leave it. "I don't think you're very judicious. You're very self-confident. You decide right away how you want to rule and then sort of patch together some law to support your ruling." The judge looked stricken. "But," Sally added, "you have a warm heart and maybe that makes it come out all right in the end."

Judge Ericson's reaction to this critique was to reach out to embrace Sally, who, however, seeing what was about to happen, put her hands, palms flat, on his chest and firmly pushed him back. "Un unh," Sally grunted, breaking what threatened to be a bear hug. "Sally! Oh, Sally! You are the most beautiful, the most intelligent, and the most exciting woman I've ever known! Please, may I make love to you?" "What!?" Sally abruptly straightened her arms, sending the judge staggering back. "You are, without doubt, the most conceited man I've ever known! Not just a brilliant judge but God's gift to women, is that it? No, you may not make love to me! Now or ever! Forget about it." "Sally, I apologize. That didn't come out right. What I wanted to say was, will you marry me?" "You mean . . . . Are you . . . proposing?" "Yes, I am." "Judge, things have gotten totally out of hand. I hardly know you. I certainly don't love you. What in the world would make you think I'd marry you?" "I don't know that I did think it. But I can hope. It's true we haven't known each other long, but Sally, I'd bet my life on you. I've seen how you are with everyone in city hall—the law clerks, secretaries, court officers. You're not just beautiful and bright. You're gentle and sweet. I don't need any more time to know that no man could have a more wonderful wife." Suddenly Judge Ericson's face turned crimson, something Sally had never seen happen before. He looked intensely uncomfortable. "I guess I've just said I think you don't need any more time to know I'd be a good husband. That is conceited, isn't it? Insulting, too. 'I'm a great guy. Just take my word for it.' I don't blame you for being angry. I'm sorry, Sally. Forget about my proposal. Let's get back to the lodge. I'll race you there."

Chapter 7

A month after the court's retreat at Mountaintop Lodge, and the day before she was to go to Maine for the Memorial Day weekend with Chief Judge and Mrs. Green, Sally was working late in Judge Ericson's chambers. It was about seven o'clock. Since their exchange on the fitness trail, Judge Ericson and Sally had studiously avoided each other. Sally was in the judge's chambers to consult some reference books that weren't in the Chief Judge's chambers. The two judges' chambers adjoined each other, separated by a common reception area, where the judges' respective secretaries and law clerks worked. By agreement between the judges, the law library in one chambers supplemented that in the other, and it was not unusual when one of the judges was not in his chambers for the other judge's law clerk to do research there. Sally had just stepped inside the bathroom in Judge Ericson's chambers to wash up before leaving when she was startled to hear the lock turn in the heavy oak door that gave access from the public corridor to the reception area. "I'll just be a moment. I left my notes on my desk." It was Judge Ericson's voice. Sally froze behind the bathroom door. He'd be gone in a moment, and she'd rather not see him. Then another voice. Whoever was with Judge Ericson had followed him in. "We won't have much chance to talk at the dinner," the other voice said, "so I may as well ask you now, why hasn't the petition to reconsider the decision in *The Lead Paint Case* been denied?" It was a suave voice, controlled, with a hint of menace beneath it. Arthur Black! What was he doing here? Not having emerged from the bathroom when Judge Ericson had entered, Sally felt trapped.

She couldn't come out now, she thought. "One of the judges still hasn't voted." "Who's that?" "Judge Weinstein." "Is there any chance he'll change his vote?" "I don't know. Llewlyn and Marcone are solid, but Weinstein has been doubtful from the start. He almost flipped when he read the dissent, which you've got to admit makes a powerful argument that only the legislature can change the law to get rid of proof of causation. And he's probably even more doubtful after reading the insurance companies' amicus brief all about how many businesses will be ruined and persons lose their jobs." "Well, I'm counting on you to hold him in line." "Arthur, I can't promise to do that. I know you've got a lot riding on the case. What would your fee be? Fifty million? More than that? I'd like to see you get it, but Weinstein doesn't give a damn about your fee. He's talking about leaving the court in June, at the end of his term, and I expect he'll want to leave on a high note. He was persuaded once that the fairest result is to make the paint manufacturers pay. We've just got to hope he doesn't change his mind." "I leave it to you to keep him persuaded. I assume I don't have to remind you that if that judgment is reversed, I'm not the only one who stands to lose." "Of course not. I understand that. The children lose, too." "And there may be other consequences. Some one else may lose, judge." "Some one else? What does that mean? Are you referring to . . . ? Are you threatening me?" "I would never threaten a judge. I merely refer to facts well known to you. But enough of this! We're already late for the dinner. Shall I turn off these lights?" "No, no. Leave them on for the cleaning crew."

Sally remained in the bathroom, motionless, until she heard the outer chamber door close. She gathered up her notes and the books she'd been working with—had the two men noticed them on the table?—put them on her desk in the reception area, and got her umbrella (it had been raining when she came to work that morning). She waited several minutes, to give Judge Ericson and Arthur Black time to get out of the building. Then she left, closing and locking the door behind her.

Chief Judge Green's and Judge Ericson's chambers were on the fifth floor of City Hall. The nearest elevator was in the southwest corner of the hall. Sally remembered, however, that after 7:00 p.m. only the elevator in the northeast corner operated. As she hurried toward the northeast corner, her footsteps echoing in the long empty corridor, she saw, ahead of her, Judge Ericson and Arthur Black. They were standing by the elevator door, evidently waiting for the elevator to ascend. Thinking about it later, Sally realized that the two men must have gone to the southwest elevator, not knowing it wasn't working, and after waiting there awhile, had gone to the northeast elevator. "Why, Sally!" Judge Ericson exclaimed. "What brings you here?" "I had some work I wanted to finish, judge." "We just came from chambers ourselves. We didn't see you there." "Oh, well . . . well, I didn't see you either. I . . . guess we missed each other somehow." "We're on our way to a dinner," Arthur Black said, "where the judge will receive an award. I'd be honored, Miss Link, if you were to join us as my guest." "Thank you, Mr. Black, that's very generous of you, but I can't. I'm already late to meet a friend for supper." As they left City Hall, Arthur Black hailed a cab, and when it pulled up to the curb, motioned to Sally to get in. "No thanks, I'll be walking. It's not that far. Congratulations on your award, Judge Ericson. Thank you again, Mr. Black, for the invitation to dinner." Sally turned and jaywalked across the street, walking as fast as she could without breaking into a run. She felt Arthur Black's eyes boring two holes in her back.

*　　*　　*

The dinner Arthur Black had referred to was the last event of the Spring Meeting of the American Society of Trial Lawyers. Membership in ASTL was by election and included lawyers from across the country. In the members' view, at least, they were a highly select group. While there were no formal criteria for membership, it was generally understood that at a minimum a candidate should have won at least five verdicts in excess of one million dollars. A corollary of this accomplishment was that the members knew each other well, at least by reputation and often as a result of having tried cases with or against each other. All of the members were men, most of them in their early or mid-fifties and most of them white, with a scattering of African-American and Hispanic lawyers. When Arthur Black escorted Judge Ericson into the large dining room of the Four Seasons, the cocktail hour was in full swing. Many of the lawyers were accompanied by their wives, or companions. Jewelry glittered, ice clinked in glasses, waiters with trays of hors d'oeuvres threaded their way through the crowd's slow swirl. Lawyers worked the room in a smooth choreography, hugging and kissing the women, thumping their colleagues' shoulders, seizing outstretched hands. As voices rose and laughter grew louder, the cocktail hour became the frenetic celebratory occasion one would expect to result from a meeting of some two hundred highly competitive, aggressive individuals, some of them flamboyant, all of them self-confident at least to the edge of arrogance, if not beyond.

Dinner concluded, the president of the society, a courtly, tanned, silver-haired lawyer from Los Angeles, introduced the chairman of the Awards Committee, a good old boy from Texas, who acknowledged the president's introduction in Spanish, told a joke about lawyers, and announced that their honored guest had been his committee's unanimous choice, on the first ballot, to receive the society's Daniel Webster Award. He went on to explain that the award was so-named in recognition of Webster's eloquent advocacy on behalf of the underdog, which he illustrated by quoting Webster's peroration in his argument to the Supreme Court in *The Dartmouth College Case*: "It is, Sir, as I have said, a small college. And yet there are those who love it." "Just so," the committee chairman said, "we love our clients, weak as they may be, and to ensure them justice, we will fight anyone, no matter how wealthy or powerful." He then asked Judge Ericson to join him at the podium, where he presented the judge with a silver platter engraved, "To the Honorable Eric Ericson, in appreciation of his pioneering efforts to make the law more just for those who have suffered injury and loss." Judge Ericson drew from his breast pocket the notes he had taken from his desk in chambers, glanced at them, and put them aside. He would speak extemporaneously. "I am deeply grateful for your description of me as a pioneer. I grew up in the western part of this state where the real pioneers used to put their families and all their belongings in a wagon and set out to start a new life, a life free of oppression and debt, a life of danger, perhaps, but of opportunity, opportunity to see another world, to fulfill their dreams, to realize themselves. Hanging in my father's library was a painting of one of those wagons fording a stream as Indians hidden behind rocks on the other side watched. I used to wish I could have been in one of those wagons. I wanted to see new worlds. I wanted to be brave. And so, when you describe me as a pioneer, you tell me that I have realized my boyhood dreams.

"Not long ago I would have agreed with you. But I was conceited then. In my own defense, let me say that being conceited, or arrogant, is a risk that goes with being a judge. We have so much power, and are treated with such deference, that our heads—not all judges' heads but some—get swelled. That happened to me. I'm sure I'm still arrogant. It's probably true that a leopard doesn't change its spots. But I hope I've become a little less arrogant, a little wiser about a judge's responsibilities.

"This Spring the judges of the Supreme Court and their law clerks went for a three day retreat to a lodge in the mountains. We discussed many subjects, including developments in the law, but the most important discussion, at least for me, concerned the nature of the judicial function. We approached this subject from an unusual angle. We examined Herman Melville's story, *Billy Budd,* and Shakespeare's play, *The Merchant of Venice.*

"I'm sure many of you will remember that the issue in *Billy Budd* is whether Budd should be hanged for striking a superior. The answer depends on how one construes the Mutiny Act. I was exhilarated by our discussion. In the circumstances, to hang Budd seemed to me, and to some of the other judges, grossly unjust, and I argued that we should construe the Mutiny Act in a way that would avoid hanging Budd. That meant forcing the language of the Act a bit, but I said that's what a judge should do to avoid a result the judge considered unjust. Then we discussed *The Merchant of Venice,* where Portia was so horrified by Shylock's demand to be permitted to cut a pound of Antonio's flesh that, to avoid that result, she resorted to legal reasoning that simply wasn't logical.

"These discussions, and other discussions afterwards, were very important to me. They made me realize as I hadn't before that a judge couldn't, or shouldn't, consider only what the judge thought would be fair, or just. The judge should remember that his, or her, idea of fairness might be incomplete or biased. It wasn't that long ago, for instance, that some judges saw nothing unfair about slavery. Portia was like those judges. Just as those judges thought that Negroes, as they called African-Americans, were less human than whites, so Portia thought that Jews were less human than Christians. The more I reflected on Portia's judgment against Shylock, the more shaken I felt. Portia's confidence that she was being fair to Shylock was profoundly mistaken. Was my confidence in my judgment of what was fair equally mistaken?

"Now, then, all of us have prejudices we don't know we have. Does this mean that judges must accept the fact that at least sometimes their judgments will be prejudiced, without their realizing that fact? I have decided that the answer to this question is, yes, with, however, an important qualification. The qualification is that a judge can limit, if not eliminate, the effects of unconscious prejudice by basing his, or her, decision on general legal principles instead of on personal conviction of what is fair. Portia, for example, had sound legal principles available to her on the basis of which she could have forbidden Shylock to cut off a pound of Antonio's flesh. There was no need for her to resort to tricky reasoning, much less to confiscate all of Shylock's property and to make him convert to Christianity. I don't mean that Portia should have abandoned her personal conviction of fairness. No judge should do that. I never will. I will always try to reach a decision that I think is fair. But I've come to recognize that sometimes my personal idea of fairness may have to yield so that my decision will be seen as not my will but the law's will. I hope that I really have been a pioneer in making the law more just. But as a judge I'm not as free to go where I want as that pioneer in the painting in my father's library."

Judge Ericson looked out over his audience, a quiet audience, and, he sensed, an uneasy one, uncertain how to respond to his remarks. Had his ears been very sharp, he would have heard one lawyer whisper in another's ear, in a voice blurred by several martinis, "What sort of shit is this? Does he think we gave him an award because he's some goddamned statesman?" Judge Ericson picked up the notes he had put to one side of the podium and returned them to his breast pocket. "I hadn't planned to speak to you like this," he said, "but as I listened to the chairman of your Awards Committee and heard him read the inscription on this very handsome platter, I decided that what I had planned to say was inadequate, even possibly misleading. Without any question, the lawyers in this room are among the most skillful and effective advocates in the United States, in fact, in the world. You do indeed, as your chairman said, fight anyone to get justice for your clients, and all of you have won verdicts commensurate with the injuries your clients have suffered. I admire and applaud your skill and determination, and I am proud to receive your award. But you and I are different. We both can fight for justice, but we must fight in different ways. I am under constraints that you're not. You know that, of course, and like all great lawyers, you wouldn't have it any other way. I accept your award, and pledge to you that within the constraints imposed on me as a judge I will fight as hard to make the law more just as you, in your different way, fight for your clients."

The lawyer who had whispered in his tablemate's ear barely flapped his hands, but on the whole, the applause was courteous if not enthusiastic. Individual comments, offered as the crowd jostled out of the dining room and to the coat rooms, varied. "That was a very moving statement, Your Honor." "You gave us a great deal to think about." "We will all watch your continued fight for justice with great interest." "May I offer you a lift home?" Arthur Black asked. "No, thanks. I'll go back to the hall. My car's parked in the garage there." "That was a remarkable discussion of judicial responsibility, judge. I hope I will be happy with its application to that matter we were discussing before dinner."

*　*　*

Judge Ericson did return to city hall after the dinner, but not to the garage. "Pretty late, isn't it, Your Honor?" the security guard at the northeast entrance asked. "Well, yes, it is, I guess. But there's something I must attend to in chambers. I should be down in about an hour."

Judge Ericson unlocked the outer door to chambers, flipped on the lights, and went directly to his desk. There, using a yellow legal pad, he wrote three memoranda. Two of these he put in separate envelopes, which he sealed and addressed. Then he wrote a note to his secretary. "Suzy, I won't be in Tuesday. I plan to spend the Memorial Day weekend here in the city. Some day later in the week I'll drive up to The Aerie. When you get in Tuesday please fax the memo to the Chief Judge to his summer home in Maine, with a copy to each of the other judges. Just mail the two addressed envelopes, although you might hold the one to Sally Link a couple of days to give her in case she comes in."

Chapter 8

Sally Link thought lying was wrong, even little white social lies, and in other circumstances she wouldn't have lied by telling Arthur Black that she couldn't accept his invitation to dinner because she had to meet a friend for supper. She would have said something like, "Thank you but I really can't. I'm not properly dressed for a lovely dinner at The Four Seasons." But the sight of Judge Ericson and Arthur Black waiting for the elevator had so frightened Sally it was all she could do to keep her composure, much less think quickly enough to be both honest and gracious.

When Sally was a girl, the family's massive male golden retriever, Trawler, slept in her room, as he had since he was a puppy. Very early one morning, when it was still black outside, Sally suddenly awoke and sat up, her back stiff and straight, her chest tight. Trawler was looking out the window. She heard nothing—at first. Then, coming from Trawler's chest, she heard a rumble so low in pitch as almost to be beneath her range of hearing. "Trawler!" she whispered, "what is it?" Another rumble, like the jaguar's growl on Sally's Natural Science Museum record, "Sounds of the Jungle." After a while Trawler left the window and jumped back onto the foot of Sally's bed. Sally pushed her feet against him and went back to sleep. In the morning Sally and her father found footprints in the muddy ground outside Sally's window. "That was one lucky burglar," her father had said. Lurking within Arthur Black's suave voice Sally had heard Trawler's rumble, she had felt the vibrations of that jaguar's growl.

When Arthur Black interviewed her, Sally had been frightened but at the same time fascinated by his controlled ferocity. Hiding in the bathroom of Judge Ericson's chambers, she had felt only fear. A $50 million dollar fee! For such stakes what would a man like Arthur Black do? What hold did he have on Judge Ericson? What did "consequences" mean? And how would the judge react to Arthur Black's veiled threat? He had sounded defiant. Would he hold his ground? If he did, some sort of storm would break. And what about her? Did they suspect she had overheard their conversation? Standing with the two men, waiting as the elevator slowly clanked up the shaft, all Sally wanted to do was to get away, away from Arthur Black's somber, piercing eyes, his dark and sensuous voice. "I have to meet a friend for supper." She didn't have to. He knew she didn't. But he couldn't hold her. She was gone, out of his reach.

On one point Sally had told the truth: she didn't have far to go. Sally's apartment was only four blocks from City Hall, in a slightly rundown but still elegant old apartment building, which, as it lost tenants to newer, glitzier apartment buildings, had filled up with young professionals able to pay its more modest rents. "Good evening, Miss Link. You're late tonight." The doorman, an older man in a wrinkled green uniform, swung open the lobby door. "Good evening, Henry. Yes, I am." Sally clattered to the elevator and pushed the button for the fifteenth floor, her floor. Then, half way up, she pushed the button for the twelfth floor and got off there. The twelfth floor was where Ted Schroeder's apartment was. "Oh, I hope he's home!" Sally knocked, not quite pounded, on Ted's apartment door. And there he was! A blue-eyed young grizzly bear, with a tousled mop of brown hair and a shaggy moustache, he might have been a rumpled model for an L.L. Bean's catalogue—turtle neck and corduroy pants, bulky sweater— which, however, he'd gotten in Ireland, where he'd spent a year at Trinity College in Dublin—and hiking shoes. "Sally! How nice to see you!" "Oh, Ted! I've just had the scariest experience!" Sally buried her face in Ted's sweater.

*　　*　　*

Sally had known Ted Schroeder for something over three years. A requirement to graduate from law school was performance of community service for five hours a week for thirteen weeks, in other words, for one semester. To help students satisfy this requirement the law school maintained a file of approved community service organizations. The one Sally selected was ARC, which, its notice explained, was short for Adult Rehabilitation Center. ARC's logo was a bent bow, the drawn-back string holding an arrow pointed skyward. ARC provided shelter, food and counseling to persons who had, at least temporarily, fought off an addiction to drugs or alcohol, or both, and wanted help to avoid a relapse. ARC's director was identified as Ted Schroeder, who was quoted as saying that he could use any kind of help anyone could give him.

After getting a master's degree in social work, Ted Schroeder had knocked around for several years working in shelters for the homeless, where he became interested in counseling addicted persons. In the course of his work he learned of an organization called Business for a Better City. One of the problems that concerned BBC was the distressing sight of homeless persons huddled in doorways and sprawled over heating grates, a sight, BBC believed, that offended and drove away visitors who might otherwise have patronized the city's shops, restaurants and theaters. In a letter to the chairman of BBC's board, Ted Schroeder proposed a way to address this concern. The chairman was intrigued and invited Ted to talk to the board at its monthly luncheon. Ted put on a shirt and tie and his only suit, an indestructible, unpressable, rust-brown Harris tweed given him by his grandfather, and told the board what he had in mind.

The board was enchanted by the tender-hearted young bear of a man with a banker's head. Who would be the residents of his shelter? "Anyone who's gotten clean and sober and wants help against relapsing." Anyone? "Yes." Ted recited from Vachel Lindsay's "General William Booth Enters Into Heaven."

> Walking lepers followed, rank on rank,
> Lurching bravos from the ditches dark,
> Drabs from the alleyways and drug fiends pale—
> Minds still passion-ridden, soul-powers frail—
> Vermin-eaten saints with moldy breath,
> Unwashed legions with the ways of Death . . . .

Did his admiration of Booth's Salvation Army mean that the shelter would condition its help on acceptance of Jesus? "No. I think Jesus was a hell of a man, but he's not the only way out for an addict." So what is the way out? "First, a warm bed, a roof over your head, and decent meals. Next, respect. I agree with the Quakers. There is something of God in every one. Failure doesn't mean you're worthless or bad. I've had clients who were as successful as anyone in this room, and lost it all to booze. And last, discipline. Obey the rules. Treat the other residents decently. No fighting. No sex with other residents. No stealing. Fail your urine test and you're out. And earn your keep." And how would a bunch of unemployable addicts earn their keep? "They're not all unemployable. Someone who's kicked the habit and has been clean, even for a long time, continues to think of, and describe, himself or herself as an addict. Many of my clients are like that and are working. I try to help them keep working. Some of my clients are unemployable. They'd have jobs in the shelter, keeping it clean, helping in the kitchen, and running the thrift shop." Where would the money to run the shelter come from? "The shelter would be self-supporting. It would take a while to get established, but I think a thrift shop could provide the necessary revenues. The Salvation Army has been able to support its rehabilitation center by running a thrift shop. Minding the shop, sorting, mending and cleaning the clothes brought in would be done by residents of the shelter." Wouldn't it be better to raise the money you need from private contributions and the government? "I hope there will be private support. In fact, that's why I wrote your chairman. We would need considerable start-up money and then we'd need money to pay for operations until the shelter was self-supporting. I hope that BBC will provide that help. But I don't want to rely on government money. The state doesn't have it. The feds do but they're stingy. They don't really want to help the helpless. They believe that if you fail it's your fault. They don't want to say that. It doesn't sound like compassionate conservatism. So instead the official line is, we'll support organizations that prove they get results, which sounds reasonable, but then they set the standards so high that only a few persons can meet them; which means the feds don't have to spend much money. What happens is, that to get federal money, a lot of organizations only admit people with a good chance of successfully completing their program. I don't want to get into that bind. That's why I recited Vachel Lindsay's poem. I want to be able to admit the drabs and drug fiends—anyone who really wants to break an addiction, even if the odds are against it. If they've gotten clean even if only for a little while, and want to try to stay clean, I want to let them in, give them a hand. Another thing. Accept government money and you have to do an awful lot of paperwork. That costs money. I'd rather use that money to help people."

In the end, BBC did what Ted Schroeder asked. The Masons were moving out of an old center city building to a new building in the suburbs. BBC persuaded them to sell their old building for one dollar to a non-profit corporation, to be called ARC, which would operate the building as a shelter. A board of directors, including BBC board members, was appointed to oversee ARC's operations; start-up money was contributed; and Ted Schroeder was employed as director. "What the hell," BBC's chairman said, summarizing his colleagues' decision, "nothing else has worked. Let's give him a chance."

When Sally Link completed the law school form, applying to work at ARC, Ted Schroeder was desperately trying to make the chance that BBC had given him work. He slept at the shelter. He almost never left it. Between counseling sessions he administered urine tests, helped in the kitchen, checked the thrift shop's books, swept the floors, mediated disputes—did anything and everything to keep the place going. When Sally applied he seemed to be making it. He didn't respect his clients, he loved them, and most of them loved him back. "Rockman," they called him, because he permitted a member of a discussion group to talk only if the member was holding a shiny black rock that Ted had found in the city park.

Sally's first assignment at ARC was to write a biography of every resident of the center and of everyone who lived and worked outside the center but came there to participate in one of its counseling programs. Then Ted asked Sally to prepare a report to ARC's board, using the biographies she had written to illustrate ARC's successes and failures. And then he made her responsible for improving the operation of the thrift shop. Sally persuaded an accountant to design simple accounts for the shop and to teach the residents how to keep them. She persuaded a cleaner to donate a press and to teach the residents how to clean and press clothes brought to the shop and how to make simple repairs. She criss-crossed the city, distributing fliers describing the center, and she told anyone who would listen all about the center's work. Within weeks the volume of clothes brought to the thrift shop, repaired, cleaned, and sold, trebled, and the board's wary skepticism that the center could support itself began to dissolve.

Sally continued to work at ARC after she had met her graduation requirement. She worked there throughout her second and third years at law school, her summer internship at Littleton Jones, and her clerkship with Chief Judge Green. The day before she knocked on Ted Schroeder's apartment door she'd helped in the thrift shop. Sally couldn't tear herself away from the center. It was a world in which she could help save a life, a world she had never known.

Norman Rockwell could have illustrated Sally's childhood. She and her brother Karl grew up in a large frame house with a white picket fence and a golden retriever woof-woofing to greet you. Her father, a family doctor, was the small town's most respected citizen. Her mother was a nurse in the emergency ward of the county hospital, where she met the man she married when the police brought him there after he dodged a squirrel but hit a tree. Conscientious, organized, and bright, Sally made her schoolwork look easy, regularly bringing home report cards with nothing but A's and little gold stars on them. Cheerleader for the football team, captain of the girl's track team, class president and valedictorian, she had boys galumphing after her like frisky colts. Her four years at college were high school writ large, and law school, for so many an intimidating and gloomy place, she found a place to solve a pleasantly complicated series of problems.

Sally was like a sunny garden in a sheltered spot, where the caretakers have been tender and nature kind. No pelting rains or icy storms have beaten down the flowers, no brawlers' heavy boots have trampled the beds. Or one might compare Sally to a new boat, carefully built and sturdy, with sea-kindly lines, mirror-smooth paint, and gleaming bright-work, but sailed only in the bay. ARC was the open sea, not the open sea in a storm perhaps, but nevertheless, the open sea.

The Alcoholics Anonymous and Narcotics Anonymous meetings at ARC, and Ted Schroeder's prevention relapse meetings, were open, and at Ted's suggestion, Sally sometimes attended. She met black Muslims in dreadlocks and with Arabic names; unshaven white construction workers with big biceps and bigger bellies; a defrocked priest; a doctor who had lost his license; ex-cons still prison-pale; ex-street walkers the men in the group tried to hit on. One night a Jewish pharmacist, "the rabbi," who had drunk away his business, went to the podium and started the meeting by blessing the group in Hebrew. Afterwards he went to the piano and played, flawlessly, one Scott Joplin rag after another. A Cuban Carmen, Maria, in a volley of Spanish, which Ted translated for the men at whom she was firing, explained that she didn't like black men or white men, especially not when they were fat, bald and old. She liked Latinos, she said, like her husband— although, Sally noticed, her affection for her husband did not prevent her rolling her eyes and hips at a Latino rock musician in the group. There were always musicians. Often they played and sang, sometimes gospel music, sometimes the blues, and then Sally sat transfixed, the waves of their pain washing over her.

Over this exuberant, passionate, aching mix of persons trying to rebuild their ruined lives Ted presided, impresario, school principal, parent, friend and cop. His method, Sally noticed, was to start discussion by "priming the pump," as he put it, by passing out a sheet of paper on which he had typed a quotation from the Bible, a verse of poetry, an epigram, followed by a list of questions. Then, holding the shiny black rock, each member of the group in turn responded. After awhile Sally started to collect Ted's pump priming sheets, then she organized them in a looseleaf notebook. "Have you ever thought of using these to write a book for other counselors, Ted?" "One more idea from the restless mind of Sally Link! Would you write the first draft for me? Please." "Sure. I think they're wonderful." Sally almost added, "like you," but she caught herself, thinking that would be disloyal to Thatch Putnam, with whom she was living at the time. Thatch or no Thatch, however, Sally had felt a twinge of jealousy when she saw one of the women residents throw her arms around Ted in appreciation of something he'd said. Ted really was quite wonderful, Sally thought to herself. Many of his pump priming sheets, Sally was sure, were not original to him but quoted inspirational material used by other counselors—passages from Romans, for example, or from Martin Luther King's "I have a dream" speech. But others were pure Ted, and it was these, Sally had observed, that triggered the most searching discussions. On one sheet, for example, Ted wrote that his father had taught him that before making a move, a chess player should ask "three little questions:" What is my opponent threatening? What is my best response to the threat? If I make that response, what will my opponent do? The sheet then went on to state:

> Good chess requires such intellectual virtues as rational thinking, anticipation of your opponent's probable and possible responses to your moves, intuitive grasp of the possibilities latent in positions and accurate analysis of the weaknesses in your opponent's position. It also requires such moral virtues as self-control, equanimity, stoicism, modesty and courtesy in the face of victory or defeat (good sportsmanship), resilience or resourcefulness. Sound familiar? You bet! Relapse prevention requires the exact same virtues! ! !

The sheet then concluded with four questions:

> Q. Have you learned how to stay calm and rational both in times of success and failure, victory and defeat? Are you a chess player? If so, what have you learned from chess? If not, what have you learned about how to live wisely from other games, sports, arts, interests and/or hobbies?

Over and over, on his pump priming sheets and during his counseling sessions, Ted used himself, his own struggles with self-doubts, discouragement, disappointment, defeats, to show the members of the discussion groups how they could prevent relapse into addiction. He developed a "checklist" of sixteen symptoms leading to relapse, such as impatience ("Things aren't happening fast enough"), making excuses for what you know you shouldn't do, dishonesty, self pity ("why do these things happen to me?"), expecting too much from others ("It's still your problem"). Then he asked, "Which of the symptoms listed above are you suffering from right now? What are you going to do to prevent yourself from relapsing?" He outlined "three basic strategies" for "navigating the ocean of emotions": "intimacy," which he defined as "fishing in the ocean of one's emotions" by finding out, through introspection and meditation, what one really feels, and then sharing it; "transcendence," which meant "discovering ways to rise above unhappy feelings . . . to soar above the ocean of emotions like a beautiful seabird . . . . Envision a kite flying high in the heavens on a windy day"); and "abstinence"—"I will not drink or drug today because doing so would involve a very high probability of drowning in the ocean of emotions! Courage in the face of adversity, stubborn determination to stay clean and sober, carrying the message of recovery to other addicts, building self-esteem upon the granite of sobriety [are like] setting foot on dry land rather than allowing oneself to be swept overboard."

When Sally applied to be a volunteer at ARC, she had imagined herself as one who would provide help to addicted persons, but as she listened to the residents describe misfortunes she had never experienced or even imagined, as she watched their efforts, guided by their beloved Rockman, to remake their lives, she came to feel part of the group, not an outside visitor or observer; she began to apply Rockman's principles to herself, not simply compile and organize them for application to others; she found heroism in persons unknown to, or scorned by, her world, and before their achievements she knelt in admiration, sometimes in awe.

One of the persons Sally interviewed, to write her biography, was Alice Jones, who had been a resident at ARC and then was employed there as a house manager. "I started smoking weed when I was sixteen. The boys chased everybody else. I was fat. I felt ugly. When I started going with my son's father, he introduced me to crack. I started using it every day. My drug was more important than my kids so I gave them up to my mom. Prostitution was part of my life. I'm not proud of it but I'm no longer ashamed of it, because I'm not that person anymore." Finally, Alice said, she got tired. "I couldn't take no more. I looked at myself in the mirror, six months pregnant, and asked, 'What are you doing?' After God gave me that moment of sanity, I never looked back. I have almost four years clean with a job and a home and my children. I'm dependable, something I never was even before the drugs, and I'm grateful to God because without Him I would not be sitting here today."

One night at ARC Ted pointed to Chuck Feely, who was holding the rock. Chuck Feely was an ironworker, biceps and forearms tattooed with dragons and naked women, black leather jacket hung on his chair. "Chuck, you've just completed Phase I. For three weeks you've stayed clean and sober, and Bertha's baked you a cake, which we'll have when we're through with our meeting, to celebrate your entry into Phase II. Would you be willing to tell us who helped you most get through the last three weeks?" "Yeah, it was Ali." Chuck pointed to an enormous black man, who'd been busted from an NFL training camp for drunkenness and repeated failure to make curfew. "You're surprised," Chuck continued, "me too. Where I grew up you belonged to a gang. White gang. Black gang. Hispanic gang. We fought each other. Bad fights. I saw one kid knifed. They killed him. I never had nothing to do with blacks. Except fight them. I got here, first night Ali took me aside, gave me some tips. I'm surprised. Why's he helping me? Must be something he wants. Some angle. But there wasn't. He was just helping me. Helped others, too. Helped a lot. Got me through." Chuck Feely walked across the room, and held out his hand. "Thanks, Ali." Ali rose and threw his arms around Feely as though he were sacking a quarterback. When Feely had returned to his chair, Ted asked, "So, Chuck, did you learn something that might help the rest of us?" "Well, I learned that Ali is a helluva man, and, like you always say, Rockman, if we help each other, we can make it."

Writing Alice Jones's biography, Sally wondered whether she would have shown such courage and resilience. And at the court's annual retreat, as she listened to the judges' discussion of Portia's anti-Semitism, Sally saw in her mind's eye Chuck Feely holding out his hand to Ali. Was her mind capable of opening the way Chuck's had?

*　　*　　*

Ted Schroeder stepped out of his apartment into the corridor and put his arms around Sally's shoulders, holding her against his chest until he felt her relax and her breathing became quiet. "Come on in, and tell me about it." One arm still around her, Ted guided Sally into his apartment. "Please excuse the mess." He hung up a coat that had been draped over one end of the sofa, took a pair of running shoes into the bedroom, moved a newspaper, which had been spread open to the sports page, and a pile of books from a table where, Sally assumed, he ate, to another table, which apparently functioned as a desk. His rearrangement was more a matter of making room than of straightening up. "I wasn't expecting anyone. I know, that's not an excuse but . . . anyway . . . . Sally! I have an idea. I went to the farmers' market on the way home and picked up some of Dick's sauerkraut—do you know Dick's? The German deli?—two knockwurst and two smoked pork chops. Why don't you just sit here while I make a choucroute? I won't take long and then we can talk over supper. I've had a couple of bottles of Gewurstraminer sitting in the fridge for weeks just waiting for the right time to open them. We can have them with the choucroute." "Oh, Ted, that would be lovely. But I can't just sit here while you work. Can't I help?" "Well, when you have a choucroute you should follow up with a tarte tatin. I got some Granny Smith apples on the way home, too. Would you like to make the tarte while I make the choucroute?" "Sure, but you'll have to tell me how."

And so they made their Alsation dinner together. Ted's kitchen was barely large enough for two persons to work in, but they didn't seem to mind bumping into each other occasionally. Ted dug out from beneath the sink a massive iron Dutch oven, filled it with the sauerkraut, dumped in a can of beer—"Yuengling's lager. A good beer"—added the pork chops, and clapped on the lid. "There, we'll let that cook over a low heat for about forty minutes and then, about eight o'clock, put in the knockwurst. If you cook them too long their skins burst, which doesn't matter except they don't look as nice. Meanwhile, we can make the tarte. This is what we'll do. I'll fill this deep dish"—which more clattering and rummaging had produced— "with the apples, and you make a pie crust." "Okay," Sally laughed, "I'll need flour, an egg, butter and a rolling pin. Will you get them or shall I go on a treasure hunt?" "I'll get them. Who knows what dark secrets you might uncover if I just turned you loose." While Sally rolled out a pie crust, Ted buttered the deep dish, peeled and cored the apples and sliced them into the dish, dotting each layer of apple slices with butter and sprinkling it with sugar, until the dish was full. "Now comes the hard part, Sally, putting the crust over the apples without breaking it. I leave that to you." "Out-maneuvered again. Just watch me. There!" Sally crimped down the edges of the crust and then, with the tip of the knife, pricked "TS" onto the crust. She regarded her handiwork with admiration. "Mother would be proud of me." Picking up the knife again, she pricked the shape of a heart around the TS. "There," she said, looking at Ted out of the corner of her eye, to see, with delight, that he was blushing. "Now," Ted said, "if you'll remove yourself to the sofa, I'll open a bottle of wine and put out some cheese, which I'm quite capable of finding myself, thank you."

When they were both seated on the sofa, with the opened bottle of wine, two sparkling Waterford wine glasses—"I saw these in that antique shop near the center"—and a Gouda cheese on the coffee table in front of them, Sally asked, "Ted, did you do that deliberately or by intuition?" "Do what?" "When I came here I was cold and frightened. Now I'm warm and happy." Ted poured the wine. Turning a little to face Sally squarely, he lifted his glass. "Here's to you, Sally. May you always be warm and happy." Sally gently clinked her glass against Ted's. "Thank you, Rockman. Now may I tell you what scared me?" "Please do."

Sally started by describing the conversation she had overheard while hiding in the bathroom in Judge Ericson's chambers, but she soon realized that by itself, that didn't explain why she had fled to Ted's apartment. So, she found herself retracing her last three months. She went backwards in time, back through the court's annual meeting, back through her interview with Arthur Black, back to her break with Thatch Putnam. She tried to be frank, but some facts she omitted. She didn't tell Ted about Judge Ericson's proposal of marriage, even though it continued to echo in her mind. Nor did she say she'd been living with Thatch, which she guessed Ted knew anyway—Thatch had often picked her up at the center. She knew these facts were important to understand what had frightened her so. Like shadows in a picture, or changes of key in a piece of music, they provided dimension. But to tell Ted Schroeder, in effect, that other men had made love to her, or had wanted to, seemed to Sally not simply in bad taste but exhibitionistic, and anyway, unnecessary to making her point. What then was her point? As Sally struggled with her narrative she realized she didn't know. She had to think her way through to it, and so far she hadn't done that. Her conversation with Ted thus became a dialogue of self-discovery, which began with Ted next to her on the sofa and continued through dinner, her pain and groping punctuated by bursts of delight—Ted lifting the iron lid from the steaming choucroute; the apple juice leaking through the holes she'd pricked in the tarte's pie crust top; the cork's pop when Ted opened the second Gewurstraminer.

Sally described her disappointment at the glibness and arrogance of the judges' discussion of *Billy Budd*. She summarized her argument with Judge Ericson, her interview with Arthur Black, her quarrel with Thatch Putnam. "I don't mean to whine or be unreasonable, Ted. I know, not every judge is an Oliver Wendell Holmes, and not every lawyer is ruthless. Thatch is still inexperienced, a decent guy, not really mean. And certainly I learned at law school that the theory of our legal system is that fights umpired by judges are a good way, maybe the best way, to get justice. But at law school we only read about the fights as they were described in courts' opinions. Oh, we had moot court oral arguments and mock trials, but they were pretend exercises. It all seemed bloodless, sort of like watching TV or playing a video game where you kill people without hurting them. And I was good at playing the game. I loved law school. But, Ted, especially in the last few months, I've found I don't love the real thing. When lawyers talk about zealously serving their clients, they mean it's all right for them to hurt people, ruin them, humiliate them, put them in prison, maybe send them to the electric chair. I don't want to do that."

"Sally, you never would. I can't see you handling that deposition the way Thatch did. I don't mean you'd be a soft touch. I can't imagine anyone being more devoted to her clients. But you'd never fight dirty. Didn't you tell me your father's father was a lawyer? I'm sure he never fought dirty."

"He never did. No one was ever fairer or more honest. When he died, everyone in town, it seemed, came to the memorial service. One person after another spoke of how kind and wonderful grandfather had been, and how much he'd helped them when they were in trouble. But Ted, I don't think I could be the sort of lawyer grandfather was." Sally hesitated. "I don't know how to say this without sounding snotty. Maybe it is snotty. But I can't see myself as a single practitioner in a small town. Part of me likes the fast track, the big cases. When Arthur Black described his practice, it was like climbing to the top of the mountain. I admit, I was excited. And I've seen a bit of Littleton Jones's practice. Fortune 500 client list. Offices in Paris and London, other capitals. And I know I'd be good. But . . ."

"But?"

"But . . . . oh, Ted, you'll think I'm the most self-centered person, thinking only about myself. But I'm afraid of what would happen to me. I've watched Thatch change. I don't know what hold Arthur Black has on Judge Ericson, but whatever it is, I'm sure Black won't hesitate to ruin the judge if he thinks that would mean he'll get his $ 50 million fee. Fifty million dollars! Ted, I've been a pretty good person, I think, but I'm not sure how strong I am."

"Sally, Sally, you're very strong. You'd be a great lawyer, for anyone, a poor prisoner or one of the fat 500."

"Thank you, Ted, but I'm inclined to think the Founding Fathers were right. They were cynics. They thought everyone, except maybe George Washington, was corruptible. I'm more vulnerable than you think. Partly, it's a feminist thing. Smash through the glass ceiling. Become the first female managing partner. Lead counsel for defendants in a billion dollar class action filed by Arthur Black. Argue before the United States Supreme Court. I think I'd like that. Anyway, I didn't come running to you just because I was suddenly afraid I was about to sell my soul. Mostly it was because I feel lost. You have a world, Ted. It's ARC. I don't. At least, I don't know which world my world is. Do you remember that night a couple of weeks ago when Chuck somebody—the man with tatooed arms who grew up as a gang member fighting blacks—pointed to Ali and said, 'This is the man who helped me most?' That sort of thing doesn't happen in the world of law, where I've spent most of my time, the world of courtrooms, judges' chambers, sheriff's holding cells. Law can allocate, compensate, reward and punish, sometimes even provide revenge. But it can't heal. Healing happens in your world, Ted, the world of love. Do you know Emily Dickinson's poem, 'I Heard a Fly Buzz when I Died?' ' . . . and then/ There interposed a fly,/With blue, uncertain, stumbling buzz,/ Between the light and me;/ And then the windows failed, and then/ I could not see to see." That's the way I felt when I heard Arthur Black tell Judge Ericson, oh so smoothly, that if the petition to reconsider wasn't dismissed, there would be 'consequences.' Ted, it was horrible! I saw a movie once where a beautifully mannered officer tells a man strapped to a chair that if he doesn't tell them what they want to know, there will be 'consequences.' The officer sounds as though he's inviting the man to dinner. When the man refuses to talk, the officer orders one of the man's fingers cut off. Arthur Black could have been that officer. When I came running to you, I was running away. Suddenly the world I was about to enter, the world I've been working to enter since my first year at law school, looked dark and cruel. And when I pushed the elevator button to your floor and pounded on your door,

I was running to your world, Ted, ruled by the law of love, not the law of courtrooms and judges' chambers. Maybe, I thought, maybe I have a choice."

Ted got up from the sofa, went to the kitchen, and returned with two white bone china demitasse cups into which he poured jet black coffee. "This is what you'd have in a Vienna coffee house, except I should have whipped cream to give you with it." He sat down. "Sally, I don't know what . . . ." Sally put her head on Ted's shoulder. "Ted, would you give me a job if I applied at ARC?" "It so happens, which I suspect you know, Miss Nevermissanything, that last week the board authorized me to hire an assistant director. The salary will be about one fourth of what Littleton Jones would pay you, not to mention that the fat 500 and the Supreme Court would be denied the benefit of your advice and analysis. Having you as assistant director of ARC would be like buying a Ferrari for city driving." Sally abruptly took her head off Ted's shoulder, sat straight up, moved away from Ted, and swept back her hair. "Well, so much for that advice: 'When you apply for a job, make love to your prospective employer.' Ted, how come you're so good?" "Sally, what a question! I'm not good, I'm just doing what I like to do. No one deserves extra credit for that. In fact, my father thinks I deserve discredit. 'A loser working with losers,' as he puts it." "What an awful thing to say!" "No, no. He has a point. We do have a lot of losers at ARC, you know. Just yesterday, for instance, Eddie left. His girl has been bugging and bugging him to come back to her and Eddie finally gave in. She's on drugs. He knew going back to her was a bad move, but he did it anyway. I give him two weeks, max, before he's hooked again. I just finished a report to the board. We lose about half the people we admit. As for me, in Dad's eyes, if you don't try to win, you're a loser, and I admit, I don't try to win, not the way he means anyway. Sally! You know that sheet I pass out about my father teaching me to ask three little questions before making a chess move?" "Yes, you use it to discuss the importance of thinking ahead." "Well, that sheet is true. Dad did teach me to play chess. But there's more to the story. It wasn't long before I was a better chess player than Dad, but I hated to beat him. So, after a certain point in a game I'd make a weak move. Not an obviously bad move, which might make him suspicious. Sometimes I'd win anyway but usually he would exploit the weak move and he'd end up winning. I don't know whether he caught on, but by and by he lost interest in playing me. Said it wasn't any fun, I wasn't trying to get better. And that pretty much sums up the difference between us. Dad's a competitor. So are my brothers. I have four brothers, I'm the youngest. Every one was a winner at sports. Phil in particular. Show him once, and he doesn't need to be shown again. How to kick a soccer ball, swing a golf club, you name it. And they're all doing well, climbing the job ladder, division manager, assistant vice president. That isn't me. I hate competition. I've hated it ever since I broke Billy Martin's nose, and I always will." Sally moved back close to Ted. "I was a big strong kid and when I was in the sixth grade the gym teacher at school suggested I take up boxing. I liked the training part. Skipping rope, learning to punch the bag in rhythm to keep it bouncing back at you, putting a snap at the end of your punch, backing it up with your whole body. Then, the first time I boxed, I boxed Billy, who was a good friend. I snapped a left jab into his nose and broke it. Blood all over his face. He put his gloves over his face and cried. I never will forget his look. Me, his good friend, had deliberately hurt him. I've never hit anyone since. I quit boxing, and I pretty much quit competitive sports. I liked being strong and fit. I used to go on long bike rides by myself. But I didn't like using my strength to beat people. What I did like, I found out, was helping people. One summer I went to a work camp in Appalachia—West Virginia—where we helped rebuild a town that had been flooded. And at college I worked at renovating houses in a poor neighborhood. And that led me to get a degree in social work, and that led to ARC. But Sally, none of that makes me good, or gooder than Dad or my brothers. It's just me being me. Some people would say—I think this is what Dad thinks—that really I'm a sissy, or coward. That I don't like to compete because I'm afraid of being beaten. I've asked myself whether that's true, and I don't think it is. I agree that competition may bring out the best in people and lead them to excel, but it's not the only way. Trying to help people can be pretty demanding. I particularly disagree with Dad about who's a loser. When I think what a lot of ARC residents have overcome, to me they're heroes. Furthermore, how do you define 'loser'? In one sense, someone who doesn't break an addiction and ends up in the gutter, or prison, or killed in a drug war or robbery is a loser. But the money an addict steals, the number of persons he hurts, is penny ante compared to what some of our so-called leaders do. You remember Gray's 'Elegy Written in a Country Churchyard?' Gray makes my point better than I can. After saying that the poor villagers buried in the graveyard never had a chance to realize their full abilities, Gray says:

> Th'applause of list'ning senates to command,
> The threats of pain and ruin to despise,
> To scatter plenty o'er a smiling land,
> And read their history in a nation's eyes,
>
> Their lot forbade: nor circumscribed alone
> Their growing virtues, but their crimes confined;
> Forbade to wade through slaughter to a throne,
> And shut the gates of mercy on mankind.

"I want to keep the gates of mercy open, Sally. That's what ARC is all about. If that means I'm a loser working with losers, so be it."

"Does your mother know the sort of son she has?"

"Mom? She's tougher than Dad. All her other sons are married, to fine women. They all have kids. What's with me? The last time we talked she asked me whether I planned to marry one of those whores of mine. I told her some of those whores would make a good wife for any man, but she shouldn't worry, I wasn't going to marry anyone. I didn't make enough money to support a family and I wasn't about to leave the center to make more money. Besides, some one who spent all his time with whores and other losers wouldn't be a good husband or father anyway. So why didn't she just forget about me? She looked at me as though I'd hit her. Then she said, 'OK, I will.' And we haven't talked to each other since. It was a bad scene, Sally. I'm very ashamed of what I said. No son should talk to his mother the way I did, no matter what she says."

"Oh, Ted, I'm sorry. Please excuse me. I didn't mean to . . . to open any old wounds. But you're wrong. You are good, in spite of what you say. And you're wrong about another thing. You'd make a wonderful husband and father." No sooner had she said this than Sally felt her cheeks burning, and it didn't help cool them that Ted was looking at her with a quizzical twinkle in his eyes. "Ted Schroeder, don't you look at me like that! That didn't come out the way I meant.

Besides, I'm furious at you for not offering me a job." Ted reached an arm around Sally's shoulders and pulled her next to him.

"Sally, I'm the one who needs to be excused. I didn't mean to dump on you. I don't know what got me started. I guess I needed to get it off my chest. Thank you for listening." He let Sally go. "What we ought to be talking about is what brought you here. Are you going to tell someone about the conversation between Judge Ericson and Arthur Black? Aren't there rules that lawyers and judges are supposed to follow? It sounds to me as though something pretty wrong happened, and maybe it should be reported." "There are rules, Ted. I'm not sure what they are though. I'll have to look them up. Meanwhile I think maybe what I should do is tell Judge Ericson what I heard. I know that ex parte conversations between a judge and lawyer are forbidden, and I'm sure the judge shouldn't have told Black about the status of the petition to reconsider, and I'm very sure Black shouldn't have threatened the judge. But still, I think I should tell Judge Ericson before I tell anyone else, like Judge Green for instance. I was an eavesdropper after all. Maybe Judge Ericson would like to take the initiative to talk to the Chief Judge himself."

"Sally," Ted said, standing up, "it's late. Didn't you tell me you have to be at the Greens' house tomorrow morning to drive up to Maine with them? Come on, I'll ride you up to your apartment." Sally put down her coffee cup and stood up beside Ted. "I don't want to ride up to my apartment." She turned and looked up at Ted. He was, of course, helpless, as Sally knew he would be. Gently, shyly, his lips touched hers, and then withdrew. Surprised, excited, a bit intimidated by the sudden surge of desire that raced through him, Ted pulled Sally against him and held her there, squeezing hard. "Oof," Sally said, laughing. She pushed away a little, and standing on her toes lifted her lips to Ted's. This time the kiss was much longer. He was awkward. None of the assurance or technique of Thatch Putnam. But Sally helped him with the buttons of her blouse, and pulled down her pantyhose herself. "Now it's my turn,"she said, and took off his shirt. As she continued, suddenly the shaggy young bear let out a sort of laughing roar. "Oh, Sally, you're wonderful!" And from then on he was just fine.

Afterwards Sally curved herself into the curve of Ted's body and backed up against him. One of Ted's big arms flopped around her, and Sally was at peace. The pain and anger of her breakup with Thatch; her disillusion with the court; Arthur Black's somber eyes; her sense of being lost—all softened, diffused, retreated. In the morning Ted made her French toast with strawberries and drove her to the Greens' house. Hopping out of the car, Ted got Sally's duffel bag from the back. As he closed the car's door and turned to hand the bag to Sally, he stopped, stunned to stillness by how lovely she was. Spun gold hair, sapphire eyes, easy grace. Handing Sally her bag, Ted kissed her, decorously, on the cheek. Judge Green had opened his front door and was walking out to meet them. "I love you, I think," Ted whispered. "That's what I like," Sally whispered back. "A decisive man." She kissed him back, on the lips, decisively. "Good morning, Sir." Judge Green had reached them. "Good morning, Ted. Everything OK at the center? Sally behaving?" "I think everything's OK. Last night, though, Sally said she was furious at me." "Her fury seems to have subsided. Thanks for bringing her. Perfect timing. We're just about ready to go." Ted turned to Sally. "See you when you get back? Have a wonderful time. I know you will."

Chapter 9

After his meeting with Chief Judge Green, Roger Littleton had called Albert Johnson, the Executive Director of the Commission on Judicial Discipline. After identifying himself as the judge's lawyer, Littleton told Johnson that he would welcome the chance to discuss what he understood Johnson had told the judge. The two men agreed to meet at 10:00 a.m. on Thursday, June 5. Johnson said he would come to the Littleton Jones building and asked what floor Roger Littleton's office was on. "No, no, I'm the one who asked for a meeting. You're in the Lafayette Building, aren't you? Good. I look forward to meeting with you on Thursday next."

When it was built, the Lafayette Building was first class. Heavy bronze doors opened onto a small but elegantly proportioned lobby with marble floors. Bronze elevator doors were of Art Deco design. The elevators were paneled inside in dark wood, mahogany or walnut with the patina of a sideboard in an English country home. But, partly because it was so solidly built, the building hadn't kept pace. The elevators were small and slow; interior walls were massive, making enlargement of offices difficult; air-conditioning was provided by ugly window units. The tenants matched the building: respectable, modest—either they didn't want flash or couldn't afford it—they included small firms of lawyers and accountants, employment agencies, engineering consultants, and a miscellaneous collection of state agencies. Consulting the directory in the lobby, Roger Littleton noted that the offices of The Commission on Judicial Discipline were on the tenth floor.

"Good morning. My name is Littleton, Roger Littleton. I have an appointment at ten with Mr. Johnson." "Yes, Mr. Littleton, Mr. Johnson will be right with you. He asked me to show you to the conference room and to ask you whether you would like a cup of coffee." "That would be very nice, thank you. Black, please."

Roger Littleton was seating himself at the conference room table when Albert Johnson bustled in, an accordion file tucked beneath one arm. As the two men sat down, facing each other across the table, the receptionist put a Styrofoam cup of coffee beside Littleton. "It's good of you to see me," Littleton said to Johnson. "I'm interested to learn what information you have."

"Well, Mr. Littleton. There's been a rather unusual development. In the end I don't think it affects our decision that a complaint against the Chief Judge has to be filed—much as I regret that fact, I may say— but I feel obliged to tell you about it." The closest observer would have detected not the slightest change in Roger Littleton's expression. The old lawyer had seen his star witness crumble into contradictions, his principal expert admit to falsifying a report, had heard a judge, for no coherent reason, change a critical ruling. He had long ago decided that there was no such thing as a lost document—it would turn up, at the worst possible moment. Being prepared against surprise, he had concluded, was a condition one must seek but couldn't achieve. One could, however, never show surprise—at least, one could if one were seasoned by hundreds of trials and thousands of negotiations. "I appreciate your candor, but it doesn't surprise me. Your reputation for fairness precedes you."

"Well, thank you. When I met with the Chief Judge, the information I gave him was based on an affidavit, which I have here." Albert Johnson took a paper from his file. "Here is a copy for you, Mr. Littleton." "May I take a moment to read this?" "Of course. Please do."

Roger Littleton saw that the affidavit had been signed before a notary by a man named Gene Kelly. The contents were not in the same detail as Chief Judge Green's account in chambers had been, but they were unequivocal that young Green had paid the affiant $5,000 to take the bar examination for him, that the affiant had taken the exam, and had passed. The only discrepancy was in the affiant's name; the judge had given Roger Littleton a difficult Polish name, which

Littleton had written down but didn't remember. Roger Littleton looked up. "Yes, you were going to say . . . . ?

"After receiving that affidavit," Albert Johnson continued, "I called Kelly. He confirmed that he was the author of the affidavit and told me that he would testify to its contents. Then I met with the Chief Judge. Well, the day before yesterday—Tuesday morning—Kelly called me. He said he was calling from Maine, where he was visiting his sister, and that he wished to withdraw his affidavit. He also said that if I subpoenaed him, which he didn't think I'd be able to do because he was moving and he wouldn't tell me where, he would plead the fifth amendment. I'm frank to say I was angry and suspicious. I asked him whether he understood the definition of obstructing justice and told him that sooner or later I'd find him and would have him arrested and charged with obstruction. I also told him he was only making things worse for the Chief Judge, that I assumed the judge had asked him not to testify, and that that made the judge guilty of obstruction, too. He became very, very upset. He said he had never talked to the judge, who, he was sure, didn't know he'd filed the affidavit. When I said I didn't believe him, he almost cried, it seemed to me. Finally, he said that he was withdrawing his affidavit because he was ashamed of it. He said the Chief Judge had decided an important case against him and he filed the affidavit to take revenge, but that as he had thought about it, he realized the judge's decision was correct. The judge was a good man, he wished he'd never filed the affidavit, and he wasn't going to do anything to hurt the judge, even if he had to go to jail. Then he hung up."

Albert Johnson pushed his file a little to one side and leaned back in his chair. "Now, as I said, I don't think Kelly's call makes any substantive difference. He never said his affidavit was false. We don't need his testimony. His affidavit by itself is sufficient evidence to support a complaint. But still, I thought you were entitled to know about the call."

"Mr. Johnson, may I suggest a somewhat different view. I'm sure you will agree with me that the Commission is obliged to prove the allegations of a complaint by evidence that would be admissible in a court of this state. The provision of the state constitution that established the Commission explicitly so provides. I'm also sure you will agree with me that the affidavit is hearsay. It is a statement by someone who won't be testifying before the Commission, and as you've just observed, you will be arguing to the Commission that the statements in the affidavit are true. The question, therefore, I respectfully submit, is whether the affidavit is admissible within some exception to the general rule that hearsay evidence is inadmissible. You are right, of course, that the affidavit is signed under oath, but hearsay under oath remains hearsay. What exception to the rule against hearsay evidence do you have in mind?"

"It fits the exception for declarations against penal interest like a glove. The declarant—Kelly—is unavailable because he won't testify, and his statement certainly tends to subject him to criminal liability."

Roger Littleton tented his fingers on the table in front of him. An almost boyish smile shone for a moment on his gaunt face, the way a shaft of sunlight may break through a bank of heavy gray clouds. Sometimes one got a nice surprise. "When you are as old as I am, Mr. Johnson, you will find that sometimes your sins return to reward you. Two years ago I argued to the state Supreme Court that it should reject the view you have just expressed—that a declaration against penal interest should be an exception to the hearsay rule. The proposition I urged on the court was that the statement of a criminal you couldn't see and cross-examine was too likely to be false to be admitted in evidence. I was gratified that the court agreed, in a unanimous decision written by"—just the barest suggestion of a smile— "Chief Judge Green. The commentators were very critical of the court's decision, and I agree, it is a minority view. Nevertheless it is the law of this state, and the Commission is bound to follow it. If I may add one more comment: Even in jurisdictions which recognize a declaration against penal interest as an exception to the rule against hearsay evidence, very often admission in evidence depends on the existence of corroborating evidence. That is true under the Federal Rules of Evidence, for example. Do you have any evidence that corroborates Kelly's affidavit?" "Frankly, Mr. Littleton, I haven't looked for any. Until yesterday I assumed that Kelly would testify. I imagine, however, that the examination paper would be powerful corroboration, for it certainly won't be in the judge's handwriting." "Last week was a beautiful week," Roger Littleton said. "We do have lovely Springs, don't you agree? And having nothing better to do, I drove up to the capital and visited the office of the Board of Law Examiners. Fortunately, the

Executive Director was there and I was able to talk with him. I explained that I was unable to disclose the identity of my client but that I wanted to know whether my client could see his bar examination paper. The director said that he could, simply by coming to the office and identifying himself, unless, that is, he had taken the examination more than ten years ago, in which case it would be impossible for him to see his paper because every ten years the board destroys its files of examination papers. The only records the board keeps are the applications to take the bar examination and a copy of the letter informing the applicant whether he or she passed the examination. If there is any evidence that corroborates Kelly's affidavit, I'm not aware of it." Roger Littleton drew a large starched white handkerchief from his pocket, breathed gently on his glasses, and wiped them with his handkerchief. "Damn!" Albert Johnson thought to himself. "The old man is good." Now he understood his assistant's low whistle, when informed that Roger Littleton would be representing Chief Judge Green. "Went right to the top, didn't he?"

"Look, Mr. Littleton. I think we've gotten off the track. You know, and I know, and certainly the Chief Judge knows, that he never took the bar examination. He should be ashamed of himself. He's not a judge, he's a fraud, a fraud on the public, not to mention on everyone who appears before him. We can't tolerate a legal system where the highest judge in the state has cheated his way onto the bench. Let me make a suggestion. If the Chief Judge will promise to resign at the end of this term, after he's finished his pending cases, the Commission won't file a complaint."

Roger Littleton sat motionless, his dark eyes hooded. After a considerable period of silence, he sighed and said. "Mr. Johnson, that is a responsible suggestion. I have in fact considered it myself, and have discussed it with the Chief Judge. I will, of course, inform him of your suggestion but I will recommend that he reject it, although the final decision will, of course, be his. May I explain my reasons?"

Albert Johnson, who was becoming used to Roger Littleton's courtly rhetoric, made no response but waited, wondering what the old man would pull out of his sleeve next. Littleton continued:

"My first reason, as you would suppose, is that I don't believe you can make out a case. Now, then, I've never told a client that I know how a court will rule. I acknowledge that it is possible that you could persuade the Supreme Court to overrule its last decision on the point and hold that your hearsay evidence is admissible. But I think it unlikely the court would do that. In this regard there is one factor we haven't discussed. As I am sure you will agree, when the Commission seeks a judge's removal, it must prove its allegations beyond a reasonable doubt. I appreciate that you feel very strongly about this case but, I respectfully submit, an uncorroborated declaration against penal interest, made many years after the alleged event, from motives of revenge, simply cannot support a finding beyond a reasonable doubt. Some prosecutors would file a complaint they couldn't prove on the theory that the respondent, in their opinion, deserved to suffer the expense and worry of defending the complaint. I make no allowance for that possibility. As I've said, your reputation for fairness precedes you.

"My second reason for advising the judge not to resign also involves an aspect of the case we haven't discussed. Mr. Johnson, no one in this state has had more experience with judicial discipline than you have had. I am sure that at least once, and I suspect more often than that, you have exercised your discretion not to file a complaint that you thought was true and that was supported by competent evidence. On balance, you decided, the importance of proving the complaint was outweighed by other factors. The case against the Chief Judge, I submit, is such a case. Let's suppose you had competent evidence and were able to have the Chief Judge removed from the bench. What would the consequences be? Uncertainty and confusion. A flood of petitions for habeas corpus and petitions to vacate judgments. Before he was appointed to the Supreme Court, Judge Green was a trial judge. In all, he's been a judge for a good many years. I don't know how many persons he has sentenced to prison. What would be your answer to a prisoner's petition that his sentence should be vacated and he should receive a new trial because Judge Green wasn't a judge and had no authority to try or sentence him? And would judgments for damages have to be vacated? Suppose they have been paid. What then? I'm not sure that every opinion of the Supreme Court in which the judge participated would be invalidated, but I am sure that every opinion he wrote and every judgment in which his vote was the deciding vote would be challenged. It's not clear to me how those challenges would be answered. Perhaps you would argue *de facto* authority, but if you were able to prove that the judge never took the bar exam, you would have proved his absolute lack of authority to act as a judge. We know that no party can waive the court's lack of subject matter jurisdiction. Either the court does or does not have the power to decide the case. And on your theory Judge Green never had the power to decide any case, either as a trial judge or appellate judge. Punishing Judge Green would therefore cause an enormous amount of disruption in the legal system and in the lives of thousands of people and hundreds of companies by upsetting matters everyone had thought settled. That would seem to me out of all proportion to the wrong you say the judge did. I don't for a moment minimize the gravity of paying someone to take the bar exam, but if, as you claim, that happened, at least no one was hurt in any very clear way. The purpose of the exam, after all, is to determine legal competence. You may not consider the judge another Brandeis or Cardozo, but I don't think you would deny his legal competence.

"Finally, Mr. Johnson, may I suggest a third factor for your consideration. Over a good many years I have come to know Judge Green and his wife, Emily, quite well. The judge and I belong to the same club and I've often attended evening programs that he and his wife have attended. If you were to insist upon the judge's resignation, he would have to tell Emily the reason. Publicly he could say he was resigning for personal reasons, or make some similar general, uninformative statement. But Emily would have to know why, and I'm not sure he would tell her. He adores Emily. In his words, she is 'the light of his life.' I can't imagine the judge doing anything to hurt her. I believe he would rather end his life. Now, I'm quite aware that this is a personal judgment on my part, which you may regard as melodramatic and sentimental, and which I have no way of validating. And I readily concede that every day in the criminal courts a wife or mother is shattered by proof that her husband or son has committed a crime. But in those cases the prosecutor has little discretion and cannot avoid inflicting pain. Here, it can be avoided."

"Are you asking that I simply drop the charges and file no complaint?"

"Yes, I am."

"You are asking a great deal."

"Not so much, really. Only that you drop a case you almost certainly cannot prove; a case where the alleged crime was not so grave but the consequences of proving it would disrupt the legal system and many settled matters; and a case where you risk causing a tragedy in the lives of two gentle people who adore each other. Mr. Johnson, together the two of us have practiced law for a good many years, I longer than you, it is true, for I am an old man, but you're not exactly inexperienced. Would you agree with me, as you look back, that most of what we have seen was dark and ugly? Formal endings to crimes and quarrels: judgments of sentence, judgments awarding damages, judgments of dismissal. I don't say our work hasn't been worthwhile. Better our clients fight in court than on the streets. Sometimes, though, I wish I hadn't spent so much time fighting. I wish I'd planted some gardens instead of only trying to create order so that others could plant them. Mr. Johnson, I admire Auden's poetry. Perhaps you know— I expect you do know—his poem 'September 1, 1939.' Auden, you will remember, is in a dive on Fifty-Second Street, watching 'a low dishonest decade' sink into war. At the end of the poem he cries out that 'no one exists alone . . . . / We must love one another or die.' And then he closes with this verse:

> Defenseless under the night
> Our world in stupor lies;
> Yet, dotted everywhere,
> Ironic points of light
> Flash out wherever the Just
> Exchange their messages:
> May I, composed like them
> Of Eros and of dust,
> Beleaguered by the same
> Negation and despair,
> Show an affirming flame.

Mr. Johnson, I consider this case you and I have been discussing as an opportunity to show an affirming flame, to light with a little kindness the dreary landscape of the law. Of course, you may say, I am arguing on behalf of an individual, Judge Green, whereas you have a different kind of client. And that's true. You represent the sovereign people of this state. But may I remind you of Portia's response, when Shylock

asked her by what compulsion he should be merciful? Because, Portia
said, mercy

> . . . blesseth him that gives and him that takes,
> 'Tis mightiest in the mightiest; it becomes
> The throned monarch better than his crown.
> His scepter shows the force of temporal power.
> The attribute to awe and majesty,
> Wherein doth sit the dread and fear of kings . . . .
> But mercy is above this sceptered sway;
> It is enthroned in the hearts of Kings;
> It is an attribute to God himself;
> And earthly power doth then show likest God's
> When mercy seasons justice.

"Judge Green and his wife have been in Maine to open their
summer home. They will return sometime today and I expect to see
the judge tomorrow morning." Roger Littleton handed his card to
Albert Johnson. "I've written my home phone on that. You may call
me at any time, at the office or at home. I hope you will let me know
your decision so that I may report it to the judge tomorrow morning.
Thank you for meeting with me. And now, good day, Sir."

Chapter 10

While Roger Littleton and Albert Johnson were discussing the complaint against Chief Judge Green, the judge and his wife were driving home from Maine, having spent the night in Hartford. As the judge drove on to the Merritt Parkway, tires squealed behind him and a horn blared. "Jimmy!" Emily exclaimed, "didn't you see that car?" "No, I didn't." "When we get to the next gas station, please pull over. I think I better do the driving. We don't want another terrible accident. Jimmy, what's troubling you? Ever since we left for Maine you've been in a shell." "I'm sorry, darling. It's got to do with the court." "Can't you tell me?" "I'll know more tomorrow, after I've met with Roger Littleton. I've asked him for his advice. Until then I really don't know what to say. I know I've been a zombie the last two weeks. Please bear with me, sweetheart. I love you." "I love you, too. You must know that. Whatever it is you're keeping from me won't make any difference." A few moments later the judge pulled over, Emily took the wheel, and they drove home in silence without stopping for lunch, Emily deeply hurt and even more deeply worried by her husband's secretiveness, the judge aching to confide in his wife but desperately afraid to do so.

*   *   *

On returning from her weekend on Squirrel Island, Sally Link had checked the Rules of Professional Conduct and the Code of Judicial Conduct, as she had told Ted Schroeder she would do, and had concluded that she should report the conversation she had overheard, between Judge Ericson and Arthur Black. Maybe, she thought, the rules didn't apply to her because maybe she wasn't a "lawyer," as the rules used that word, since she hadn't been formally admitted to the bar. She had, however, passed the bar examination, and while she had no "client," she had served as a law clerk for almost a year. Even if she were simply a private, non-lawyer citizen, Sally decided, the rules provided a standard of conduct she should follow.

Rule 8.3 of the Rules of Professional Conduct, Sally found, provided, in part, that:

(a) A lawyer having knowledge that another lawyer has committed a violation of the Rules of Professional Conduct that raises a substantial question as to that lawyer's honesty, trustworthiness or fitness as a lawyer in other respects, shall inform the appropriate professional authority.

(b) A lawyer having knowledge that a judge has committed a violation of applicable rules of judicial conduct that raises a substantial question as to the judge's fitness for office shall inform the appropriate authority.

Rule 8.4(d) provided that it was "professional misconduct" for a lawyer to "engage in conduct that is prejudicial to the administration of justice." Surely no conduct could be more prejudicial to the administration of justice than Arthur Black threatening Judge Ericson with dire consequences if the judge didn't rule in his favor. True, Sally thought, Black hadn't specified just what consequences the judge would suffer, and in fact, he had denied that he was making any threat at all, saying he was just referring to facts well-known to the judge, but no one could doubt his meaning. He was not engaged in polite conversation on the way to dinner. In any case, Sally decided, it didn't matter whether Black's veiled statements qualified as a threat. Rule 3.5 provided that

A lawyer shall not:

(a) seek to influence a judge . . . by means prohibited by law;

(b) communicate ex parte with [a judge] except as permitted by law; or

(c) engage in conduct disruptive to a tribunal.

The only lawful way to influence a judge was by presenting evidence and argument to the judge, in the presence of opposing counsel. (In an emergency, when there was no time to do this, a lawyer might be permitted to appear before the judge without opposing counsel, but even then, under Rule 3.3(d), the lawyer had to tell the judge all the material facts the lawyer knew, including those adverse to the lawyer's client, and as soon as possible the other lawyer had to be told about the ex parte proceeding.) All in all, Sally had no doubt that Arthur Black had engaged in conduct that "raise[d] a substantial question as to [his] honesty, trustworthiness or fitness as a lawyer in other respects."

The impropriety of Judge Ericson's participation in the conversation was perhaps not quite as clear as was Arthur Black's. The judge had seemed to defy Black's threat. But, Sally decided, it was clear enough to require her to report it. Canon 2.A of the Code of Judicial Conduct required that a judge "should respect and comply with the law and should conduct himself at all times in a manner that promotes public confidence in the integrity and impartiality of the judiciary." The rule forbidding Arthur Black to engage in an ex parte communication with a judge was part of the law. While Judge Ericson hadn't initiated the conversation, he should have cut it off when Black initiated it. He certainly should not have answered Black's questions about the status of the petition for reconsideration or have discussed Judge Weinstein's doubts about how to vote. In fact, Sally thought, the judge should have reported Black's misconduct, just as she was apparently going to have to do—although, she supposed, he didn't because that would reveal his own misconduct. And the more Sally thought about it, the more serious the judge's misconduct seemed. While she didn't know what hold Arthur Black had on the judge, he had some sort of hold that he at least thought was tight enough to persuade the judge to vote against the petition for reconsideration. Canon 5.C (1) provided that a judge "should refrain from financial and business dealings that . . . interfere with the proper performance of his judicial duties . . . ." Was Judge Ericson under some financial commitment to Arthur Black? Was Black threatening to call a loan, for instance? Canon 3.C (1) provided that a judge "should disqualify himself in a proceeding in which his impartiality might reasonably be questioned . . . ." If Judge Ericson was under some financial or other obligation to Arthur Black, how could he be impartial in deciding a case in which Black was counsel? He shouldn't have participated at all in *The Lead Paint Case*, much less have written an opinion in favor of Black's clients. Indeed, Sally thought, the judge had violated the most fundamental principle of judicial ethics. As Canon 1 recited, "An independent and honorable judiciary is indispensable to justice in our society." Therefore, the canon continued, a judge "should . . . observe . . . high standards of conduct so that the integrity and independence of the judiciary may be preserved."

Sally came away from her examination of the Rules of Professional Conduct and the Code of Judicial Conduct deeply discouraged. Tattle-taling on a Supreme Court judge and on an eminent member of the bar was not how she had anticipated starting her legal career. She understood that the reason for the rules requiring that professional misconduct be reported is that an essential feature of a profession is self-regulation. Or so the commentators said. But did the American Bar Association, in proposing the rules, or the courts, in promulgating them, really believe that lawyers would report each other, or would report the judges before whom they appeared and whose favor they curried? To Sally, the reporting rules seemed a piece of the hypocrisy that infected the rules generally—a hypocrisy, she reminded herself sardonically, she had only a little while ago discussed with Arthur Black when he interviewed her: enact rules that sound noble but you know won't be obeyed. Nor would her obedience of the rules win her honor. Enemies of Judge Ericson and Arthur Black would gloat at their disgrace but wouldn't applaud her, and friends of the two men would despise her. No doubt a few persons would support her, but a whistle-blower's lot is rarely happy. And yet, there the rules were. She couldn't ignore them because others did.

Finally, after fretting a few days, Sally decided she needed help. As early in the morning as she thought polite, a little after nine, she called Roger Littleton. Sally had worked on one of his cases during her summer at Littleton Jones. Intimidating but approachable, vastly experienced, he was the wisest man she knew. Mrs. Eleanor Eastburn, who, Sally understood, had always been and presumably always would be his secretary, answered. When Sally said she had "something personal" she was anxious to discuss with Mr. Littleton, Mrs. Eastburn responded, "I'm sure he'll be delighted to see you, dear. How would Thursday, June fifth at two o'clock be?" "That would be fine. Thank you, Mrs. Eastburn."

*   *   *

Sally bounced out of bed Thursday morning. She was sure Mr. Littleton would solve her problem. May and June were her favorite months, flower-filled with gentle breezes, and it was a perfect morning. Sally brushed her teeth, splashed through her shower, jumped into some sweats, ripped down the elevator and around the corner to the deli, bought a morning paper, a cinnamon and raisin bagel, toasted, easy on the butter, a large coffee, regular blend, ripped back up the elevator and settled down by her apartment window, from which she could just glimpse the boulevard leading to the park. She barely glanced at the front pages of the paper. She despised the moralistic President and was sick of reading about him and the craven Congress. En route to the comics and crossword, she came to the business section. "Judge allows shareholders to sue law firm," a headline read. "Oh?" Sally thought, and sure enough, the story was about a law suit in which Arthur Black was identified as counsel for plaintiffs. "A federal district judge in Chicago has ruled that shareholders of a bankrupt corporation, Pioneer Pharmaceuticals, may sue the corporation's lawyers, James, Roberts & James, on their claim that the lawyers knew or should have known that the corporation's officers were engaged in illegal transactions from which they realized personal gains of hundreds of millions of dollars but which diluted the value of Pioneer's stock and caused its bankruptcy. According to the plaintiff shareholders, not only did Pioneer's lawyers, James, Roberts & James, not inform Pioneer's board of directors but they aided and abetted the officers in their illegal transactions. The shareholders are demanding $500,000,000 compensatory damages and $500,000,000 in punitive damages. The judge emphasized that her ruling did not mean that the defendant lawyers were liable to pay any damages but only that the shareholders were entitled to try to prove their allegations. 'This is a landmark decision,' Arthur Black, counsel for the shareholders, said. 'It tells lawyers that they must be faithful to the interests of the corporation and its shareholders. They can't stuff themselves with fat fees while closing their eyes to what's going on.' The lawyers for James, Roberts & James declined to comment until they had analyzed the judge's lengthy opinion." "So," Sally thought, "he's drawn first blood." She resumed turning pages. After the stock market quotations came the obituary section. "Oh, no!" "Eric Ericson, 52, Supreme Court Judge, Killed." Sally went numb, as from a sudden blow. Spreading out the obituary page, she raced through the story. Early Wednesday morning, about 4 A.M., Judge Ericson's automobile had run head-on into an abutment at the entrance of a tunnel on the turnpike. The state police said that the damage to the automobile indicated that it had been traveling at a high rate of speed, and that death had been instantaneous. The police speculated that the judge may have dozed for a moment. Also, they said, the area was notorious for its early morning fogs. Chief Judge Green of the Supreme Court, called at his summer home in Maine, expressed shock and dismay. "Judge Ericson was the most vigorous and imaginative judge on the court," the Chief Judge said. "He was passionate in his dedication to the law"—not the Judge Ericson I knew, Sally thought to herself, but then, she would expect her boss to say something nice—"and the court will miss him, as will everyone concerned with justice." The Chief Judge said that as soon as he could confer with the other judges, a date would be set for a special session of the court in honor of Judge Ericson. The newspaper story quoted other tributes to Judge Ericson, by the president of the state bar association among others. It was noted that shortly before his death the judge had received a special award from a nationwide association of trial lawyers, honoring him as a pioneer in making the law more just. The judge's career before he was appointed to the Supreme Court was described. The President Pro Tem of the State Senate was quoted as remembering that Judge Ericson had been an unusually effective member of the legislature, a tireless supporter of the underdog. While in the legislature, the judge had studied law at night at the state university and the president of the university was quoted as announcing that a night law school scholarship would be established in his honor. The judge's only surviving relative was a brother, who lived in Montana on a cattle ranch and who said he expected to take the judge's ashes to the ranch, where the judge loved to ride in the mountains. Services would be private.

Sally put down the newspaper. She felt as though Judge Ericson were standing beside her, invisible but there. She heard again, word for word, their quarrel on the fitness trail at Mountaintop Lodge; his fervent declaration of love; her furious, contemptuous rejection; his question to Arthur Black, "Are you threatening me?" She remembered his searching look as he wondered, by the elevator, how he'd missed her in chambers. Had he guessed she had overheard them? How would he have explained the conversation? Now she would never know. Now she would never understand some one she suddenly realized she very much wanted to understand, a painful, incomplete relationship would remain that way, her half-sensed hope that it might be somehow resolved would never be realized.

Sally put on her bicycle helmet and wheeled her bicycle, which she kept at one end of her living room, to the elevator. Out! She wanted out, out into the sun, the breeze on her cheeks, her legs pushing hard. As she entered the lobby, she heard a voice call, "Miss Link?" It was the mailman, sorting the mail into the postal boxes near the elevator. "Here's your mail. Might as well give it to you now." He handed Sally a copy of *The New Yorker* and two letters. "Thanks. Oh!" "Is something wrong?" "No, no, it's just that I wasn't expecting . . . . But never mind. Thanks again." As she took the letters from the mailman, Sally had noticed in the upper left corner of one of the envelopes the gold seal of the Supreme Court, and printed beneath the seal, "The Honorable Eric Ericson, Judge." "He must have written before . . . ." Sally thought, leaving the thought unfinished because "he was killed" was too painful. "But why would he write me?" Sally had also noticed that the addresses on the other envelope were handwritten. The return address was "Green, Squirrel Is. ME 04570." It must be the Chief Judge's answer to her letter asking his advice on whether she should be a lawyer. She had indicated that she hoped he would answer promptly, and he had. "Typical of him," Sally thought.

Sally put the magazine and letters in the basket on her bicycle and as Henry held open the lobby door—"Thank you, Henry, I should be back about lunch time."—wheeled the bicycle out to the street. The next instant she was off, beating the traffic lights, zigging between cars, pedaling hard, as reckless as any New York City messenger, off to the azalea garden behind the city art museum.

The art museum was a great pile of pale yellow stone on top of a hill. Built to look like a Greek temple, it faced east to center city and west up the river that wound through the park. The azalea garden was on the western side of the museum, its beds curving around a broad sunny lawn. When Judge Green, steering the *Emily* between Fisherman's and Darmariscove, had said he was entering the sacred sector, Sally had thought of the azalea garden. Now, early in June, only a few of the azaleas—some of the yellow and orange ones—were still blooming. But the rhododendrons were in their glory, white, lavender, red, the euonymus was heavy with its waxy fruit, wisteria dripped from a massive wooden arbor, and borders of roses were in pink bloom. In the middle of the lawn two young women—college students, Sally judged from the books scattered beside them—were soaking up the sun, blouses pushed off their shoulders, skirts pulled up to short short. A burly young man, carved chocolate muscles, jogged by, a German Shepherd heeling beside him. Two mothers pushing strollers, one with twins in it, chatted with each other. Sally headed for the cat.

The cat was a larger-than-life statue carved from a single block of black stone with pale mica chips embedded in it. It wasn't any particular species of cat but a sort of Platonic cat, a cat of cats. It sat on its haunches, on the edge of the garden close to one of the curving borders, tail curved around its feet, sightless stone eyes surveying the lawn where the two young women were sunning themselves. Near the cat was a bench. Sally leaned her bicycle on the bench, sat down, and opened the letter from Judge Ericson. It was dated "Friday night' and was written—better, perhaps, scrawled—in pencil on yellow sheets from a legal pad.

"Dear Sally: I'm writing this in chambers. I came back here after the dinner we went to when we left you outside city hall. I plan to drive to a house I have in the mountains, sometime during the week, I haven't quite decided when, and I want to tell you about the dinner before I leave.

"It was terrible, Sally, but now I feel like new. Free. You know how in comic strips, when a character suddenly understands something, an electric light bulb turns on over his head? That's what happened to me. The dinner was supposed to be in my honor, but the lawyers weren't honoring me as a judge. They regarded me as sort of a mascot, or cheer leader, as someone supporting their team. I was 'their judge.' Just before the dinner one of them—a famous lawyer and an officer of the association—said something that showed he thought he could control how I decided a particular case. In the middle of the main course I decided I would tell them I was not their judge.

"Sally, I think you would have been proud of me. Anyway, in my remarks, when I accepted the award, I was talking to you, not to the lawyers at the tables in front of me. I wish you had been there to hear me. I told them that while I would always try to do what I thought was fair, I could not, as a judge, do what I would like to do. I had to do as the law required. My decisions had to be based on legal principles even if that meant that sometimes I could not decide as I—by which they knew I meant they—would have liked. Not what they expected. Their applause was quite tepid. But I didn't care.

"It must seem strange to you, my excitement at having said something so banal. Doesn't everyone know that a judge is supposed to do what the law requires, not what the judge or anyone else would like? How could saying that make me feel free and new? Because, Sally, since we argued with each other on the Mountaintop Lodge fitness trail, my idea of how a judge should decide a case has changed. I didn't say this to the lawyers, but what I did say reflected the change.

"I don't think a case should be decided by principles laid down by God—if there is a God. I can't define what sort of God would create or permit our world—or decided by principles laid down by reason—which has so often justified what is wrong as right. I remember a trial judge who used to tell the jury, 'You must follow the law as I explain it to you, for I am the law.' When I became a judge, that's how I felt. The law, I thought, was made by those with the power to make it, and now I would make it.

"Sally, more than anything else I love freedom. My brother and I grew up in Minnesota on my parents' farm My parents weren't poor exactly. We always had a tight roof over our heads and good food, which they grew. But there wasn't anything left over. No trips to the theater, no records, no soccer balls or baseball gloves. My parents worked all the time, and between going to church and school, my brother and I helped them. My brother is still a farmer—rancher—but when I graduated from high school, I ran away and never went back. I worked my way through the state university. During the summers I signed on as a seaman on freighters and saw the world. After graduation I was down and out in Paris and London for a year—like George Orwell. Then I settled here and became a state legislator, a lawyer, and a judge. I made a lot of money as a lawyer. With some of it I bought a huge old Mercedes Benz phaeton. If you were older you would remember seeing one like it in news reels of political events in Europe, especially Eastern Europe, and Scandinavia. It's the kind of car kings and visiting heads

of state rode in. I still have my old Mercedes. I call it The Monster.
After I became a judge I bought a house in the mountains, which I
call The Aerie. I love driving the Monster, very early in the morning,
to The Aerie. When I get there, I sit on the deck with a cup of coffee
and watch the rows of hills emerge, blue and gray, one row behind
another, as the sun climbs the sky.

"That's what I live for, Sally, that's what I've worked for since I was
a boy—to be free, and for awhile, as a judge, I felt free. I could decide
my cases the way I wanted. What happened at dinner tonight, when
the light bulb went on over my head, was that I suddenly realized I'd
been fooling myself. I wasn't free. I was like a spoiled kid indulging
himself. Freedom isn't doing what you want, I thought. Freedom is
doing something by following rules. Mozart was free. He had so
mastered the rules of music he could express whatever feelings he
wanted. Michelangelo could find Mary and the crucified Christ, or
David, or a slave in a block of marble. Capablanca played chess the way
Orpheus played his harp. And that's what a judge, a real judge, a free
judge, does. The rules of law are like the rules of music, or sculpture,
or chess. Or the rules of poetry, Sally, poetry. Think of Robert Frost's
'Stopping By Woods On A Snowy Evening.' Four verses, each with
four lines, each line with four beats, the verses tied together with
interlocking rhymes. Frost was free!

"Most judges are parrots, in my opinion. They utter the rules of
law the way parrots utter words: without understanding. Some judges
are peacocks: conceited and lazy. Conceited because they're sure they
know what is fair. Lazy because they don't make the effort to prove
that it's the law. They just strut and preen. 'See how brilliant I am,
how clever! See my generous heart!' That last was me, Sally, as you
told me on the fitness trail, when I asked you what you thought of me
as a judge. Then there are judges—only a few—who think, but aren't
sure, they know what is fair, and ask themselves whether the law
supports what they think. They respect their material. They carve with
the grain. And just as their thinking shapes the material, the material
shapes their thinking. When Frost started to write 'Stopping By Woods
On A Snowy Evening,' he couldn't have foreseen his closing couplet.
That couplet wasn't pre-ordained, it wasn't 'right' because it was laid
down in Heaven and Frost found it. Frost created it. But not by himself.
He created it by overcoming the resistance of rules—rules thousands

of poets before him had also struggled to overcome. That's the way the law is, Sally, or so I've decided. A judge's decision is 'right.,' or 'in accordance with the law,' to the extent to which, using rules, it expresses a vision of our humanity. If a judge's vision of humanity is rooted in ignorance, the judge's decision will die. But if it is rooted in an understanding, which will always be incomplete, of what we need to realize ourselves, the decision will lead to broader, deeper decisions. I think this is what Coke meant when he said, 'Out of the old fields cometh the new corn.'

"Oh, Sally! How I wish I had understood this earlier! Then I would have been an artist instead of a peacock! Then perhaps I could have written an opinion in *The Lead Paint Case* that you wouldn't have torn apart. Because I still believe I'm right that letting the paint manufacturers off scot-free is wrong. I simply don't have the artistry to show that the law requiring proof of causation should be changed.

"I know I've gone on and on. But that's what happens when a light suddenly turns on and the world looks different. You want to tell people, to ask them, 'Don't you see how different the world looks?', to persuade them that that's the way the world really is. Anyway, Sally, I wanted to tell you, because you're the one who started me thinking, and reading (Coke, for instance), and thinking some more. Without you, I wouldn't have been ready—it wouldn't have occurred to me— to tell the lawyers at the dinner that I wasn't 'their judge.' And I've done something else. When I got back to chambers, after the dinner, before writing you I wrote a memo to the Chief Judge. I'm not going to tell you what's in it, Sally, because I want you to be surprised. But it will show that my talk to the lawyers wasn't just an after-dinner speech. And now, it's very late and I must stop.

"I'm sure you never expected a letter like this—or any letter from me, for that matter. It is, I suppose, a sort of love letter, for you must be able to tell from it how much you have meant to me. But I assure you, I'm not trying to persuade you to let me see you. I do love you, as I told you on the fitness trail, but I recognize, and accept, the fact that that doesn't mean we should have a relationship with each other. It often happens that two lives cross for a little while and then must go separate ways. You will do something wonderful. As for me, I'll fold down the top of The Monster, and in the small dark hours before dawn I'll fly past the apple orchards, away to my mountains. No artist, perhaps, but, thanks to your beauty, sweetness and idealism, a free man, his self-respect regained. Thank you.

Eric Ericson

As Sally read Judge Ericson's letter she had felt her eyes filling with tears. Now they brimmed over to trickle down her cheeks. "That stupid car! Why did he drive so fast? Couldn't he have waited until morning before he left? Just when he had what he wanted, he threw it all away!" Sally was surprised by how hard she wept. It wasn't as though some one she loved had been killed. And surely he didn't really love her, even though he protested that he did. He just thought he did.— a typical, impetuous, romantic judgment. Still, she wept. She asked herself whether somehow she had behaved badly. Should she have refused to argue with him, when they were on the fitness trail together? He didn't seem to think so. According to him, their argument led to his regaining his self-respect. And then Sally's thoughts suddenly lurched, and losing their balance, plunged down to darkness. Was his letter a farewell letter? He seemed to say he'd never see her again. Why not? Had he deliberately driven into the abutment? Was that the only way he could escape Arthur Black's grip—the only way he could be "free"? Had her "sweetness" and "idealism" inspired him to act in a way that led to his death?

With that last question Sally became angry, very angry, with herself. She abruptly straightened up and wiped her eyes. "You are not, repeat, not, in any way responsible for his death. And don't be stupid and imagine a melodrama. He would not have said he was looking forward to watching the sunrise over his mountains if he was planning to kill himself. No one can be sure, but all the evidence is that the state police are right: he dozed, or ran off the road in the fog." Having thus scolded herself, Sally regained her composure, although she was very subdued. After awhile she stood up from the bench by the cat. Closing her eyes, she spread her arms and faced the sun, letting it pour over her. Then she chained her bicycle to the bench, walked over to a boathouse, where there was a take-out food stand, and bought a cup of coffee, an orange, and a blueberry muffin. She returned to the bench with these and peeled the orange, which she broke into sections. After neatly arranging the muffin and orange sections on a napkin, Sally took out Chief Judge Green's letter. "My dear Sally," the letter began. Sally smiled at the old-fashioned style. Whatever else the Chief Judge was, she thought, he wasn't a parrot judge, or peacock judge, or artist judge. He was a caring man, doing his best in a job for which he didn't seem quite suited. It would, Sally was sure, be a nice letter. She was anxious to read what it said. She took a bite of her muffin, ate an orange section, sipped her coffee, and read:

"Since you have asked for my advice on whether you should be a lawyer I will tell you what I think. You were a wonderful law clerk, as I've told you before, and a tremendous help to me. In addition, and more important, you are a sweet and generous person. I would feel selfish and rude if I were to refuse to advise you. But really, I think I probably should refuse, for I'm not competent to advise you. Please, therefore, consider what I'm about to say with great caution.

"As you may know, I spend a good deal of time coaching boys, and some girls, too, on how to play baseball and basketball. When I was younger I was a good baseball and basketball player, and so when I coach them, I know what I'm talking about, and I can show them how to do it—throw a curve, for instance. If one of my star players asks me whether he should go into pro ball—and some of them have asked me—I feel competent to advise him. But Sally, I can't tell you what it's like or how to be a good lawyer. I never was one. I barely got through law school, and although I was an assistant district attorney, I never learned how to try a case well enough to be entrusted with any important prosecution. I became a trial judge and then a judge of the Supreme Court not because of my legal ability but because my father had a great deal of political influence.

"I hate it when people talk about themselves. It's boring and self-important, and may embarrass those who have to listen. But here I am, talking about myself. Please forgive me, Sally. The only reason I do it is my hope that something in my experience of deciding to be a lawyer may prove helpful to you, as you make your decision.

"You don't say in your letter why you've 'begun to wonder' whether you want to be a lawyer. I suppose something about your experience with the court has been disappointing or disillusioning, but I'm guessing, and as guessing isn't a good basis for advice, I'll try to state some general principles that seem to me valid (I have a sinking feeling that I'm about to be pompous and pretentious, but here goes!).

"One might say that there are three ways to decide whether to do something—to become a lawyer, or make any decision that is important to us: the way of Right, the way of Reason, and the way of Love.

"First, then, the way of Right: To become a lawyer is certainly a *good* thing to do. Our society is so complex that without the advice of lawyers we can't do many things essential to an orderly, responsible life—buy a house, or write a will, or start a business, for instance. Lawyers keep society's wheels turning. And lawyers help us in other ways—to recover compensation for injuries or breach of contract, to ensure that if we are accused of a crime we get a fair trial, and so on. Some of the assistant district attorneys I served with believed very strongly that by prosecuting criminals they were protecting the community. But because becoming a lawyer may be *good* doesn't mean it's *right*. If doing something is 'right,' then not doing it is 'wrong.' Keeping a promise is right, breaking it is wrong. Not becoming a lawyer, however, isn't wrong.

"When I was thinking about whether to become a lawyer, I didn't make this distinction as clearly as I should have. I was different from you: I wasn't *doubtful* about whether to become a lawyer; I was *sure* I *didn't* want to be one. What I *did* want to be was a baseball coach. My father, however, thought life was too serious a matter to be frittered away playing games. Also, he believed, he knew, that the law was often oppressive and cruel and arbitrary. His parents had emigrated to the United States from Ireland. He had seen first hand what it was like to be on the outside looking in. When I told him I wouldn't be any good as a lawyer, he said, 'Don't sell yourself short.' He knew I liked all sorts of people and was good at persuading them to work together, and he thought that as a lawyer I might be able to make the legal system a little kinder, a little more reasonable. I respected and loved my father, and I was an obedient son. I decided that he was right—that the right thing for me to do was to be a lawyer. But it wouldn't have been wrong for me to become a coach.

"Next, the way of Reason: I may well have been unreasonable when I decided to become a lawyer. It was at least doubtful whether I had the analytic ability a good lawyer needs. At one point I decided to tell the dean I was withdrawing from the law school, but I didn't follow through. My persistence resulted in considerable unhappiness. I often considered myself a failure. As I've said, I was never entrusted with an important prosecution, to cite one example. On the other hand, to some extent I compensated for my weaknesses by developing rehabilitation and settlement programs, which did what my father had hoped I'd do—made the law less oppressive.

"You're just the opposite of what I was. It would be eminently reasonable for you to become a lawyer. As your teachers told me, and as I've seen for myself, you have outstanding legal ability. If you accept the Littleton Jones offer, you will be on a very fast track very soon. That firm has major cases. You'll be assigned to one, you'll perform superbly, and you'll move right up the ladder until you are a partner appearing as first chair representing the firm's most important clients.

"I do have one possible reservation about whether it would be reasonable for you to become a lawyer. As a law clerk, you have *looked* into the legal world, but you haven't *been* in it. In many ways, Sally, it's a nasty world. Especially when the stakes are high, lawyers may do almost anything to win. Cheat, lie, double cross. And in the fast track world you would inhabit, the stakes get very, very high. The best lawyers take such matters in stride. They know how to fight without fighting dirty. I've no doubt you'd be among the best, but in our adversary system, Sally, people get hurt, by lawyers. You may wish to ask yourself to what extent you want to play the game. Of course, in some fields of practice lawyers aren't so driven, but there, Sally, you may be trapped. Your legal engine is very high powered. High powered engines don't idle well. Which brings me to my last general principle.

"The way of Love: Every year for a good many years now, Emily and I have gone to Washington, D.C., to see the cherry blossoms and to visit some of our favorite places, chief of which is the Phillips Gallery. If you haven't already gone there, Sally, I hope you will go soon. One of the pictures in the Gallery's own collection is Renoir's 'The Luncheon of the Boating Party.' I'm sure you know it, if not from having seen the original, then from a reproduction. I never tire of looking at that picture. The young men and women gathered around the table beneath the red and white striped awning. The bottles of wine, the crystal glasses, the fruit, the white linen tablecloth. The young woman in her flowered straw bonnet talking to her little dog, another young woman in the background covering her ears with her gloved hands to shut out the blandishments of two men flirting with her. And so on. The picture is flooded with sunshine and love. Can you imagine how Renoir must have felt when he finished it? I think, Sally, that when you ask yourself, 'Should I become a lawyer?', you should ask, 'If I become a lawyer, will I feel about my work as Renoir must have felt about his?'

"If I had asked myself that question, I think I would have stood my ground against my father and have become a coach. I loved working with boys and girls. To see them change from gangly, uncoordinated kids to athletes; to watch them learn sportsmanship, to play as a team, to be gracious winners and gallant losers, who meant it when they congratulated their opponents; to know that my teaching had introduced some pride, and joy, and self-respect in their lives—I hadn't created a masterpiece, as Renoir did, but I'd done something good, something filled with sunshine, which I loved.

"One of my law professors revered Cardozo, and recently I've read some of his writings. Cardozo admitted that sometimes he felt lost, as on a "trackless ocean," he said, but you can tell from the way he describes how he went about deciding a case—the different factors he considered and how he weighed them against each other—that lost or not, he loved the law. I'm sure he stepped back from a finished opinion with the same joy that Renoir felt when he stepped back from a finished picture.

"Sally, this letter has become even more personal than I expected, when I said I was going to talk about myself, in the hope that you would find my experience helpful. You may think from what I've said that I am bitter about having decided to become a lawyer, that I feel I've been a failure, and that it's my father's fault—that I'm trying to discourage you from becoming a lawyer. That isn't so. Especially, I'm not bitter. No man in love with Emily and loved by her as I am could be bitter. And I don't fault my father, who was a good man and loved me. He may after all have been right in wanting me to be a lawyer. In any case, my decision to be one was mine, not his. I don't mean to encourage or discourage you from becoming a lawyer. I think you would be a superb lawyer, but there are other fine careers. Whatever you decide to do you will do very well. I don't mean to advise you *what* to decide, only *how* to. I believe in the old song, it's love that makes the world go 'round. By all means, Sally, listen to your head. Don't deprecate your very considerable legal abilities. But even more, listen to your heart. Think of Renoir, of sunshine and love, Sally. Be true to yourself. And when you've made your decision, don't second guess yourself. You are very young. The world in all its wonderful variety lies before you.

I know Emily joins me in sending very best wishes.

Love, James Green

*   *   *

In his poem, "Musee des Beaux Arts," Roger Littleton's favorite poet, W. H. Auden, wrote:

> About suffering they were never wrong,
> The Old Masters: how well they understood
> Its human position; how it takes place
> While someone else is eating or opening a window or just
> walking dully along . . . .

And so it was with Arthur Black. While Chief Judge and Mrs. Green were on the last lap of their trip home from Maine; while Roger Littleton and Albert Johnson were discussing the complaint against the Chief Judge; while Sally Link was reading her letters on the bench by the cat in the azalea garden; while pedestrians jostled across City Hall courtyard and stoical cabbies waited for The Four Seasons doorman's whistle; while the city's life surged and eddied about the rows of office buildings, the Dunkin'Donuts, pizzerias, cleaners, jewelers, and discount dress shops, Arthur Black plunged from the pinnacle of his profession and circled slowly down to death.

As was his habit, Arthur Black woke up at five. A perfect June day was dawning. He started the day, as he always did when in town, by swimming twenty-five laps in his pool. Arthur Black's apartment occupied the entire top floor of a high rise apartment house built on the foundation of what had been a wharf on the waterfront. The pool, two lanes wide and fifty yards long, extended along one side of the apartment. It was surrounded by tropical plants, including gardenias in bloom, orange trees, and orchids, and was covered by a glass roof. Panels in the roof opened and closed and sprinklers misted the plants in response to a computer's calculations of temperature and humidity. As he swam, Arthur Black sometimes rolled over on his back to watch puffs of white clouds float across the sapphire sky. His laps done, he walked a mile on the treadmill, in twenty minutes, shaved and bathed, selected one of a dozen suits, all dark, a tie, always silver or pale gold with a small pattern, and a set of cufflinks—this morning, turquoise set in silver, from Mexico. When he had finished dressing, he sliced a banana over a bowl of plain yogurt, popped two croissants into the microwave, and filled a cup with coffee from a coffee maker timed to have completed brewing its coffee at 7 A.M. By now the newspapers had been delivered to his front door. He took them and his breakfast out onto the terrace. It was too nice a day to eat inside.

Arthur Black lived alone. He always had—even as a child, it seemed to him. He had never known his father, who had left his mother before he was born, he was told, and his mother wasn't home much. She worked all day and at night went out with a series of men, none of whom Arthur liked. For the last ten years Arthur Black's secretary, Francesca Barbieri, had been his companion. Sometimes she spent the night with him. One of the bedrooms in the apartment was hers, and she kept some clothes and toilet articles there. In the Spring and Fall they traveled in Europe together for several weeks, using as their base a palazzo he owned in Venice. Once at dinner, watching the sun set over the Grand Canal, Francesca had said: "Arthur, I think we're right for each other. We both love luxury, but what we really want is freedom. We're too proud to fall in love, but once in a while we want it and need it. Me more than you. You're Arthur Black, after all, Mr. Class Action." She took a sip of Limoncello, ice cold, pale yellow in a deep blue Murano crystal glass. "When you're fighting, Arthur, you scare me. But then you dismount your huge black warhorse, put aside your sword, take off your plumed helmet and massive armor, and I see a gentle man. A man I could love." They watched the sun sink, staining the water and sky with its color. "Francesca, I don't know why I'm the way I am. But I hate the world. It's a rotten world run by rotten people. I don't want to join them and I don't want to try to make their world better. I want to fight them. I'm like the mongoose in Kipling's story, I guess. I live to kill cobras. Sometimes I wonder, is that all I am, a killer? I don't think so, Francesca. For one thing, I love beauty, especially wild beauty, like you. But falling in love? I've never done that. I don't think I ever will. I'm like some god damned wild animal, always ready to spring." Francesca Barbieri leaned back on the banquette, sighed, took another sip of her Limoncello. "Yes, you are, Arthur. Stretched out on a branch, watching everything below. Very beautiful, but not something you'd want around the house. As for me, if it's OK with you, I'll flit around every so often and show off my tail feathers."

After Arthur Black had eaten his yogurt and bananas, he took his pills. Avapro, toprol, imdur, coumadin. He felt like a drug store. Carruthers didn't like his electrocardiogram, or his blood pressure, or his heart beat, but there hadn't been any episodes for a year now. "Your weight is good. Keep up the exercises. I want you to walk at least two miles a day. Walk to your office when you can. I wish you'd slow down." Reminded by his pills of his doctor's instructions, Arthur Black called the garage. "I won't need the limo this morning, George. I'll walk to the office." He turned to the papers, looking for the business pages. He wanted to see if there was a story on the Pioneer Pharmaceuticals decision. "That was certainly a gratifying decision. I wish she hadn't gone on and on, though. Littleton will make mincemeat of some of her arguments—which she thought of all by herself, and which I don't need. As I will tell Roger." Arthur Black smiled happily. He had an appointment to see Roger Littleton in the afternoon. Within hours of the district court's decision refusing to dismiss the shareholders' action, Littleton had called to say that he had been retained by James, Roberts & James. "Arthur, perhaps it would be useful if we chatted a bit about your clients' novel theory." "Well, Roger, I see it didn't take the defendants long to realize they needed you. I'd be delighted to chat. Would three o'clock this afternoon be good?"

As it happened, Arthur Black never found the story on Pioneer Pharmaceuticals. Looking for it, he saw the story on Judge Ericson's death. "What the hell!!?" He raced through the story, got his briefcase, and left. The maid would clean up the breakfast.

Arthur Black had a favorite route when he walked to his office. Avoiding the main streets, he zigzagged by cobblestoned alleys to a small park with boxwood hedges, an herb garden, and a magnificent magnolia tree kept warm by sun reflected from the stone wall of a church. Sometimes he lingered in the park a little while to enjoy its fragrance. From there he had a straight route to his office along a busy but interesting street of brownstone residences, fashionable shops and restaurants, and professional offices. This morning, though, there was no lingering. He barely glanced at the herb garden, or the shops' displays, or the fine doorways and flower boxes of geraniums of the Colonial residences. What had the court done about *The Lead Paint Case*? Had Ericson voted on the petition for reconsideration before he was killed? Had the other judges? A three-three tie should mean the petition would be denied, wasn't that right? Or would they take another vote? The sunny June morning might as well have been gray and gloomy. Arthur Black had shut it out. Faster and faster he strode. He had to get to the office.

"Good morning, Francesca." "Good morning, Arthur." Francesca Barbieri stood up behind her desk and followed Arthur Black into his office. "A couple of bummers." "Oh?" He felt his chest tighten. "The Clerk of the Supreme Court called a few minutes ago to say that the court had decided *The Lead Paint Case* and should he fax me the order. I said he should." She handed him two sheets of paper. Still standing by his rosewood table, Arthur Black read:

> To all counsel:
>
> Enclosed find true copy of order entered by the Supreme Court in the above-captioned matter.
>
> AND NOW, June 5, 2002, on defendants/appellants' petition for reconsideration, Judge Ericson having withdrawn the opinion for the court authored by him, and having stated that he joined the dissenting opinion authored by Chief Judge Green; Judge Weinstein having withdrawn his joinder in Judge Ericson's opinion for the court, and having stated that he joined the dissenting opinion authored by the Chief Judge; Judge Llewlyn and Judge Marcone having stated that they remain of the views expressed in Judge Ericson's withdrawn opinion, and Judge Carlisle and Judge Hull-Jackson having stated that they continue to join the dissenting opinion authored by the Chief Judge; said dissenting opinion is withdrawn and is re-filed as the opinion of the court, Judge Llewelyn and Judge Marcone dissenting; the judgment in favor of plaintiffs/appellees is vacated; and the record is remanded to the trial court with instructions to enter judgment in favor of defendants/appellants notwithstanding the verdict.
>
> SO ORDERED.

"And here's something else." Francesca Barbieri handed Arthur Black a letter from the Lawyers' Disciplinary Board, dated June 4, 2002:

Dear Mr. Black:

This is to inform you that the Board has received a formal complaint from the Honorable Eric Ericson of the Supreme Court charging you with professional misconduct. The original of the complaint is on file with the Board. On your request, you may examine it at the Board's offices at such time as agreed by you and the undersigned. In relevant part, the complaint alleges:

That on May 23, 2003, at or about 6:30 p.m. in Judge Ericson's chambers, you did ask Judge Ericson the status of a petition for reconsideration pending before the Supreme Court in a matter captioned *The Lead Paint Case*, in which you represented the plaintiffs/appellees; that when Judge Ericson informed you that the court had not yet ruled on the petition, you replied that you expected him to ensure that the petition was denied, and that if it was not, he should be prepared to suffer the consequences; that on December 1, 1995, on your intervention, the Farmers' and Mechanics' National Bank loaned Judge Ericson $500,000 on his demand note, with which money he built a mountain retreat known as "The Aerie"; and that by your aforesaid reference to "consequences" you intended Judge Ericson to understand that if the aforesaid petition for reconsideration were not denied, you would cause his aforesaid demand note to be presented for payment, which you knew he would not be able to make.

The Board has made no determination of the truth of the aforesaid allegations. The Board has concluded, however, that they state a prima facie case of violation of the Rules of Professional Conduct, in particular, Rule 3.5(b) (forbidding certain ex parte statements) and Rule 8.4(d) (forbidding conduct prejudicial to the administration of justice). The Board, therefore, requests that you answer the allegations within thirty days. A failure to do so will be considered an admission of the truth of the allegations.

Very truly yours,
James Scattergood, Executive Director

When Francesca Barbieri saw that Arthur Black had finished reading the letter from the Lawyers' Disciplinary Board, she said: "Arthur, why don't you just hang it all up? Write them that you are retiring from the practice of law and resigning from the bar. Then go with me to the palazzo. We could live there. Do some traveling."

Arthur Black continued to stand by his rosewood table. He was rigid, his face white as paper. When he spoke, it seemed as much to himself as to Francesca Barbieri. "I didn't need the money. Oh, I wanted it. I was going to found a law school for trial lawyers. But what I really wanted was that decision. Do you realize what that decision did, Francesca? It didn't just mean millions of dollars for those kids. It meant that from now on, plaintiffs would only have to prove that the defendants' product *might* have hurt them, not that it did. Can you see how that would have revolutionized manufacturing? How it would have forced manufacturers to make their products safe?" Arthur Black's tone was even, but Francesca Barbieri felt the fury concealed beneath it. He had taken her by the shoulders, as an angry parent might grab a child, and she winced in his grip. Then, abruptly, he let her go. "Francesca, I'm sure you know the seven sins. I have committed four." He spoke like a judge enumerating the defendant's crimes before imposing sentence—cold, objective, without compassion. "Number one, greed. I wanted to pile the money up, count my millions, finger them like a miser. Number two, lust. I would force the law to change. Not seduce her. Number three, anger. I hated the pipsqueaks who stood in my way. And Number four, pride. Most of all, pride. I, only I, could succeed. I was strong, above the rules. Who would tie me down? Well, I have my answer. Never force your adversary into a corner, Francesca." Arthur Black's chiseled white face, aquiline, marble, crumbled. His manicured hands disheveled his gleaming black hair. "How could I have been so stupid?" he whispered. "That's the greatest sin. Stupidity. I'll never try the *Pioneer* case now, Francesca. Just when I have that squinty-eyed sanctimonious bastard who runs this country and his buddies almost in my cross-hairs, I throw it away!" Arthur Black's face turned purple. He clutched his chest, let out a cry Francesca Barbieri would hear the rest of her life, and fell forward, down onto his desk.

"911? I'm calling from the tenth floor of two thousand and six Mulberry Place, the law offices of Arthur Black. I am Mr. Black's secretary. About two minutes ago, Mr. Black had what looked to me like a massive heart attack. He's unconscious and his pulse is very weak. I could barely feel it. Please send a rescue squad right away. The tenth floor elevator opens into Mr. Black's office."

Francesca Barbieri walked around to the back of Arthur Black's desk. She reached beneath it, seemed to fumble a moment for a switch or spring of some sort, then pulled out a shallow drawer, from which she took a brown, legal size envelope. Arthur told her that if anything happened to him, she was to have this. Well, something had happened. She took the envelope to her desk, with the letter from the Discipline Board. Tomorrow morning she would herself return the letter to Mr. Scattergood. She would tell him that Mr. Black died before receiving it—she was sure he was not going to survive his attack—and that she supposed the complaint could be considered as withdrawn, especially since, she had read, Judge Ericson also was dead. She clicked onto the firm's e-mail. "To all addressees. A few minutes ago Mr. Black had a massive heart attack in his office. He is unconscious. I've called 911."

And then Francesca Barbieri settled back in her chair to wait until the elevator doors opened, when a flood of people would fill Arthur Black's offices. And take him away. She was forty-nine. They'd ask her to stay, but she wouldn't. Tonight she'd go to his apartment and get her things, and as soon as she decently could, she'd get away. To the palazzo, she guessed. To watch the sun drown in the Grand Canal.

* * *

"I'm here for my two o'clock appointment with Mr. Littleton, Mrs. Eastburn." "And on the dot, Sally. He's on the phone but I know he's expecting you. He said I should show you right in."

As Sally entered Roger Littleton's office he put down the telephone and rose to greet her. "Sally, how very nice to see you again. It's been quite a while. Mrs. Eastburn told me you had a matter you'd like to discuss. Please, how can I help? Shall we sit here?" He gestured to a leather sofa.

Sally carefully described how she had overheard Judge Ericson and Arthur Black talking about the petition for reconsideration pending in *The Lead Paint Case.* As nearly as she could, she quoted the two men's words. She also described how she had met them by the elevator, adding that she wondered but didn't know whether they suspected that she had overheard them. "I've read the Rules of Professional Conduct and Judicial Canons, Mr. Littleton, and it seems to me that both men engaged in serious professional misconduct. I don't know whether the rules apply to me. I've passed the bar exam but I haven't been formally admitted to the bar of any court. Also, I read in the paper this morning that Judge Ericson was killed in an automobile accident and I don't know whether that makes a difference as to whether his conduct should be reported. But as to Mr. Black, Rule 8.3 seems to provide that the sort of conduct he engaged in must be reported. I'd very much appreciate your advice on what I should do." Sally considered for a moment telling about the letter Judge Ericson had written her but decided not to; it wasn't relevant to whether the judge had engaged in misconduct.

Roger Littleton had listened with the intensity so many clients found unnerving: motionless; eyes hooded; fingers tented; silent. When Sally had finished her account, he stirred himself, straightening from his slightly hunched over position. "Sally, thank you for such a clear statement. If I may, let me add some facts that by pure chance I have only learned today.

"The first fact is that this morning the Supreme Court handed down its decision in *The Lead Paint Case*. This firm didn't represent any of the parties in the case, but the entire bar is talking about the decision and one of the lawyers called me and faxed me a copy. It is really quite an unusual decision. What happened is that Judge Ericson withdrew his opinion and he and Judge Weinstein joined the Chief Judge's dissent, which then became a majority opinion. Accordingly, with Judge Llewlyn and Judge Marcone dissenting, the court vacated the judgment for plaintiffs and remanded with instructions to enter judgment n.o.v. for defendants. I agree with your analysis. Judge Ericson, in my opinion, did engage in serious misconduct in discussing the petition for reconsideration with Arthur Black. If the petition had been denied, so that Judge Ericson's original opinion in favor of Arthur Black's clients had remained the majority opinion, we would have to decide whether, even though you're not a lawyer yet, you would have to report Judge Ericson, because then it would seem that the judge had succumbed to Arthur Black's pressure, or threat. But, as we know now, the petition was granted, and it was granted, at least in part, because the judge defied Arthur Black's threat.

"The second fact is that at noon today, Arthur Black died in the University Hospital from a massive heart attack he suffered earlier in his office." Sally gasped. "He and I had an appointment to meet this afternoon to discuss a case," Roger Littleton continued, "and just a little while ago his secretary telephoned me and told me of his death. One can't help but wonder whether the shock—for it must have been a shock—of the court's reversal in *The Lead Paint Case* caused his heart attack, but I suppose we'll never know.

"So, Sally, let's see where we stand. Judge Ericson shouldn't have talked to Arthur Black, but in the end he acted independently, which is what a judge is supposed to do. Arthur Black shouldn't have threatened the judge, but the threat did him no good—in fact, maybe it drove the judge to do just the opposite of what the threat was intended to accomplish. In the circumstances, I don't see any need to report the judge. He made up for his misconduct. And he's dead. Arthur Black's case is different though. A lawyer shouldn't be excused from threatening a judge because the judge ignores the threat, and if Black were alive, he would, in my opinion, be subject to being disbarred. But he isn't alive. I don't see what purpose would be served by disbarring him post-humously.

"Except," Roger Littleton paused, "I do think I have to qualify what I've just said. Suppose, Sally, there was another case in which Arthur Black appeared before the Supreme Court with Judge Ericson sitting, and the court decided in his favor, with Judge Ericson voting with the court, maybe, even, writing the opinion for the court. I should think the losing parties would have a good argument that the judge's failure to recuse himself denied them their right to an impartial tribunal. What do you think?" "I suppose it would depend on whether at that time Mr. Black had some sort of hold on Judge Ericson, as he apparently did later, when he argued *The Lead Paint Case.*" "Quite. And the conversation you overheard doesn't give us that information. Well! Don't worry about it, Sally. I think it's very unlikely that Arthur Black did argue any other case before Judge Ericson. He almost never appeared in the state courts. As I understand it, the only reason *The Lead Paint Case* was in state court was that the defendants bungled their petition to remove to the federal court. Anyway, I"ll ask the library to tell us the cases Arthur Black has appeared in before the Supreme Court, and when he did. Meanwhile, I suggest you jot down the facts while they're fresh in your mind and that we sit tight. When I hear from the library, we can chat again."

"Thank you, Mr. Littleton. I confess I hope I won't have to report what I heard. But of course I'll do whatever you advise. I do feel like a sneak. I shouldn't have hidden in the bathroom. Also, I'm sure Judge Ericson didn't write his opinion to favor Mr. Black. After the Chief Judge circulated his dissent, Judge Ericson told me why—it was at the court's annual retreat, and we happened to be exercising together and we argued about his decision—anyway, he insisted he was right that causation didn't have to be proved. Judge Ericson was a very proud, really passionate man, Mr. Littleton."

Roger Littleton's old hawk's eyes did not miss the slight pinking of Sally's cheeks. "Why do you think he changed his mind?" No response from Sally. "Perhaps you persuaded him." His guess confirmed by Sally's flush, the old man quickly moved on. "I'm sure you're right, Sally, and as I just said, I don't think you'll have to report the judge."

"I'd . . . I'd rather not report Mr. Black either." "Sally, you do have a soft heart! A good many of my colleagues of the defense bar despised him. I don't say they'll dance on his grave, exactly, but they certainly won't miss him. Or Judge Ericson either, for that matter—although his *Lead Paint* vote must have surprised them. What do you know about Arthur Black?

"Not very much, really. He did interview me. He said he hoped that when I finished my clerkship. I would apply to be an associate in his office." "Oh? And what was your impression of him?" "I had very mixed impressions, Mr. Littleton. I know a lot of people think class actions are abusive but Mr. Black said that the actions he planned to bring against lawyers and accountants who had advised dishonest corporate officers would raise professional standards. I'm sure his critics would say he was being hypocritical, that what he cared about was collecting huge fees, not raising professional standards. But to me, he seemed sincere. In fact, he seemed so fiercely sincere he frightened me. He made me think of Robespierre or Savonarola. I . . . I'm afraid that's pretentious . . . ." Sally's voice trailed off.

"No, no, it's not. It's right on the mark. I've known Arthur Black for a good many years. We've appeared as opponents on several occasions. In my opinion, he is—well, now I have to say, was—the finest trial lawyer in the United States. No jury was able to withstand him.

Arthur loved and trusted juries, and they responded accordingly. But he hated the law. The law, he thought, is made by the powerful to hold down the weak, the ordinary citizens who sit on juries. His basic argument to juries was that they should confound the wicked. And they did. Arthur's weakness, if I may say so, was the fierceness you detected. Lawyers live a contradiction, Sally. They may hate the law—sometimes they should hate it, because sometimes the law is oppressive—but they must work through the law. They must use the law to change the law. That may take time. It may require patience. Most of us are too patient. Arthur was impatient. He was passionate, always forcing the pace. I think that's what he was doing when he threatened Judge Ericson. He had just achieved a revolution in the law—because that's what Judge Ericson's first opinion was—and he felt it slipping away." Roger Littleton sat in silence, it seemed to Sally in memorial tribute to his dead adversary. "I shall miss him, Sally. If he had survived his heart attack, I would have testified on his behalf before the Lawyers' Disciplinary Board. I would have represented him, if he'd asked me to. Of course, he shouldn't have threatened a judge. But the law *is* oppressive. It *should* be challenged. And no one challenged it more effectively than Arthur. I never felt more a lawyer than when he and I crossed swords. Requiescat in pace, Arthur. I do hope the library doesn't turn up any other cases, but I'll let you know either way."

Sally got up to leave. "Thank you very much, Mr. Littleton." "Sally, since after all I'm not going to meet with Arthur Black, may I ask you to stay a moment longer?" "Of course, Mr. Littleton." "The Hiring Committee will be meeting this afternoon at five. I expect I'll be asked whether I know your decision on the firm's offer. Are you able to tell me whether you'll be joining us?" "No, no," Sally thought to herself. "Not fair to surprise me that way. I'm not ready." But then she realized it was fair. She owed the firm an answer. In fact, she was overdue. She might just as well decide. Now. "I know I've been slow answering Mr. Littleton. I do appreciate the offer, very much. It's just . . . just . . ." "May I ask, are you considering some alternative?" "Yes, I am. When I was at law school and since then, up to now, I've been a volunteer at ARC—Adult Rehabilitation Center. I had lunch today with Ted Schroeder, the center's director. He asked me to be his assistant. He also said, however, that he knew that Littleton Jones had made me an offer, and I should first decide what to do about that." "I'm familiar with ARC, and I know Ted Schroeder." Roger Littleton smiled. "Not, I'm sure, as well as you do. This firm is counsel to BBC and as it happens, I heard Ted's presentation when he asked BBC to provide start-up support for the center. I'll never forget Ted's answer, when one of the board members asked if the center would be operated on Christian principles. 'Jesus was a hellluva man,' Ted said, 'but he's not the only way.' That board member, on the spot, became the center's strongest supporter. BBC gets quarterly reports from the center, and every so often I drop in. It's a wonderful place. Oh, Sally! What a choice! I'm sure you know Frost's poem about the two roads that 'diverged in a yellow wood/And sorry I could not travel both/ . . . I took the one less traveled by,/ And that has made all the difference.' The firm's world and Ted's world are at least as different as the worlds Frost had to choose between. Ted's world is ruled by the law of love, the firm's world, by the law of power. The two don't mix, Sally. Like Frost, you have to choose one."

Sally felt her eyes fill up. What a magnificent old man! There he sat, at one end of the leather sofa, gaunt, angular, elegant. She felt sure she knew the choice he hoped she'd make. The Hiring Committee evidently already regarded her as his protege. But not a featherweight of pressure had he exerted on her. He had asked her to choose, but to choose as she wished. He would not intrude. Sally stood up, and as she did, Roger Littleton stood up, matching her movement. She turned to face him. "Mr. Littleton, the reason Ted wanted me to see you before I decided whether to accept his offer was because I told him once that if I decided to be a lawyer, I wanted to be like you. Thank you for the chance to work for you. Thank you for all you have taught me, not just about the law but about what it means to be a professional. I will never match your standards, but I will always try to. Please tell the Hiring Committee that I deeply appreciate their offer but I've decided to accept Ted's offer to be the Assistant Director at ARC." The old hawk's black eyes flashed gold for an instant, then returned to their usual inscrutable opacity. Like a counselor before his queen, Roger Littleton bowed from the waist. "I will report to the Committee." Afterwards Sally wasn't sure whether she had extended her hand or whether he took it. In any case, very gently he lifted her hand to his lips and kissed her fingers. "Sally," he said, still holding her fingers, "if I had married I would have hoped for a daughter. And if I'd had one, I would have hoped she would be like you." His gaunt face exploded in a smile, a little boy's smile, a boy who has just hooked a fish or kicked a goal. "I have a suggestion, Sally. I don't have any appointments this afternoon. How about walking across the street with me to The Four Seasons? We could have sherry and a little cake to celebrate your new position." Sally brushed away her tears. "Oh, Mr. Littleton. That would be lovely!" Still holding her hand, Roger Littleton led Sally from his office. "Mrs. Eastburn, I expect Ron James and the rest of the Hiring Committee will be here at five. If I'm not back, please tell them that Miss Link and I have escaped their clutches, and that I may or may not be back."

Chapter 11

Chief Judge Green hadn't touched the mail that had accumulated while he was in Maine and that lay before him, neatly sorted by Mrs. B into little piles on his desk. He felt light-headed—"disoriented," a neurologist might have said—giddy from relief, exultation, and uncertainty about what to do next. When he and Emily had gotten home last night, there was a voice mail message for him from Roger Littleton, saying that it was most important that they meet in the judge's chambers the next day. An hour ago Littleton had left. Since then, Chief Judge Green had sat and stared at the little piles of mail.

At their meeting, Roger Littleton had described in detail his discussion with Albert Johnson: the contents of Gene Kelly's affidavit; Johnson's account of Kelly's telephoning to withdraw his affidavit; Littleton's argument that the affidavit was inadmissible hearsay; his additional argument that in any event, no complaint should be filed because successful prosecution would invalidate who-knew-how-many-decisions in which Judge Green had participated. Littleton and the judge had speculated about why the affidavit was signed "Gene Kelly;" the judge didn't know anyone by that name and couldn't identify any particular decision for which some one might want to seek revenge. Finally, Littleton had reported Johnson's offer to file no complaint if the Chief Judge would resign. "I think that's a very reasonable offer," the judge had replied. "I agree, it is reasonable. I told him, however, that I would recommend that you reject it. In my view, when you don't have a case, you shouldn't bargain, you should just drop it. The way we left matters was that Johnson would telephone me his decision. Late yesterday afternoon he did telephone. He told me that he still thought you should resign but that even if you didn't, no complaint would be filed." Then Roger Littleton had smiled. Not a triumphant, gleeful smile. A gentle, kindly smile.

"Roger, I don't know what to say. You're a magician. What do you think I should do?" Roger Littleton's smile faded, his gaunt face resumed its usual inscrutable expression. "When we first discussed the matter, judge, I said I would like to see you remain on the bench. That's still true. But it doesn't answer your question. As your lawyer, I advise you that you are under no obligation to resign. But whether to resign for non-legal, personal reasons is for you alone to decide. In making that decision you will no doubt wish to consider what to tell Emily. Again, as your lawyer, I advise you that you are under no obligation to tell her anything. If you do tell her about not taking the bar and about all that's happened the last week or so, I suggest you swear her to secrecy. But what to tell her depends on your answer to the question, 'How much should we share with someone we love?' I don't think I should try to answer that question. I think I know the law's commands. I don't know love's."

Neither did he know love's commands, Chief Judge Green thought. What would Emily say, if he told her? "Oh, Jimmy! And you never told the Governor when he appointed you? You sent all those men to prison? How could you do that? How could you deceive so many people, for so long? And I was so proud of you!" Better just not tell her. Go on as though nothing had happened. But something had happened. His secret was out, even if Albert Johnson had told Roger Littleton he wasn't going to do anything about it. So, get it over with. Resign. Johnson wouldn't do anything then. He could tell Emily he was tired of being a judge. That would be partly true anyway. But only partly. Sally Link had given him a sense of confidence in his judgment. Also, the State Constitution gave the Chief Judge of the Supreme Court the authority to supervise the state's judicial system, and he had been looking forward to using that authority to initiate reforms other states had put in place—working with the schools to explain the legal system; requiring continuing education for judges and lawyers; that sort of thing. But now?

Roger Littleton watched his silent client. "You don't have to decide right away," he said gently. He rose and put one hand on the judge's shoulder. "As you think about it, don't sell yourself or Emily short. Good people make good decisions. I'm sure it will work out. As for a statement for my services, I wouldn't dream of submitting one. It was a professional privilege to represent you. More than that, it was a joy— a sentiment we lawyers don't often feel." And then, Roger Littleton had left.

"Judge?" It was Mrs. B, a concerned expression on her face. He apparently had not heard her knock and she had opened his chambers door to look in. "Judge? A Mr. Kelly is here. He said you would know him by another name, which I didn't quite get—Kwinski or Kocinski, something like that—and that it was very important that he see you." "Yes, yes. It is. Show him in Mrs. B." The man who entered was not the assured, smoothly persuasive Genik Kwiecinski who'd ordered drinks for himself and Jimmy Green in Duffy's Bar and Grill. Sherlock Holmes would have taken his measure in a glance. His way of walking showed he'd been in judicial chambers before. Penniless, or close to it. His suit was well made but hadn't been to a cleaner for weeks. Shirt wasn't dirty but wasn't fresh, either. Cuffs were frayed. Tie was worn. Shoes were scuffed. Shaved but flabby face, watery eyes, little broken blood vessels in his cheeks. "A lawyer, Watson. Prosperous once but has lost his practice. Alcoholic. Probably disbarred."

As Genik Kwiecinski entered, Judge Green rose behind his desk. He did not move forward, or extend his hand, or smile, or offer any sort of welcoming word. He just stood and looked at the slightly seedy figure standing about halfway between the door and the desk, obviously uncertain whether to come closer. "Good morning, Your Honor." "Good morning. You wanted to see me?" "I think I owe you an explanation, if you're willing to hear it." The Chief Judge sighed and sat down heavily. Then, realizing that Genik Kwiecinski was still standing, waved vaguely toward a chair. "Well, why did you report me, after so many years? And how come you signed your affidavit 'Gene Kelly?'"

Genik Kwiecinski sat down. His hesitancy, his sheepishness, disappeared. He told his story with assurance. The ability of an advocate who could capture and hold the jurors' attention had rusted but was still sharp.

"Not long after we met at Duffy's, I legally changed my name. I had won some pretty big cases and my practice was growing. The name 'Genik Kwiecinski' didn't help, though. No one knew how to pronounce it, or spell it, and no one could remember it. 'Gene Kelly' was much better. From the beginning, my practice was criminal. My big break came when one of the major law firms in the city had a conflict of interest and referred their client's CEO to me. Their idea was to get their client, the corporation, off, and to throw my client, the CEO, to the wolves. It didn't work out that way. I showed that the CEO was a fall-guy, who had been duped by the corporation's board of directors. After that, I had more cases than I could handle. I hired a couple of associates, and really got rolling.

"I must say, I loved it. They were good associates, I paid well, they worked hard, I was in court almost every day doing my thing. And if I do say so, I was good. By then, most of my cases were federal cases. The feds prepare well, but even so, I won more than my share, and often, I was able to negotiate a favorable plea agreement. I had fame, of a sort. I had money. I had women. Life was sweet.

"Too sweet, as it turned out. At least for me. I got cocky, and lazy, and started trying cases by the seat of my pants. Intuition and street smarts will take you a long way, but when you don't know the file, unpleasant surprises occur. I lost a case, a big one I should have won. What I should have done was clean up my act and get back to basics. I didn't. I continued to try to get by on instincts—and mine were good enough so lots of the time I did get by. But I wasn't what I used to be. I knew it, and so did my associates. First one, then the other left. I cut more corners, I started to drink, I mean, really drink. I'd always liked a drink. When I was in my glory days, after a day in court I'd stop in at the Ritz Carlton bar. There were other bars but that was my favorite. I'd never have more than two drinks, though. Then it was back to the office to see my associates, review my notes, and prepare for the next day. When my associates left, I stopped going back to the office. I had another drink. And another.

"I won't go into detail, judge. It was pretty ugly. The prosecutors and judges all knew me and most of them liked me. But they couldn't cover for me forever. The last straw was when I showed up for trial obviously drunk. The judge declared a mistrial, and not only held me in contempt but reported me to the Lawyers' Disciplinary Board. I was suspended and ordered to attend a rehabilitation program, which I promised I'd do. After a couple of weeks, I stopped going. The board revoked my suspension and ordered me disbarred. I appealed to the Supreme Court.

"You wrote the opinion for the court, judge. I argued that alcoholism was a disease. I asked the court to treat me as a sick person and to give me another chance. You rejected my argument and affirmed the order disbarring me. In your view—and all the other judges agreed, except Judge Ericson, who said he thought disbarment was too severe—anyway, in your opinion for the court you said that whether alcoholism was or was not a disease was irrelevant. Whatever it was, I knew I had it, and I could get rid of it. You admitted that breaking an addiction to alcohol might be very difficult, but it could be done, and if I wanted to be a lawyer, I had to do it, because unless I did, I couldn't be faithful to my clients and serve their interests effectively. You agreed with Judge Ericson that disbarment was severe, but, you noted, I'd promised to try to break my addiction and I hadn't kept my promise. The court, you said, should ensure that lawyers fulfilled their obligations.

"I thought it was a pretty tough opinion, judge, and the more I thought about it the more bitter I became. I didn't think about the fact that you wouldn't know that the Gene Kelly you were disbarring was the Genik Kwiecinski who took the bar exam for you. What I did think about was how high and mighty you sounded, how holier-than-thou, whereas I knew"—Genik Kwiecinski paused, and with an expression that mixed equal parts of dignity and defiance, looked squarely at the Chief Judge, who looked squarely back, his face a wooden mask—I knew you were a fake. At least I could be disbarred. I'd earned admission to the bar. You never had. And so I decided to take Your Lordship down a notch. You'd ruined me. I'd ruin you. I wrote out an affidavit that you'd paid me to take the bar exam, got it notarized, and mailed it to the Commission on Judicial Discipline.

"I don't remember much of the next few weeks. I'd get drunk, pass out, wake up somewhere with vomit all over my clothes, get drunk again. One night a cop found me unconscious in a gutter—yes, literally, a gutter. He called a wagon, which took me to a hospital emergency ward. The nurse found a card in my wallet identifying my sister as the person to call in an emergency. They called her. She lives in Boothbay Harbor, in Maine, but the next day she and her husband drove down and took me back to their home, where they cleaned me up, had a doctor examine me, fed me, and put me in a pretty bedroom looking out onto the ocean. It was the first kindness I'd experienced in two years.

"While I was staying with my sister, her son went sailing, on Memorial Day weekend. He didn't anchor his boat properly and when he saw it drifting, he swam after it. Well, he couldn't catch it and probably would have drowned except a man and a woman in a motor boat came along. They got him in their boat and called the Coast Guard, who took him to the local hospital. My sister and her husband naturally wanted to thank the persons who had rescued their son but they didn't know who they were. 'You're a lawyer,' my sister said, 'how about if you find out who they were.' Well, I didn't exactly have to be Perry Mason. The Coast Guard told me the rescuers' boat was named 'Emily,' and they let me review the registration records, which showed only one 'Emily,' which, lo and behold, was owned by you. I also talked to the crew of the cutter that had taken the boy to the hospital, and their description of the man running the boat fit you to a T. They also, by the way, described a young woman they said was with you. As nearly as I could make out, she was a combination of Marilyn Monroe and Greta Garbo. They couldn't care less when I said I knew who you were. Did I know who she was? How could they find her? I had to tell them I had no idea."

"She was my law clerk," Chief Judge Green said, a bit stiffly. "She was spending the Memorial Day weekend with Emily and me on Squirrel Island. We have a summer house there."

"Well, she certainly made an impression on three Coast Guard sailors. In any case, when I told my sister I knew you, she got all excited. How could she write you? If she hasn't yet, I'm sure she will be writing."

"I noticed a letter from Maine in one of these piles, but I haven't had a chance to go over the mail yet."

"What a wonderful man you must be. To rescue her boy and not even leave your name. A good Samaritan if ever there was one. It got a little much, and so, to correct the record, so to speak, I told her you were the judge who wrote the opinion disbarring me. Did that tarnish her image of you? Ha! Now she thought you were not only good but wise. If Sis's tongue had been a whip, I'd have been flayed alive. She explained in exquisite detail why you were right to disbar me. And then she burst into tears.

"Judge, it was a turning point, maybe the turning point, in my life. I suddenly realized that Sis was crying because she loved me. Because she believed I could again be the brilliant lawyer I'd once been. And because she was afraid I wouldn't make it. I was going to die a drunk, and there was nothing she could do about it. She cried and cried, and I stood there, watching her heart break. But I didn't see just her holding her hands to her face, her shoulders shaking. I saw myself. A shit. A cowardly, self-pitying, useless shit. I'd stolen my clients' money. I'd lied to them that I was prepared to defend them. I'd hurt my sister, the only person in the world who still loved me. And I had ruined the man who had saved her son's life, which was especially contemptible because I was the one who set you up. I didn't tell you then, but I desperately needed that $5,000 to get out of a jam. If I hadn't come along, you'd have taken the bar exam, probably failed, and gone on to something else. Instead, to save my own skin, I persuaded you to be a cheat. Then, years later, behind your back, I turn you in. Why? Because you'd ruined me? I'd ruined myself. You hadn't done it. I had.

"I'll never forget the pain I felt seeing myself as I really was. I got down on my knees beside my sister. I begged her to stop crying. I promised her that if she'd stop I'd make her proud of me again. She did stop, finally. The next morning, when she and her husband had left for work, I telephoned the Commission on Judicial Discipline and told the Executive Director that I wanted to withdraw my affidavit and that I wouldn't testify against you. Then I telephoned a lawyer I knew. He used to be an alcoholic himself. He told me that if I stayed clean and sober he would try to get me admitted to a program called ARC, here in the city. My sister staked me to a bus ticket, I have stayed clean and sober, and I'm living at ARC now. It's a wonderful place. I'm not kidding myself. I know I've got a long, long way to go. But I also know I'm going to make it. I write or call my sister every day. She just sent me a box of cookies. I am not going to break her heart again."

Genik Kwiecinski paused. He seemed to steel himself to continue. "Judge, I came to tell you what I'd done, and to apologize. I know it's too late. The Executive Director told me my affidavit was a sufficient basis on which to prosecute you. He said he didn't need my testimony— that if I refused to testify, he'd use the affidavit. I am deeply ashamed. Reporting you was one of the rottenest things I've ever done. I don't expect you to accept my apology. But I do apologize. Now, sir, if you will excuse me, I'll go back to ARC. Under the rules I've got to be back by twelve."

Chief Judge Green motioned Genik Kwiecinski not to leave. "Before you go, you may be interested to learn that my lawyer has told

CHOICE OF LAW · 195

me, this morning, in fact, just before you came, that the Commission will not prosecute me. It turns out that without your testimony, your affidavit is not admissible in evidence. So, Genik"—and here the judge stood up behind his desk and reached out his hand—"I accept your apology. You were a shit. But, I was a cheat." Slowly, hesitantly, as though he were expecting an electric shock, Genik Kwiecinski extended his hand toward the judge's. "You mean . . . there won't be any complaint? You're in the clear?" "That's what the Executive Director of the Commission told my lawyer." Whereupon, instead of taking the Chief Judge's extended hand, Genik Kwiecinski leapt from his chair and broke into a wild dance.

At this moment, Mrs. B opened the door. Judge Green had inadvertently pressed a button that activated a buzzer on her desk. She and the judge watched in astonishment as Genik Kwiecinski circled the judge's conference table, tapping it as though it were a great drum. Finally, panting a bit, he subsided. "Mrs. B," the judge said, "may I introduce Genik Kwiecinski, or Gene Kelly, as he's known now. We were at law school together and were discussing something that went back to when we last saw each other. Genik, this is Mrs. Breresford, a k a Mrs. B, who knows all and without whom I couldn't function." "Nice to meet you, Mrs. B." "By the way, Genik," the judge continued, "have you met Sally Link at ARC? She used to work here." "Sally Link?! Have I met her? I'm in love with her. Every man at ARC is in love with her. She's my inspiration." "Well, she's my former law clerk, the young woman who was with me when we picked up your sister's boy."

With this, Genik Kwiecinski broke into dance again. Tipping an imaginary hat over his eyes, twirling an imaginary cane, he proceeded to do a sort of soft shoe shuffle around the judge's chambers, accompanying himself with a street rapper's banter. "Oh happy day, hurray, hurray. I'm free, Mrs. B, free at last. The past is past. Just you wait. I'll go straight. Not the law. It's too raw. No more for me the snickersnee, the cut and thrust, the lex, the sex, the bloody wrecks. I'll find some day a better way. I'm okay. I've been to hell but I've come back. Ring the bell, I'm on the track. And now to ARC and sweet Sally." A final tip of his hat, a twirl of his cane, and Genik Kwiecinski was through the door, and gone.

"Not long ago, Mrs. B, a police officer pulled that man out of a gutter. What do you say to that?"

"Never give up. Never."

"That's a rule I haven't always followed, but I'm going to follow it now." Chief Judge Green touched the speed dial button on his desk telephone. Brief wait. "Emily? I don't want to go through all this mail. I want to see you. How about if I come home early and we drive up to Carver's Mill, have dinner, and spend the night?" Brief pause. "I'll be home in about half an hour." The judge took his Panama hat off the hook on his door—no one in the city wore Panama hats anymore, except, come June first, Chief Judge Green. "I'm on my way. I'm okay, Mrs. B. Soon I'll see my Emily." Hannah Breresford watched her boss go. She'd been his secretary twenty years. "I never thought I'd see him dance. Not bad."

Chapter 12

For over a hundred years, starting before the Revolution, the Inn at Carver's Mill was a grist mill, its mill wheel turned by a stream that plunged down the river valley's steep slope. As farms turned to suburbs and farming became agribusiness, the mill became an anachronism, its wheel stopped turning, its roof collapsed, and weeds clogged its mill race. When the township commissioners declared the mill a nuisance and talked about razing the stone barn and the miller's house, a sharp-eyed young couple bought the entire property at sheriff's sale and persuaded the local bank to lend them the money to convert the buildings to a fancy establishment that would attract tourists, who would drive down river to patronize the township's antique dealers and artists' galleries. The young couple, and the bank, had the good sense not to scrimp. The barn became a restaurant, its wooden floor boards and roof beams cleaned and waxed. For looks, a massive stone fireplace was built at one end of the barn; for comfort, invisible heating and air conditioning units were installed. Wood from the barn doors was used to make a bar. Wine bottles nestled in racks, the tables were far enough apart to ensure diners that their conversations would be private, the menu was elaborate, the prices high. But it was worth it. The chef and sous-chefs had been lured from famous restaurants, and many people drove many miles to sample their cuisine, a blend of French, Italian, and Thai.

Before dinner, when the weather was pleasant, one could—and many did—sip a drink while strolling the grounds, to admire the herb garden within its boxwood borders and toss pennies to the giant gold fish fanning their tails in the mill race. After dinner, a few diners, as Chief Judge and Mrs. Green would do, crossed a slightly Japanesey bridge to the miller's house to spend the night in one of the four small but luxurious rooms upstairs, perhaps after a nightcap before the fire place in the miller's living room.

"Emily," the judge said, lifting his glass of wine to his wife across the dinner table, "you are very beautiful tonight." And though she demurred—"You say that because you love me"—she was. She still had her slim figure and fresh face. She wore a long loose dress of some exotic design—"It's Peruvian," she had told the judge—large but delicate gold earrings, and a necklace the judge had bought for her in Maine, of semi-precious stones found there—pink and white quartz, topaz, and amethyst.

"Some sort of artist," an observer might have said, and the observer would have been right. For Emily had become more than a librarian. Fascinated by the demonstrations of artists who every so often gave talks to her children at the library, Emily had decided to take lessons herself, and she had become an accomplished, and published, illustrator of children's books. Meanwhile her career as a librarian had expanded. While she insisted to her supervisors that she would never leave her branch library and the children she taught there, she had an office in the main library from which she directed city-wide programs of summer reading clubs, poetry readings, play readings, and creative writing. Last year the Mayor had presented her with a citation describing her as "Friend and Teacher of our Children." Judge Green was very proud of his wife—and tight as a fiddle string about what he would say to her after dinner, and how she would respond.

What worried the judge was his wife's uncompromising sense of right and wrong—a characteristic he attributed to her upbringing. Emily's father and mother had both been ordained ministers. She accepted her husband's atheism, or paganism, as he had once described his attitude when they were discussing how many people in the United States went to church, but she herself was a devout Episcopalian. In any case, whether because of her upbringing or for another reason, there were things Emily would never do. She would never lie, or take advantage of some one. She could, and quite often did, become angry, especially at politicians whose policies she considered selfish or cruel, but even then her criticism was dignified, it stuck to the facts, and she would address the merits of a proposal, not, at least not usually, its proponent's motives. And she would never resort to violence, nor support its use by others. She was a veteran of marches for peace. For her there was no such thing as a just war. The consequences of war were inevitably bad. Betting that the consequences of not going to war would be worse was a bet Emily was unwilling to make. Naive? Unrealistic? Foolish? Many, including some of her friends, thought she was. But that was Emily, in her husband's eyes an angel who wouldn't hurt anyone. And yet, he thought as he looked at her across the dinner table, he was about to hurt her, and, perhaps, lose her. For he had decided to tell her that he had never passed the bar examination, and to describe all that had happened since Albert Johnson had visited his chambers, just before they left for Maine.

Emily knew some sort of revelation was coming. When the judge had left for City Hall that morning he had been as close-mouthed and withdrawn as he had been while they were in Maine. His only comment had been that he "had to see Roger Littleton"—about what he didn't say. Then, later that morning, had come his exuberant telephone call suggesting they drive to Carver's Mill, which suggested he wanted to celebrate some good news. At dinner, though, his mood wasn't celebratory He seemed, rather, nostalgic, wistful, sad. "I wish he'd come out with it," Emily had thought to herself at one point. "I don't think I can take this moody broodiness much longer."

Finally, the judge did come out with it. They had checked into their room in the miller's house and were sitting on a little balcony, looking out onto the broad, black river flecked with rapids and glinting with the reflections of lights on the farther shore. He had begun at the beginning, with his meeting Genik Kwiecinski at Duffy's Bar and Grill, and had continued through Albert Johnson's visit to chambers and his two meetings that morning, first with Roger Littleton and then with Genik Kwiecinski. Throughout her husband's narrative Emily said nothing. "What should I do now, Emily?"

"Oh, Jimmy, why didn't you tell me long ago you never passed the bar exam?"

"I couldn't face up to it. By the time we met I'd buried it so deep inside me it was part of me. I couldn't imagine pulling it out any more than I could imagine pulling out my guts."

"Then why did you tell me now?"

"Because it isn't a secret anymore. I didn't want you learning from any one else what I'd done. It was hell not telling you while we were in Maine. Roger Littleton persuaded me I shouldn't tell you until he'd had a chance to talk to Johnson, and I guess he was right. No reason to worry you until I knew what I was up against."

"But sweetheart, I don't understand. What you're 'up against' doesn't seem to me to have changed all that much. It doesn't seem likely, after the way he acted this morning, that Genik Kwiecinski will tell anyone, and Albert Johnson seems to have promised Roger Littleton that he isn't going to do anything. So why didn't you just keep your secret and go on the way you were doing?"

"Well, I'd almost decided that that was what I should do. I'd deceived you, and everyone else, for so long, why change now? What good would it do? According to Roger Littleton, I don't have any legal obligation to tell anyone I never passed the bar exam. When I asked him whether I should tell you, though, he said that was a decision I had to make on my own. He'd tell me the law but not what to say to some one I loved. And then Genik Kwiecinski came along and made the decision for me. He danced, Emily! Danced! And you could tell, his heart was as light as his feet. 'I'm free at last' he said, 'the past is past, I'll find a better way!' He wasn't Fred Astaire dancing around Ginger Rogers. He was a man who had wiped off the vomit, looked in the mirror, and was celebrating his discovery that he was strong enough to build a new life. If he can do it, I thought, so can I. That's why I told you. How much do you tell some one you love? You tell her whatever she needs to know to decide whether she loves you. Even if that means you lose her. I suppose it's something like when a man decides to confess to his wife he's had an affair."

"Oh, Jimmy! No more confessions! I don't think I could manage that. If it was Sally Link, I forgive you." Judge Green, who had turned to stare at the black river, turned back to look at his wife. Her eyes were filled with tears, and laughter, her lips were curved in a smile. She was teasing him! It was going to be all right! He pulled her against him, put his head on her shoulder, and sobbed.

"Did you really think I would leave you?"

"I didn't know. I thought you might. I knew how proud of me you were, and I thought that once you knew what a cheat I'd been you'd be so disappointed, or disillusioned, that . . . that . . . you'd stop loving me."

"Jimmy, I will never stop loving you." Emily took her husband's hands. Holding them in her lap, she looked squarely in his eyes. "Listen!" she commanded. "'Love is not love/ Which alters when it alteration finds . . . O, no!/ It is an ever-fixed mark/That looks on tempests and is never shaken . . . . /Love's not time's fool, though rosy lips and cheeks/Within his bending sickle's compass come;/ Love . . . bears it out even to the edge of doom!' Those aren't my words, of course. They're Shakespeare's. But they say what I believe about love, and how I feel about you. Am I disappointed in you? Well, in a way, yes, I suppose. I mean, I wish you'd never done it. But I'm glad you told me. I've known, or sensed anyway, for a long time that there was something you were hiding, something that made you feel inferior, or unworthy, or insecure. And now it's out, out in the light where we both can look at it, and that's good. You made a mistake, a bad one, but you were young and foolish and strongly tempted. You're not unworthy, Jimmy. You're a good man, and I'm very proud of you, and I love you very much."

For a long time James and Emily Green sat watching the black river murmuring its way to sea. They were silent, drained of words. Emily put her head on James's shoulder. He drew her close against him, then closer still, as though by holding her he could fill the gap that had been between them for so many years.

* * *

"Well, now I have to decide where I go from here. Do I resign from the court or not? What do you think I should do? You're my moral compass, you know."

"I liked it better when you told me at dinner I was beautiful. 'Moral compass' sounds pointy and angular. You'll have to explain the law to me. You know I've never been able to get inside the legal mind. How did Roger Littleton get you off?" Emily flushed. "I mean, how did he persuade the Commission not to prosecute you?"

Chief Judge Green chuckled. "No, no. 'Get you off' was the right expression. First, he pointed out that under the law the Commission had the burden of proving its allegations by admissible evidence, and then he persuaded Albert Johnson that the only evidence the Commission had— Genik Kwiecinski's affidavit—wasn't admissible evidence."

"Why wasn't it?"

"Let's suppose you want to prove that the yellow Cadillac went through the red light. The general rule of law is that you must offer the testimony of a witness who can say that he saw the Cadillac go through the light. There are some exceptions to this general rule but none of them is relevant. The reason you must call an eye witness is because that will enable the jury—or the judge or whoever is the fact finder—the Commission in my case—to decide whether to believe the witness's testimony. The jury will see and hear how the witness answers questions, especially on cross-examination. Does the witness squirm, or hesitate, or seem evasive? Or is the witness forthright, assured? Also, the jury will have the chance to learn how much the witness really knows. For instance, the lawyer for the driver of the yellow Cadillac might be able to show by the witness's answers on cross-examination that the witness wasn't in a good position to see the color of the traffic light. Now suppose that instead of calling the witness to testify you offer in evidence a letter the witness wrote in which he told his wife that on the way home from work he saw a yellow Cadillac go through a red light. The jury would have no way of testing how truthful the letter was, or whether the witness was in a position to see the color of the light. You can't question a letter. All you can do is read it and wonder whether what it says is true. And so, the law of evidence is that you can't use the letter in evidence, you have to call the witness. Genik Kwiecinski's affidavit is like the letter. To prove that he took the bar exam for me, the Commission had to call him to testify. They couldn't just use his affidavit."

"But that seems upside down. Roger Littleton wasn't objecting to the affidavit because he couldn't test its truthfulness by cross-examining Genik Kwiecinski. He knew the affidavit was true. You had told him so. Is it ethical for a lawyer to object to evidence he knows is true?"

"Most lawyers think so. Their argument is that if the prosecution is required in every case to prove its allegations by admissible evidence, the administration of justice overall will be fairer."

Emily looked skeptical. "You mean, Roger Littleton was teaching the Commission a lesson? Because it lost your case it would do a better job getting evidence in its next case?

"I think that's a fair summary."

"That sounds to me like a rationalization. 'It's all right for me to steal this cookie because, when grandmother sees that it's missing, next time she'll keep the cookie jar out of reach.' Maybe she will, maybe she won't. Meanwhile, the child has his cookie. Anyway, couldn't the Commission just have asked you whether you had paid Kwiecinski to take the bar exam for you?"

"They could have, but I wouldn't have had to answer." Anticipating that Emily would ask, "Why not?," Judge Green continued. "Our Constitution provides that no one can be forced to incriminate himself, which is what I would do if I admitted paying someone else to take the exam for me. I don't know its exact name but I'm sure paying someone to impersonate you is some sort of crime. There are two reasons the Constitution says an accused doesn't have to incriminate himself. First, if the accused has the right not to confess, the prosecutor can't—at least, can't lawfully—resort to torture to make him confess. And second, since the prosecutor can't rely on the accused confessing, he has to search out other evidence. Requiring the prosecutor to do that ensures that when a crime is prosecuted, there will be a sound basis for the prosecution."

"But the accused can always choose to confess, can't he, or she?" "Yes." "Tell me, sweetheart, if the Executive Director of the Commission—what's his name? Albert Johnson—had asked you whether Genik Kwiecinski's affidavit was true, would you have answered him?" While her husband cleared his throat and shifted his position on the wicker sofa, as though to gain time, Emily continued. "Because I was brought up to admit it when I'd done something wrong. Like, 'Did you cut down the cherry tree, George?' No one ever suggested to me that George could say, 'Father, I don't have to tell you. You must prove whether I did.' If Albert Johnson had asked you, what would Roger Littleton have advised you to do?"

"Well, I think I can answer that. He would have told me I had a legal right not to answer Johnson's question. Then he would have said that in his opinion, with only Kwiecinski's affidavit, Johnson couldn't prove that I hadn't passed the bar exam. And then he would have said that whether to answer Johnson's question was my decision." Judge Green sighed and leaned back in the wicker sofa. "I know I haven't answered your other questions. I'm not sure Roger Littleton was right in objecting to Kwiecinski's affidavit as inadmissible in evidence, and I don't know what I would have done if Albert Johnson had asked me

204 · EDMUND B. SPAETH, JR.

whether Kwiecinski's affidavit was true. I'm not sure I'd have had the courage to say, yes, it was, and accept responsibility for what I'd done. I'm ashamed to admit that, but there it is. I'm grateful—I guess—that Johnson never did ask me because Roger Littleton had persuaded him that even if I was guilty, it would do more harm than good to prosecute me."

"Roger Littleton sounds to me like a sort of Merlin. He utters some magic words, points his wand at something, and poof! it's gone. We know you didn't take the bar exam. We know that therefore you're not qualified to be a judge. But, because the Commission can't prove you didn't take the exam, and anyway, shouldn't try to prove it because that would upset a lot of decided cases, it's as though what you did never happened—as though you really did take the exam. So, after all, you are qualified to be a judge. Ah me! The legal mind!"

"And that's why I need your advice, my beloved, angular, pointy moral compass. I can keep on being a judge, but should I? Since the legal mind offers no guidance, what guidance do you offer?"

*   *   *

"Let's try a different tack," Emily said. "Instead of asking what you should do, let's ask what you'd like to do. Would you like to be a judge? Because if the answer is, no, this might be a good time to resign. I know sometimes you've been discouraged."

"A year ago, I'd have been glad to hang it up. But I've changed. Yes, I would like to be a judge, now that I know, or think I know, what it means to be a judge. Do you remember when you were studying slavery and you told me the law was cruel, that kindness was better? And I said that kindness wasn't enough, sometimes you have to use force?" "Yes, I cried because you thought I said you'd be cruel." "I've never forgotten our argument. I thought both of us were right and I've often wondered whether our views couldn't be reconciled. Jesus, I know, didn't think so. He was on your side. According to him, no one should be a judge because we're so imperfect we won't understand the person we're judging. The beam in our eye is too big. Instead of judging others, therefore, we should love them, or try to anyway. But as I told you when we argued, I don't believe in heaven. I think we live only once, and that means, to me, that someone has to protect the weak, now, and that means, you have to have judges, and sheriffs, and police, who can, for instance, put murderers in prison. And yet, I knew you were right, too. Sometimes the law is cruel and judges are blind.

"Well, until recently, I just sat and stared at the problem our argument had uncovered. I was paralyzed and depressed by it, a judge who had no confidence in his ability to be a judge, or any one else's ability, and no confidence that the law he had sworn to enforce deserved enforcement. The reason I changed is that I decided to stop trying to be Cardozo and to follow Emily's Rule."

"Oh? And what, pray tell, is Emily's Rule? And what does Cardozo have to do with it?"

"When Cardozo had to decide a case, he started by reading cases that had already been decided, by his court or other courts, and that were like the case he was working on. Usually, he found, those precedents stated a rule of law that told him how he should decide his case. Sometimes, though, the precedents stated rules that were, or seemed, inconsistent with each other. Then Cardozo would derive from the precedents what he called a 'directive principle,' which he would use in deciding which of the rules of law involved were the more persuasive and should prevail in his case. Cardozo recognized that this technique, which he called the 'method of logic,' could go only so far and that in the end, the judge might have to choose among competing rules. In such a case, he would look to history, and custom, and social welfare—which for him included considerations of public policy and community standards of good or right conduct.

"Now, then, after years of trying, I found that Cardozo's method of deciding cases simply didn't work for me. When Cardozo read the precedents he was like a master fisherman reading a trout stream. He looked beneath the surface to see where the pools and hidden currents were, he balanced the forces pushing against each other, the constraining stream banks, the rocky dams, the rushing rapids. I didn't, and I don't, have Cardozo's eye.

"But beyond this—and I know, I'm being presumptuous—I was never persuaded that Cardozo's method was entirely sound. If you were right—and I thought you were—that the law is sometimes cruel, that meant that some of the precedents were cruel. How can you derive a good 'directive principle' from bad precedents? And the same with history and custom and social welfare. Examples taken from those fields will sometimes illustrate admirable conduct, but other times they'll illustrate ignorance and oppression. By what standard does a judge—any judge, including Cardozo—decide which precedents, and which examples from history, and so on, are good and which are bad? Is a judge's decision purely subjective? And if it is, what does 'the rule of law,' which we're always boasting about, mean? 'The rule of judges?'

"Cardozo recognized this problem, but he didn't consider it a big deal. He more or less assumed that different judges' different views would balance one another, and that in the long run, things would work out for the best. For me, though, it was a big deal. From my experience, I simply didn't have as much faith in judges as he did. The turning point in my thinking—forgive me, darling, I know I'm being pompous, but this is the way it happened—came at the court's annual meeting at Mountaintop Lodge, this Spring, where we discussed *Billy Budd* and *The Merchant of Venice*. Captain Vere thought he was enforcing the law, when he persuaded the court to condemn Billy to be hanged. So did Portia, when she declared Shylock's life and property forfeit because, as an alien, he had threatened the life of a citizen of Venice. But they weren't enforcing the law. They were enforcing their personal, their subjective, interpretations of the law. Vere was a Navy captain, in time of war, preoccupied with suppressing mutiny, Portia was a wealthy Venetian preoccupied with keeping a Jew in his place. If they had interpreted the law through different eyes, they would have decided differently. Vere would have decided that under the law, Billy shouldn't be hanged because he hadn't intended to kill Claggart, and Portia would have decided that the law only required that Shylock couldn't recover the money he had lent Antonio.

"And that, my beloved, is where Emily's Rule comes in. I decided to reverse Cardozo's method. Instead of starting with the precedents, I would start with my vision of what the law should be, and I would make no bones about the fact that it was my own, subjective vision. Then I would look at the precedents, and history and custom and social welfare, and decide whether they squared with my vision of what the law should be. Emily's Rule states my vision. I suppose it's really my rule, not yours, but I call it yours because it's based on what I've learned from you. It's my attempt to reconcile the different positions we took when we argued about the significance of the fact that judges used to enforce the law of slavery. Emily's Rule states that since kindness is better than force, when deciding a case a judge should define the law in a way that will make it as kind as possible.

"I don't mean to suggest that Emily's Rule is a magic rule. Close your eyes, say it three times, and presto! you know how to decide a case. Most judges, I'm pretty sure, would say it isn't a rule at all. And I can imagine the sarcasm Justice Scalia would heap on it. It only begs the question. What does it mean, to be 'kind'? Maybe granting a new trial to a convicted felon is being kind to the felon, but is it being kind to his victims? Anyway, a judge's job isn't to be kind, it's to be just. Well, I don't know what Justice Scalia's vision of the law is, but I think his decisions are cold-hearted and cocky. Anyway, I'm not trying, by Emily's Rule, to state a system of jurisprudence, only to describe an approach to deciding cases that will take me safely past some of the pitfalls I've fallen into, and will make me a better judge—a 'juster' one, if you prefer that word to 'kinder.'

"As I thought about my career as a judge, I wished I could take back some of the decisions I'd written, and some of my joinders. One was the decision I wrote disbarring Genik Kwiecinski—or Gene Kelly. Another was a decision I'd joined, holding that the court shouldn't order the legislature to change the way it funds public schools. Another I joined was a decision reversing a trial judge's order requiring changes in the prisons. I would have voted differently in all of those cases if I'd followed Emily's Rule—which I didn't because I hadn't thought of it yet. In none of them had I made any effort to define the law to be as kind as possible. To the contrary, in all of them the law was callous, indifferent at best, cruel at worst. In the decision disbarring Genik I used language implying, if not saying outright, that alcoholics are not simply physically weak but morally inferior. In the school funding case the court was utterly indifferent to the fact that thousands of children would lead stunted lives because their schools had out-of-date text books, unqualified teachers, no courses in art or music. In the prison case the court was not simply indifferent but cruel. It knew—the record was uncontradicted—that prisoners were being raped, denied their medication, kept for days in solitary. And yet, as it did in the school funding case, the court professed its belief that the responsibility for improvement lay with others—the legislature, or the prison authorities—others, I might add, who had shown no disposition to make any improvements.

"My point is, I came to realize that the law doesn't drive the judge, the judge drives the law. And that was exhilarating. For the first time I realized that as a judge I had the power to define, or redefine, the law so that it would not be cruel or oppressive, or, at least, less so. I was not a rubber stamp. I was a lawgiver, who could be kind, like my beloved wife.

"Let me give you an example of what I'm talking about. A few months ago we had to decide whether a lesbian was entitled to visit a child she and another lesbian had been raising. The two women had split up when one of them—the one who wanted to visit the child—had an affair. I thought she should be allowed to visit. It seemed to me that her former partner's refusal to let her visit was simply a way to take revenge on her for having had an affair. The child—a little girl—loved both women. I didn't think she should be cut off from one because of the other's bitterness. That was the decision Emily's Rule led me to. It would be kinder to permit visitation than to deny it. Having decided the direction I wanted to go, I had to look at the decided cases. What did they say? Well, Sally collected them for me, and none of them involved a dispute between lesbians. In addition, the judges on the court read the cases very differently.

"The rule the cases seemed to stand for was that someone *in loco parentis*—as the cases put it—could petition for visitation. Now, clearly a biological mother or father might stand *in loco parentis*. But who else? The cases weren't clear. A minority of the judges said they would permit any family member who had taken care of the child to petition for visitation—for example, an aunt or grandmother. But, they said, two lesbians did not constitute a 'family.' In the end, though, most of the judges agreed with me. I argued that biology shouldn't be decisive, the test should be whether the person petitioning for visitation, first, had lived with and cared for the child, as a parent would, and second, had a strong, loving relationship with the child. In the case before us, the lesbian petitioning for visitation satisfied that test.

"Now, as I said, it was exhilarating to feel that I'd made the law kinder. But it was also sobering, and humbling. In what sense had I upheld the law, as a judge is sworn to do? Was my reading of the cases justified? Did they contain a directive principle that warranted extending the traditional view of 'family' to include a lesbian? Who was I to say that my colleagues' support of the traditional view of family was in some sense mistaken or out of date? Had I become as arrogant as Justice Scalia? Do you see how far out to sea I'd ventured? Had I lost my bearings? "It may be that for awhile I did lose my bearings. The law, however, has an iron logic of its own designed to get a judge back on course. Some rules are so well established a court won't change them, even when it has doubts about the result. Even Emily's Rule must yield. The last case we decided this term, a few days ago, was just such a case. It was also Judge Ericson's last decision before he was killed.

"The case is called *The Lead Paint Case*, and the question was whether children who had suffered brain damage from eating lead paint that had chipped off walls and furniture could recover damages from the paint manufacturers. Eric circulated an opinion that would have let the children recover damages, and at first a majority of the judges joined him. Under Emily's Rule, I wanted to join him, too. Some of the children's lives had been ruined, and the paint manufacturers had known all along that ingesting lead paint could cause brain damage. But I couldn't join Eric. Over and over the courts, including our court, have said that a person seeking damages for personal injuries must prove that the defendant caused the injuries, and the children couldn't do that. Every child—and thousands of children were suing—could prove injury as a result of ingesting lead paint, but no one could prove who made the paint. About a dozen manufacturers had been sued. All little Suzy, for example, could prove was that one of them must have made the paint that poisoned her. Which one, she couldn't say. So, to permit her to recover damages from Manufacturer X, which Eric's opinion would let her do, might mean X would pay for injuries Manufacturer Y had caused. Since that seemed to me dead against all the cases that said that to recover damages, Suzy had to prove who hurt her, I circulated an opinion dissenting from Eric's opinion. In my opinion I agreed with Eric that it seemed unfair to make Suzy prove that X had hurt her. Why not make X prove that its paint hadn't poisoned Suzy—that some other manufacturer's had? I said that if I were writing the law, I'd provide that when a manufacturer made a product it knew was dangerous, it should have to prove that injuries that might have been caused by its product hadn't been. But then I pointed out that that wasn't the law.

The question, therefore, as I saw it, was whether we should change the law by overruling our cases requiring Suzy to prove who had hurt her, or whether the legislature should change the law. I said that if there was to be a change, it should be by the legislature. A change would likely have a tremendous impact on manufacturers, not only on the paint manufacturers, which might go bankrupt, but on all manufacturers. Perhaps, on balance, it would be better to leave the law as it was. Whether that was so, I said, was a question better answered by the legislature, which could hold hearings and conduct investigations, than by a court.

"In the end, most of the judges agreed with me. The last memo Eric wrote as a judge, a few days before he was killed, was a memo to me withdrawing his opinion and joining mine. It was a very moving memo. Eric said that my opinion had shown him how a judge should respond when required to decide whether to uphold a law the judge believes unfair.

"So there you have it, sweetheart. The story of how Judge Green finally learned to be a judge. Thank you for listening. It's a crazy business. You feel free and at the same time trapped by the logic of the law. You care passionately and at the same time you're racked by doubts. You know, despite what some philosophers of the law have argued, that for some cases there's no single right way to decide. There are too many factors to be weighed and balanced. Reasonable judges will weigh and balance them differently. And besides, we simply don't know enough, or we don't know that what we think we know is wrong. Even Holmes and Cardozo wrote some decisions that turned out to be clunkers. And so you wonder, and you worry, and you hope that flawed as you are, by a chemistry you don't understand you have created something perfect, something time will validate, some rule, some principle, some phrase or expression, that those who come after you will use to make the world a little kinder place in which to live."

* * *

It was late—far past midnight. One by one the lights across the river had been blinking off until only a handful were still reflected in the gleaming blackness streaming by the balcony where Jim and Emily Green sat. Emily realized what her husband had done. He had carefully, with great pains, explained everything he thought she needed to know to advise him whether he should resign from the Supreme Court. He had exposed the morally suspect reasoning by which he had escaped prosecution. He had described his long odyssey from an inexperienced, insecure, and unhappy judge to a judge confident in his vision of the law and unafraid to pursue it. Just as he had done in stating the lesbians' and *Lead Paint* cases, so he had stated his own case, identifying the factors to be weighed and balanced, one against the other, in deciding his future. But he had not weighed and balanced them. He was leaving that up to her. She was to be his judge.

As though following his wife's thoughts, Judge Green resumed his disquisition. "Emily, I know it isn't fair to ask you to decide what I should do. After all, what sort of judge am I if I can't even decide whether to be a judge? But truth to tell, after the last two weeks I'm not sure I've got it in me to decide. There I was, riding high. It had been a wonderful Spring. The court's annual conference had gone like gang busters. Some day, by the way, you must meet young Emerson. The two of you would make a wonderful team to develop a course on law and literature, which the library could take to the public schools. Sally Link had been a brilliant law clerk. She had given me the confidence to trust my judgment of how a case should be decided. For the first time in my life, I was glad to be a judge, and knew how to be a judge. And then, in walks Albert Johnson and tells me he's going to file a complaint against me because I'd never passed the bar exam. I had never taken such a blow before, and I hope I will never have to take another one like it. I knew I wasn't dead because I was walking around and talking. But everything inside me was dead. I felt like a sort of ghost. When I was in Maine working in the garden with you, I'd try to reassure myself that some how things would work out. And when Sally and I fished that youngster out of the drink, that gave me a lift. But when I'd snug down beside you in bed at night, all I could think of was the headlines you'd be reading soon. 'Chief Judge Of Supreme Court Removed, Never Passed Bar Exam.' Well, now everything looks different. Roger's gotten me off, so I don't have to worry about being disgraced. I finally got the courage to tell you what I should have told you years ago, and you've said you still love me. I ought to feel elated, ready to go back to work, to pick up where I left off. But I don't. I'm exhausted. I'm tired of living a lie I'd buried so deep for so long I'd almost forgotten what I'd done. And now that I've told you, I can't bury it again. That would implicate you in my deception. Well, I guess I have to resign. I don't see how else I can stop pretending to every lawyer who appears before me and to every judge I sit with that I have done what they've all done—pass the bar exam. But, I admit, the thought of having to resign shatters me. It makes me realize, not only am I a failure, I'm a fool. Talk about building a house on sand! I invest years in learning how to be a judge. I study the materials, I learn the design, I fit everything together. And then, one day, just as I finish the job, the tide rushes in. Emily, you are the most wonderful woman— the most wonderful person—I've ever known. I love you beyond my ability to say. You have been the light of my life. Thank you for every day I've had with you. But you shouldn't be stuck with a fool."

"Jimmy, I hope your nose won't be out of joint if the next time we see Roger Littleton at the City Club, I give him a kiss—quite a big kiss. I know he's a wily old scoundrel who can stand the law on its head, and everyone in the courtroom, including the judge. But I also know" —and here Emily, who was trying to keep her voice light, choked up; then, regaining her composure, she continued—"I also know that he is a great lawyer who has saved some one who will be a great judge. Since you've asked my advice, I'll give it. I don't think you should resign. Why don't you just take the bar examination now? You're Chief Judge, responsible for supervising the legal system. You've said for some time you thought the education of lawyers could be improved. Why don't you tell the Law Examiners that as part of your review of legal education you want to see what sort of examination applicants for the bar have to pass, and that you've decided the best way to do that is to take the examination yourself?"

"But Emily! Suppose I fail it?"

"That might be awkward, but you won't, my darling. I know you'll pass. Aren't there special courses you could take?"

"Yes, there are, but . . . ." Chief Judge Green slapped the arm of the wicker sofa. "I've got a better idea. I'll ask Genik Kwiecinski and Sally Link to prepare me for the exam. When Genik took the exam for me, he didn't have time for any preparation at all, but he passed with a grade of ninety something. And they don't come any brighter than Sally. Genik will know what I'm doing, but of course I won't tell Sally I've never passed the exam. I'll just say what you just said—that I want to see what the exam is like, and will she be sure I'm not embarrassed. The exam is given in September. I'll have all summer to study."

"Don't tell me you're planning to ask Sally to come to Squirrel again?"

"No, you minx! I'll have to stay at home to study. It's your fault, with your cockamamie idea that I should do what other lawyers have had to do. We could still go up to Squirrel a couple of times for short stays. Or you could go, and leave me down here alone. But that would be cruel and inconsistent with Emily's Rule."

"Speaking of Emily's Rule, there's a corollary we should consider."

"Oh?"

"Yes. It says, 'If with sober law you spend the night, when morning breaks, taste love's delight.'"

The sky had turned pearl gray. Soon the river would shimmer with dawn's pink and gold. Emily leaned back against Jimmy's chest. Gently, he brushed back her hair and traced around her ear, along the line of her jaw, down to her chin. From the shadowed edge of the river, on majestic wings, a great blue heron rose into the light. Emily tipped up her lips. Life was good.

The End

www.ingramcontent.com/pod-product-compliance
Lightning Source LLC
Chambersburg PA
CBHW031929190326
41519CB00007B/465